DELIBERATIVE SYSTEMS

'Deliberative democracy' is often dismissed as a set of small-scale, academic experiments. This volume seeks to demonstrate how the deliberative ideal can work as a theory of democracy on a larger scale. It provides a new way of thinking about democratic engagement across the spectrum of political action, from towns and villages to nation states, and from local networks to transnational, even global systems. Written by a team of the world's leading deliberative theorists, *Deliberative Systems* explains the principles of this new approach, which seeks ways of ensuring that a division of deliberative labour in a system nonetheless meets both deliberative and democratic norms. Rather than simply elaborating the theory, the contributors examine the problems of implementation in a real world of competing norms, competing institutions, and competing powerful interests. This pioneering book will inspire an exciting new phase of deliberative research, both theoretical and empirical.

JOHN PARKINSON is Associate Professor of Public Policy in the Department of Politics and International Studies at the University of Warwick.

JANE MANSBRIDGE is Adams Professor of Political Leadership and Democratic Values in the John F. Kennedy School of Government at Harvard University.

D1475074

THEORIES OF INSTITUTIONAL DESIGN

Series Editor
Robert E. Goodin
Research School of Social Sciences
Australian National University

Advisory Editors
Russell Hardin, Carole Pateman, Barry Weingast, Claus Offe,
Susan Rose-Ackerman, Keith Dowding, Jeremy Waldron

Social scientists have rediscovered institutions. They have been increasingly concerned with the myriad ways in which social and political institutions shape the patterns of individual interactions which produce social phenomena. They are equally concerned with the ways in which those institutions emerge from such interactions.

This series is devoted to the exploration of the more normative aspects of these issues. What makes one set of institutions better than another? How, if at all, might we move from the less desirable set of institutions to a more desirable set? Alongside the questions of what institutions we would design, if we were designing them afresh, are pragmatic questions of how we can best get from here to there: from our present institutions to new revitalized ones.

Theories of institutional design is insistently multidisciplinary and interdisciplinary, both in the institutions on which it focuses, and in the methodologies used to study them. There are interesting sociological questions to be asked about legal institutions, interesting legal questions to be asked about economic institutions, and interesting social, economic, and legal questions to be asked about political institutions. By juxtaposing these approaches in print, this series aims to enrich normative discourse surrounding important issues of designing and redesigning, shaping and reshaping the social, political, and economic institutions of contemporary society.

Other books in the series
Brent Fisse and John Braithwaite, *Corporations, Crime and Accountability*
Robert E. Goodin (editor), *The Theory of Institutional Design*
Itai Sened, *The Political Institution of Private Property*
Mark Bovens, *The Quest for Responsibility: Accountability and Citizenship in Complex Organisations*
Bo Rothstein, *Just Institutions Matter: The Moral and Political Logic of the Universal Welfare State*
Jon Elster, Claus Offe, and Ulrich K. Preuss, *Institutional Design in Post-Communist Societies: Rebuilding the Ship at Sea*
Adrienne Héritier, *Policy-Making and Diversity in Europe: Escape from Deadlock*
Geoffrey Brennan and Alan Hamlin, *Democratic Devices and Desires*
Eric M. Patashnik, *Putting Trust in the US Budget: Federal Trust Funds and the Politics of Commitment*
Benjamin Reilly, *Democracy in Divided Societies: Electoral Engineering for Conflict Management*
John S. Dryzek and Leslie Templeman Holmes, *Post-Communist Democratization: Political Discourses Across Thirteen Countries*

DELIBERATIVE SYSTEMS

Deliberative Democracy at the Large Scale

Edited by

JOHN PARKINSON

Associate Professor of Public Policy, University of Warwick

JANE MANSBRIDGE

Adams Professor of Political Leadership and Democratic Values,
John F. Kennedy School of Government, Harvard University

CAMBRIDGE
UNIVERSITY PRESS

CAMBRIDGE
UNIVERSITY PRESS

University Printing House, Cambridge CB2 8BS, United Kingdom

Published in the United States of America by Cambridge University Press, New York

Cambridge University Press is part of the University of Cambridge.

It furthers the University's mission by disseminating knowledge in the pursuit of education, learning and research at the highest international levels of excellence.

www.cambridge.org
Information on this title: www.cambridge.org/9781107678910

© Cambridge University Press 2012

First published 2012
First paperback edition 2013

A catalogue record for this publication is available from the British Library

Library of Congress Cataloguing in Publication data
Deliberative systems : deliberative democracy at the large scale /
[edited by] John Parkinson, Jane Mansbridge.
p. cm. – (Theories of institutional design)
Includes bibliographical references and index.
ISBN 978-1-107-02539-4
1. Deliberative democracy. I. Parkinson, John, 1966– II. Mansbridge, Jane J.
JC423.D3897 2012
321.8–dc23
2012013676

ISBN 978-1-107-02539-4 Hardback
ISBN 978-1-107-67891-0 Paperback

Contents

Contributors

James Bohman, Danforth Professor of Philosophy and Professor of International Studies, Saint Louis University

Simone Chambers, Professor of Political Science, University of Toronto

Thomas Christiano, Professor of Philosophy and Law, University of Arizona

Archon Fung, Ford Foundation Professor of Democracy and Citizenship, John F. Kennedy School of Government, Harvard University

Michael K. MacKenzie, Doctoral Candidate in Political Science, University of British Columbia

Jane Mansbridge, Adams Professor, John F. Kennedy School of Government, Harvard University

Yannis Papadopoulos, Professor of Public Policy at the Institut d'Etudes Politiques et Internationales, University of Lausanne

John Parkinson, Associate Professor of Public Policy, Department of Politics and International Studies, University of Warwick

Dennis F. Thompson, Alfred North Whitehead Professor of Political Philosophy, Harvard University

Mark E. Warren, Professor of Political Science and Harold and Dorrie Merilees Chair in the Study of Democracy, University of British Columbia

Preface

This volume began at a conference called *Democracy and the Deliberative Society*, held at the King's Manor, University of York, in June 2009. Supported by grants from the British Academy, and the University of York's Research Priming and Distinguished Visitors Funds, the plan was to bring together a mix of political theorists, philosophers, public policy scholars, empirical political scientists, and practitioners to explore an emerging 'macro' emphasis in deliberative democracy: the idea that deliberative democracy is as much a theory about how democratic societies work at the large scale as a set of blueprints for the design of relatively small-scale institutions.

In the event, it was one of those conferences that academics dream of. The atmosphere was one of intellectual generosity, fun, and goodwill, and that was due not only to the commitment of the invited participants but to an active, spirited audience as well. The sun shone, the debates were lively, friendships were made, and the conversation flowed.

We therefore want to begin by thanking everyone who made the York conference such a success, especially Matthew Festenstein who was one of the instigators along with John Parkinson, and Alex Bavister-Gould who conducted a literature review that gave the project a strong foundation. Behind the scenes Tom Flynn contributed both intellectually and organizationally. That everything eventually went so smoothly was largely due to the cheerful unflappability of Judith Pink.

The paper givers were superb, and while this particular volume has focused on a selection of the most theoretical papers, we want to acknowledge the important contributions made by other colleagues both during the conference and afterwards. Those others, who could not participate in this volume for a variety of reasons, include John Dryzek, Sophie

Duchesne, Florence Haegel, Maarten Hajer, Mathias Koenig-Archibugi, Christian List, Aletta Norval, Graham Smith, and Wytske Versteeg.

Following the conference, ideas for a book germinated for a while, until finally a proposal went to Cambridge University Press. Bob Goodin, Series Editor, was extremely generous with time and criticism, and the eventual shape of the volume and the substance of the chapters owes much to his care and attention. We also thank the anonymous referees whose comments proved invaluable in the sometimes extensive redrafting process. Some chapters are completely new, but all are much revised and much stronger as a result. John Haslam has been a supportive and enthusiastic Commissioning Editor throughout.

In between first submission and final acceptance of the proposal, a second weekend conference was held at Harvard University in December 2010 to deepen the opening theoretical statement. We thank the Ash Center for Democratic Innovation at the Kennedy School of Government for hosting and sponsoring the workshop, Bruce Jackman for administrative support, and Hollie Russon Gilman and Adriane Gelpi for assistance during the meetings. Most of the contributors to that conference have become co-authors of the introduction, and we thank them all for their enthusiastic participation. We are also grateful to David Estlund for his phone-in contributions to the first session.

Finally, we would like to thank very much those others who have helped with long discussions or quick observations over the last two years, including Selen Armityan, André Bächtiger, John Dryzek, Andrew Knops, Gerry Mackie, Simon Niemeyer, Espen Olsen, and Stefan Rummens.

So, a cast of thousands (well, dozens), in several forums over two years: a deliberative system in action.

John Parkinson and Jane Mansbridge

I would also like to thank Jane Mansbridge for all that she has done on this project. She gave generously of her time to graduate students in York, did interviews, organized the Harvard conference, and steered the collaborative writing of the introduction, all through some very busy times. It would not have come together as it has without you, Jenny. Thank you.

John Parkinson

A systemic approach to deliberative democracy

JANE MANSBRIDGE, JAMES BOHMAN,
SIMONE CHAMBERS, THOMAS CHRISTIANO,
ARCHON FUNG, JOHN PARKINSON,
DENNIS F. THOMPSON AND MARK E. WARREN

The last several decades have seen growing agreement among political theorists and empirical political scientists that the legitimacy of a democracy depends in part on the quality of deliberation that informs citizens and their representatives. Until recently, those who wanted to study and improve the quality of deliberation in democracies began with, basically, two strategies. One concentrated on deliberation in legislative bodies of all sorts and the campaigns that produce their members. The other strategy, not necessarily at odds with the first, addressed the design, promulgation, and empowerment of small deliberative initiatives in which citizens could deliberate under relatively favourable conditions.

Both of these strategies, however, focused only on individual sites and not on the interdependence of sites within a larger system. Typically, the ideal has been cast in the image of the best possible single deliberative forum. Most empirical research on deliberative democracy, accordingly, has concentrated 'either on a single episode of deliberation, as in one-time group discussions, or on a continuing series with the same group or in the same type of institution' (Thompson 2008a: 213). Yet no single forum, however ideally constituted, could possess deliberative capacity sufficient to legitimate most of the decisions and policies that democracies adopt. To

This introduction was written in a process of deliberative co-authorship led by Jane Mansbridge, who prepared the first draft from multiple contributions and oversaw the many revisions. Although each co-author, if writing independently, would no doubt present the arguments and analyses somewhat differently, the chapter represents a direction of thought to which each co-author has substantially contributed and which all collectively endorse.

understand the larger goal of deliberation, we suggest that it is necessary to go beyond the study of individual institutions and processes to examine their interaction in the system as a whole. We recognize that most democracies are complex entities in which a wide variety of institutions, associations, and sites of contestation accomplish political work – including informal networks, the media, organized advocacy groups, schools, foundations, private and non-profit institutions, legislatures, executive agencies, and the courts. We thus advocate what may be called a *systemic approach to deliberative democracy.*[1]

Thinking in terms of a system offers several advantages. First, a systemic approach allows us to think about deliberative democracy in large-scale societal terms. A continual challenge for deliberative democracy theory has been the problem of scale. Face-to-face deliberation happens only in small groups. Parliamentary deliberation is confined to those forms of deliberation organized by states or subnational units. In what sense can we say that whole societies, demoi, peoples, or even different communities deliberate together? A systemic approach allows us to think productively and creatively about this question. It expands the scale of analysis beyond the individual site and allows us to think about deliberations that develop among and between the sites over time.

The systemic approach does not dictate that we take a nation or large polity as our object of study. Schools and universities, hospitals, media, and other organizations can be understood along the lines offered by a deliberative system approach. But in allowing for the possibility of ratcheting up the scale and complexity of interrelations among the parts, this approach enables us to think about democratic decisions being taken in the context of a variety of deliberative venues and institutions, interacting together to produce a healthy deliberative system.

Second, a systemic approach allows us to analyse the division of labour among parts of a system, each with its different deliberative strengths and

---

[1] Habermas suggested a broad approach, compatible with a systemic one, in his earlier writing. In (1996) he advanced a 'two-track' view combining a relatively 'wild' sphere of deliberation among 'weak' publics with more formal legislative deliberation. For a recent view, see Habermas (2006). On deliberative systems, see Mansbridge (1999) introducing the term and concept of a 'deliberative system', Goodin (2005) on 'distributed deliberation', Parkinson (2006a) on 'legitimacy across multiple deliberative moments and the wider deliberative system', Hendriks (2006a) on an 'integrated deliberative system', Bohman (2007) on 'institutional differentiation' with 'multiple and intersecting processes of public deliberation', Krause (2008) on the 'different types of constraint on deliberation in each domain', Thompson (2008a) on the 'allocation of deliberation', Dryzek (2009) on 'deliberative capacity' in the system, on the 'systemic turn' in deliberative theory (in a book [2010a] largely on the deliberative system), and Neblo (2010) on elements of a deliberative system working together to 'serve the larger deliberative standard'.

weaknesses, and to conclude that a single part, which in itself may have low or even negative deliberative quality with respect to one of several deliberative ideals, may nevertheless make an important contribution to an overall deliberative system. For example, highly partisan rhetoric, even while violating some deliberative ideals such as mutual respect and accommodation, may nonetheless help to fulfil other deliberative ideals such as inclusion. In another example, serious discussions on European Union (EU)-wide matters take place mostly among elites, while the national media and, to a lesser degree, national politicians, organize the public debate on EU issues. Although the overall system is far from ideal epistemically, the elite discourse provides expertise, reasoned and informed mutual accommodation, and mutual respect, while the nationally instigated deliberation provides perspectives that might otherwise not be heard. By enhancing inclusion, the national media also increase the EU's normative democratic legitimacy.

Parts of a system may have relationships of complementarity or displacement. In a complementary relationship, two wrongs can make a right. Two venues, both with deliberative deficiencies, can each make up for the deficiencies of the other. Thus an institution that looks deliberatively defective when considered only on its own can look beneficial in a systemic perspective. Conversely, an institution that looks deliberatively exemplary on its own, such as a well-designed minipublic, can look less beneficial in a systemic perspective when it displaces other useful deliberative institutions, such as partisan or social movement bodies. In another instance of displacement, legislatures are less likely to take their deliberative responsibilities seriously when a constitutional court is treated as the primary deliberative forum (Gutmann and Thompson 1996: 45–7; see also Dryzek 2010a: 13).

Third, a systemic approach introduces into the analysis large contextual issues and broad systemic inadequacies that have an impact on individual sites and shape the possibilities of effective deliberation. Once we identify what a deliberative system should accomplish, we can identify gaps in a system's deliberative quality. For example, a deliberative system may fail to include in a policy deliberation individuals with legitimate claims for inclusion, owing to legal exclusion or to deficiencies of education, information, or transparency. Or a system may rely excessively on parliamentary processes that frame debate but fail to make space for deliberation, leading to decisions of relatively poor quality. Even if a legislature has a high quality and well informed debate about, for example, reducing the deficit, the deliberation looks less adequate in the context of a system that permits highly unequal campaign contributions or enables the media to frame the issue by highlighting the dangers of deficits with little mention of the harm that cuts would do to the least advantaged citizens in society or to fiscal stimuli aimed at stemming recession. A systemic approach allows us to see more clearly where a system might be improved, and recommend institutions or other innovations that could supplement the system in areas of weakness.

In the next section we lay out, in general and programmatic terms, what a systemic approach to deliberation entails, and discuss in more detail the benefits of this approach. While we may at times favour certain directions and theoretical orientations over others, we want to stress that the approach we outline could be taken up by any number of theories of deliberative democracy. Like any useful paradigm, deliberative democracy theory contains many theoretical variations, competing articulations, and contested definitions. Our aim is to articulate an overarching approach to deliberation that could signal a new and we think exciting direction for deliberative theory, but which is not itself a free-standing theory of deliberative democracy.

We take up in a separate section three elements of a democratic system that are usually not considered part of the exercise of deliberative democracy, and reconsider their place in terms of the system. We evaluate experts, pressure, and protest, and the partisan media, asking whether they do or could enhance the quality of deliberation in the system. We present these three only as examples of the sorts of directions a full systemic approach to deliberative democracy might take. Nevertheless we think that they represent central elements in almost any deliberative democratic system. They illustrate particularly well the advantages of a systemic approach, because all three are often assumed to be incompatible with deliberative democracy and do in fact create tensions with it. In a final section we identify five potential pathologies that threaten any deliberative system. Although some of these pathologies have their analogues at the level of individual sites, they are fundamentally problems inherent in a system and most clearly discerned through a broad systemic approach.

What is a deliberative system?

A *system* here means a set of distinguishable, differentiated, but to some degree interdependent parts, often with distributed functions and a division of labour, connected in such a way as to form a complex whole. It requires both differentiation and integration among the parts. It requires some functional division of labour, so that some parts do work that others cannot do as well. And it requires some relational interdependence, so that a change in one component will bring about changes in some others. A *deliberative* system is one that encompasses a talk-based approach to political conflict and problem-solving – through arguing, demonstrating, expressing, and persuading. In a good deliberative system, persuasion that raises relevant considerations should replace suppression, oppression, and thoughtless neglect. Normatively, a systemic approach means that the system should be judged as a whole in addition to the parts being judged independently. We need to ask not only what good deliberation would be both in general and in particular settings, but also what a good deliberative system would entail.

A systemic approach, in our view, does not require that every component have a function or that every component be interdependent with every other such that a change in one will automatically bring about a change in all others. If a component does contribute to a function, it is not necessary that the function be fulfilled optimally in one location, since in a deliberative system the same function may be distributed across various subsystems. The concept as we apply it is not intended to be mechanistic; nor do we require a system to have clearly identifiable boundaries. Our point is that normatively, in the systemic approach the entire burden of decision-making and legitimacy does not fall on one forum or institution but is distributed among different components in different cases.

We expect that a highly functional deliberative system will be redundant or potentially redundant in interaction, so that when one part fails to play an important role another can fill in or evolve over time to fill in. Such a system will include checks and balances of various forms so that excesses in one part are checked by the activation of other parts of the system. We also envision systems that are dynamic rather than static. Thus it may be hard to predict in advance when or why some parts of the system will respond to certain forms of public opinion or represent certain interests and publics or certain kinds of values and procedures.

It should not be surprising that a political system requires a division of labour. Political judgments are complex, and the system in which they are made should also be complex. Because political judgments involve so many factual contingencies and competing normative requirements, and because politics involves the alignments of will, both in concert and in opposition, among large numbers of citizens, it is virtually impossible to conceive of a political system that does not divide the labours of judgment and then recombine them in various ways. The concept of a system highlights these necessities.

To take an example of the systemic approach applied to a concrete policy deliberation, John Parkinson (2006a) has analysed a series of UK initiatives that promoted deliberative public involvement in health policymaking, including through citizens' juries – small groups of citizens chosen relatively randomly and convened to deliberate on the issue. As he points out, health care is 'a tough testing ground of the ability of any deliberative process to handle legitimacy deficits' (2006a: 44). He shows that understanding the deliberative process in the UK on this issue requires looking beyond the particular deliberative site of citizens' juries to a complex deliberative system with many participants – including health service professionals, unions, activists, administrators, charity groups, and more – each set of players with its own, sometimes internally competing, agendas and points of view. The processes cut across levels of government, from the local and regional to the national. Parkinson shows that it matters a great deal which groups commission forms of 'micro-deliberation' like citizens' juries and how they construct the procedures. It also matters at what level of the policy hierarchy such micro-deliberative procedures are used. These procedures 'tend to be used lower down in the hierarchy' because the lower echelons have greater legitimation needs and feel stronger pressures to be responsive (2006a: 64). A systems analysis allows us to see how on this issue the citizens' juries can themselves score relatively high on deliberative standards and at the same time have both negative and positive systemic effects. On the negative side, they to some degree displaced and weakened the existing advocacy organizations, thus reducing the impact of these groups on societal deliberation. On the more positive side, they served as a stimulating 'focal point' (2006a: 177) for organizing societal deliberation. A deliberative system approach thus takes into account not only a particular forum or innovation but also the role of that forum or innovation in the larger deliberative system, allowing us to gauge its democratic weaknesses and strengths within the larger dynamic of groups and levels.

A deliberative systemic approach also suggests looking for 'deliberative ecologies', in which different contexts facilitate some forms of deliberation and avenues for information while others facilitate different forms and avenues. Partisanship and information heuristics or shortcuts are usually contrasted with deliberation and seen as among the most serious obstacles to good quality deliberation. But a deliberative systemic approach asks when and where there is an appropriate ecological niche for partisan campaigns and heuristics. Because legislators and citizens in their busy lives will tend to rely on partisan organization and heuristics to guide their decisions, a good deliberative system will draw from the virtues of these individually deliberatively deficient devices but guard in various ways against their vices. Sometimes associations that are internally non-deliberative and homogeneous will, for that very reason, be able to assert a coherent public position and sharpen a public debate. Sometimes particular stages or sequences in a political process will embody a useful division of labour, with relatively open deliberations at the beginning narrowing to a focus as the point of decision is reached. Sometimes arguments made in one part of the system will be tested in another part. Such mechanisms enable a good deliberative system to be self-correcting.

Here are three examples of how partisanship may appear to undermine deliberation at a micro level but not at a systems level:

- The British House of Commons engages in partisan heckling that violates many standards of good deliberation. Yet that very culture of heckling provides incentives to poke holes in the reasoning of a Government that otherwise makes all the major decisions and rules by strict and overriding majority. It may also function to frame and sharpen broader public deliberations.
- Some politically partisan media are of very low deliberative quality, but in conjunction with other media of equally low deliberative quality bring out information and perspectives that television stations or newspapers aiming at the middle of the road do not raise or address.
- Activist interactions in social movement enclaves are often highly partisan, closed to opposing ideas, and disrespectful of opponents. Yet the intensity of interaction and even the exclusion of opposing ideas in such enclaves create the fertile, protected hothouses sometimes necessary to generate counter-hegemonic ideas. These ideas then may play powerful roles in the broader deliberative system, substantively improving an eventual democratic decision.

A systemic approach can also illuminate how partisanship that is functional in one part of the system becomes dysfunctional when it spreads to another part of the system that requires other virtues. For example, the attitudes and practices of campaigning – emphasizing the sharp differences with opponents, refusing to find common ground or look for ways to compromise, and concentrating on defeating rather than cooperating with opponents – are not deliberative but may be appropriate, even necessary, in a campaign. Yet as campaigns become 'permanent' and their practices come to dominate the institutions of governing, they can overpower the deliberative practices that promote desirable change, thus creating a bias in the system in favour of the status quo (Gutmann and Thompson 2010).

To clarify the systemic approach for democracies, we need to consider the boundaries of the system, the functions within the system, and the standards by which the system should be evaluated.

Boundaries of the system

What are the boundaries of a deliberative system? In our current analysis, these boundaries define a decision-making arena that is at least loosely democratic. It is of course possible to think about a deliberative system independently of democracy. Authoritarian regimes have deliberation. Much deliberation goes on within the Catholic Church. Scientific communities could perhaps be said to have deliberative systems. But because we focus here on deliberative *democratic* systems, we begin with systems that are broadly defined by the norms, practices, and institutions of democracy.

As a first cut, we adopt here an institutional approach in which the deliberative system is conceptualized and evaluated as it functions within the boundaries of nation states, supranational states, international decision-making bodies, and the international institutions with which the nation states and supranational states are linked. Our analysis applies to all governmental and non-governmental institutions, including governance networks and the informal friendship networks that link individuals and groups discursively on matters of common concern.

One can define the boundaries of a deliberative system either institutionally or by reference to a particular issue. Both demarcations, however, include societal decisions. This important dimension added by the systemic approach has often been excluded from deliberative analysis. Informal discussion can contribute to an eventual state decision and to broad societal decisions, such as the decision not to settle a particular matter through the state. Such societal decisions in our understanding are emergent rather than definite. They are binding only in a loose social sense. As decisions by accretion (Mansbridge 1986), they have no clear-cut point at which an observer can say that a decision has been taken. Yet when the majority of a society or a subgroup changes its norms and practices, bringing to bear social sanctions on those who deviate from the new norms and practices, it seems fair to say that in a general way that majority has taken a decision, especially when the change has been accompanied by extensive discussion of the pros and cons of such a change. Thus the widespread societal conclusion that discrimination in hiring by race and gender is unjust is reasonably described as a collective decision, resulting in part from certain binding state decisions but also in large part from hundreds or millions of individual and institutional decisions based on widespread collective discussion and interaction. The lack of a clear decisional point in such emergent decisions provides one more reason why looking only at a part of a system can cause one to miss significant phenomena that affect deliberation. New emergent discourses change over time the way that people conceptualize problems – from explicit social agreements not to engage in genital cutting in Africa (Mackie forthcoming) to accepting the idea of sustainable development. We conceive of such discursive interactions as part of the deliberative system.

Other decisions with significant societal effects, for e:
rations to end sweatshop conditions, are not necessaril
legal sense, but when they derive from or affect the arg
in broad societal deliberation they are part of the deli
Sometimes exclusion from the state generates a livelier dis
environmental activists, excluded from the neo-corporati
from the late 1960s to the mid 1980s, generated some of the
green critiques of political economy at a distance from the state (Dryzek
et al. 2003; see also Dryzek 2010a: 170–6). Including societal discussions
and emergent decisions in a deliberative system does not, however, mean
including all talk. Our criteria for inclusion in a deliberative system are
that the discussions in question involve matters of common concern and
have a practical orientation. By a practical orientation we mean the discussion is not purely theoretical but involves an element of the question 'what
is to be done?'.

Deliberative systems include, roughly speaking, four main arenas: the
binding decisions of the state (both in the law itself and its implementation); activities directly related to preparing for those binding decisions;
informal talk related to those binding decisions;[2] and arenas of formal or
informal talk related to decisions on issues of common concern that are
not intended for binding decisions by the state.[3]

When Jürgen Habermas (1996) employed the spatial metaphor of
centre/periphery – the centre being the place of binding decisions (will-
formation) and the periphery being the place of less formal deliberation
(opinion-formation) – his deliberative system took the modern nation state
as its subject and made the legislature its centre. Many subsequent scholars
have done the same, conceiving of the deliberative system as 'rings' around
the state.[4] By contrast, our understanding of deliberative systems includes
both informal decisions by accretion and binding decisions that take place
outside the state. It goes beyond the boundaries of the nation state to
include international, transnational, and supranational institutions, and
extends as well to societal and institutional (e.g. corporate) decisions that
do not involve the state. We take the state and its legislatures as the ultimate decision-makers in a polity, but not as the centre to which everything

---

[2] This kind of talk is often described as informal '*political*' talk (Searing *et al.* 2007), talk
about '*politics*' (Neblo 2010), talk about '*public issues*' (Chambers, Chapter 3 in this volume; Jacobs *et al.* 2009), or 'private talk that is recognizably *political*' (Parkinson, Chapter
7, this volume), our emphases.

[3] The definition of 'common concern' in these non-state arenas is contested. Mansbridge
(1999) defined it as encompassing 'issues the public ought to discuss', thus making the
contest at its heart explicit.

[4] E.g. Searing (2007), Hendriks (2006a), and to some degree Neblo (2010).

.med in the polity's deliberative system. It is true that, to the degree .1at any given constitution and set of international agreements permit, the state can in theory make binding decisions in all issue areas. We also recognize the state's central role in solving human collective action problems by making and implementing binding decisions with a monopoly on the legitimate use of violence. Moreover, the state has a unique role to play in constituting deliberative systems. Liberal-democratic constitutional states create spaces of deliberation within political institutions such as legislatures and courts. They also enable deliberation within society by protecting free speech and association. They encourage deliberation by underwriting institutions in which deliberation is itself constitutive, such as universities and scientific research establishments. But even though states play a central and often constitutive role in deliberative systems, not all efficacious and important parts in the system lead to the state. The state is not the terminus of all deliberation. For example, our institutional demarcation of the deliberative system includes societal decisions, many of which have only a very indirect impact on state legislation.

A map of nodes in the deliberative system would reveal many nodes, with multiple forms of communication among them. Those nodes would include nation state bodies at different levels of government and with their different legislative houses, administrative agencies, the military, and the staffs of all of these; international bodies at different levels and their staffs; multinational corporations and local businesses; epistemic communities; foundations; political parties and factions within those parties; party campaigns and other partisan forums; religious bodies; schools; universities with their departments, fields, and disciplinary associations; unions, interest groups, voluntary associations and non-governmental organizations (NGOs) both *ad hoc* and long-standing; social movements with both their enclaves and their broader participation; the media including the internet, blogs, social media, interactive media, books, magazines, newspapers, film, and television; informal talk among politically active or less active individuals whether powerful or marginalized; and forms of subjugated and local knowledge that rarely surface for access by others without some opening in the deliberative system.

Functions of the deliberative system

In the systemic approach, we assess institutions according to how well they perform the functions necessary to promote the goals of the system. Theorists disagree about the goals of deliberation within a democracy, and thus they may not agree about the most important functions of a deliberative system. However, we believe that the system approach can accommodate a variety of functions and goals, and its value does not depend on resolving these disagreements. For our purposes, three functions that are relatively non-controversial in their most general articulation can serve to illustrate how a system approach can be applied. We identify epistemic, ethical, and democratic functions.

The *epistemic* function of a deliberative system is to produce preferences, opinions, and decisions that are appropriately informed by facts and logic and are the outcome of substantive and meaningful consideration of relevant reasons. A healthy deliberative system is one in which relevant considerations are brought forth from all corners, aired, discussed, and appropriately weighed. Locations in which this weighing occurs may or may not manifest publicity, although the absence of publicity often limits deliberative capacity. Because the topics of these deliberations are issues of common concern, epistemically well grounded preferences, opinions, and decisions must be informed by, and take into consideration, the preferences and opinions of fellow citizens.

In addition to the epistemic reasons for listening to what others have to say, there are also ethical reasons. A primary *ethical* function of the system is to promote mutual respect among citizens. Prudentially, mutual respect helps keep the deliberative system running. It serves as the lubricant of effective communication. Ethically, mutual respect among human beings is a good in itself. Mutual respect is also an ethical requirement among democratic citizens. The moral basis for mutual respect in democracy is grounded on the idea that citizens should be treated 'not merely as objects of legislation, as passive subjects to be ruled, but as autonomous agents who take part in the governance of their society, directly or through their representatives' (Gutmann and Thompson 2004).

This moral basis is not controversial, although how mutual respect should be interpreted in practice may be. It is more contestable than the epistemic function of simply improving informational quality and learning about others' preferences, opinions, and decisions. Theorists and citizens alike disagree about what mutual respect means, what constitutes its successful achievement and how weighty it is compared with other considerations. We stress mutual respect, however, because, even more than other ethical considerations, it is *intrinsically* a part of deliberation. To deliberate with another is to understand the other as a self-authoring source of reasons and claims. To fail to grant to another the moral status of authorship is, in effect, to remove oneself from the possibility of deliberative influence. By the same token, being open to being moved by the words of another is to respect the other as a source of reasons, claims, and perspectives. Other goods are closely linked with mutual respect. Mutual respect, for example, implies non-domination, because relationships of domination have already short-circuited mutual respect and, with this, deliberative influence.

A final function of deliberation, not completely separable from the first two, is to promote an inclusive political process on terms of equality. We call this the *democratic* function. The inclusion of multiple and plural voices, interests, concerns, and claims on the basis of feasible equality is not simply an ethic added to democratic deliberation; it is the central element of what makes deliberative democratic processes democratic. Who gets to be at the table affects the scope and content of the deliberation. For those excluded, no deliberative democratic legitimacy is generated. In short, a well functioning democratic deliberative system must not systematically exclude any citizens from the process without strong justification that could be reasonably accepted by all citizens, including the excluded. On the positive side, it ought also actively to promote and facilitate inclusion and the equal opportunities to participate in the system.[5]

The successful realization of all three of these functions promotes the legitimacy of democratic decision-making by ensuring reasonably sound decisions in the context of mutual respect among citizens and an inclusive process of collective choice. Legitimacy in this strong sense maximizes the chances that people who share a common fate will agree, willingly, to the terms of their common cooperation. Of course, these different functions can come into conflict within any democratically deliberative system. There will be controversy about their relative weights. Some deliberative democrats will assign, for example, much higher priority to mutual respect than to the aim of producing epistemically sound decisions.

Normatively, we endorse all three overarching functions, recognizing their potential conflicts and expecting that many conflicts will have to be worked out through deliberation on a provisional basis in any given context. A systemic approach allows for a nuanced application of these functions, recognizing that some will be more important than others in different parts of the system.

As our preceding discussion and some of our cases below illustrate, a systemic approach complicates the question of standards. What might be considered low quality or undemocratic deliberation in an individual instance might from a systems perspective contribute to an overall healthy deliberation. For example, not every group that participates in the democratic deliberation of the whole society need be internally fully democratic. The purposes of institutions and their functions in collective decisions will often dictate differing internal constraints on

---

[5] See Goodin (2007). Including affected interests may involve formal representation and new political rights (Bohman, Chapter 4, this volume).

deliberation, such as instructions to juries about rules of evidence, blind peer review, limitations on amendments to a bill that has gone through its final reading, or closed-door negotiations on sensitive matters. Judging the quality of the whole system on the basis of the functions and goals one specifies for the system does not require that those functions be fully realized in all the parts. This two-tier approach to evaluation will become clearer as we move through three examples of a systemic analysis of deliberation.

Many practitioners in the field of deliberative democracy are in the process of examining the conditions that promote or impede the performance of these epistemic, ethical, and inclusive functions, at the same time that theorists are investigating the appropriate standards for deliberation that promote these functions.[6] On the most abstract level, we argue simply that high quality deliberation promotes these functions effectively; low quality deliberation fails to do so as effectively. The question becomes more complex when we try to specify the conditions more concretely. For example, we might agree that sound epistemic grounding for decisions is one important function of the deliberative system but disagree about what conditions of deliberation produce epistemically sound decisions. Therefore in addition to the three larger functions we would also need a template to evaluate the conditions that support the various functions of good deliberation. This is, however, not a project that we will take up here. We turn instead to three examples that illustrate the deliberative approach.

Three systemic analyses

Experts

Any democratic system – indeed any decision-making entity of even the slightest complexity – must rely on experts at all levels within the system. Even a highly participatory workplace of only forty people, in which members spend as much as a seventh of their time in collective decision-making, relies on a division of labour in which some members of the collective develop expertise on which the others depend. In democracies of any size, however, controversy arises over where and when experts are appropriate and how expert deliberations can be connected to final policy decisions or the polity's more general direction. Only a systemic approach to deliberation can make this question tractable.

---

[6] See Mansbridge *et al.* (2010) on the evolution from 'classic' standards of deliberation to more contemporary ones.

A deliberative systemic approach allows us to appreciate the division of labour within which experts operate and, for problems that arise, devise remedies that draw upon the many different stages and loci in the full deliberative process. We can then judge sequences of stages and loci on their systemic capacity to draw from the rewards of expertise while reducing the potential deliberative costs of bias, disrespect and non-inclusion. The following analysis looks at these costs, each linked to one of the functions of a deliberative democratic system, then suggests systemic ways to reduce those costs.

Epistemically, delegation to experts can promote citizen ignorance, with highly negative consequences for the deliberative system as a whole. In addition, experts themselves can be biased. The world in which they communicate can be deeply self-referential. Policy experts may orient themselves primarily towards their professional discipline, following technically attractive models that once put into practice produce detrimental results for the polity. Subtle or crass self-interest, whether in the academic or private sector, can affect their conceptions of or policy recommendations for the public good. Their own experience may be far narrower than they realize. Experts are particularly likely to ignore the experience of marginalized groups. In 1955, Cook County Hospital had to decide whether to expand its central facility or build a second facility in another area. The hospital's deliberative process involved experts on issues that ranged from parking to the costs and benefits of gathering advanced medical equipment in one place versus siting in proximity to underserved populations through a second branch. Based on extensive expert deliberation, the hospital decided to build a second branch. That decision, however, met with significant opposition from spokespeople for the Chicago African American community, because creating a second branch of the racially integrated public hospital in the chosen area would undermine a proposed campaign to force private hospitals in that area to integrate. The experts had never even considered this issue (Banfield 1961).

Delegation to experts threatens the ethical function when it produces expert disrespect for citizen contributions and even for citizens themselves as a result of the sheer complexity and importance of some policy decisions. Particularly when faced with life and death decisions, experts sometimes need deliberative protection from the ignorance, emotional volatility, and myopia of the non-expert. Yet that protection can generate deliberative disdain among the experts, which then provokes a reciprocal disdain of experts on the part of citizens.

The democratic problem of inclusion in expert rule is simply that the exclusion of non-experts from decisions threatens the foundation of democracy itself as rule by the people. Even when the people set the ends while the experts in theory address only the means (Christiano, Chapter 2), the process of discussing, experimenting with, and implementing the means often clarifies and poses new problems for the ends. Excluding non-experts from the processes of deliberating over the means undermines the public's goal-setting role in a democracy.

A systemic approach to deliberation can help by stepping back from any individual instance of deliberation in which non-experts are excluded to evaluate the place of that individual instance in the larger deliberative system. The standard approach to the problem of experts looks primarily at the legitimacy of the delegation and the relation of the final decision to citizen preferences. A systemic approach also looks at the division of labour in deliberation, at deliberative stages and forms of recursive and redundant non-expert input, at processes designed to surface the knowledge of disadvantaged and subordinate groups, at participatory innovations designed to make citizens into experts, and at the role of many forms of trusted proxies. Expertise within a system need not be constructed as a hierarchy: in some circumstances citizens can divide and distribute their labours, so that many contribute their expertise to common decisions at differing points in decision processes. In other circumstances, when otherwise competent experts are not adept at explaining the reasons for their decisions to non-experts, the system as a whole requires some agents with the capacity to translate expert conclusions into recommendations that citizens can understand.

A systemic approach also draws attention to the way that expert authority is itself often conditionally earned through deliberative means and within specialized deliberative communities. Thus experts are often subject to deliberative accountability through networks of their peers (Goodin 2003a). In such circumstances we may trust experts because we can ask them to explain and to justify their advice or decisions, if not to us directly then to a group of their peers who in turn have earned their credentials in a deliberatively trustworthy manner. Yet the entire peer network may itself be biased. In a good deliberative system, expert authority must be deliberatively generated and evaluated with safeguards against systemic bias (Warren 1996).

Deliberative stages include the selection of experts and the appropriate delegation of authority to them, the expert deliberation itself, and the processes of retrospective analysis and consent. Improvements in expert–citizen deliberative interaction can come in any of these stages. The disconnect between citizens and experts can be bridged by improving the efficacy of multiple chains of intelligibility in which 'translators' make sense of expert considerations for citizens and vice versa (Christiano, Chapter 2). Partisan adversary processes can provide a form of trusted proxy when citizens can rightly trust political parties through reputation and parties both select their own experts and hold them accountable.[7]

Participatory innovations allow citizens to develop their own expertise and provide channels through which the citizens' own expertise can influence policy (Smith 2009). For example, as the primary group that collects wood, Nepalese rural women have expertise in identifying disturbed locations in the forest. When new participatory political practices allow these women to add their expertise more directly to the deliberative system that produces policy decisions, they help correct the errors that professional experts make in understanding local forestry practices and possibilities (Agarwal 2010).

In an important recent development, democratic polities have begun to create new forms of trusted proxy by inserting in the deliberative system relatively randomly selected citizen bodies in which the citizens themselves become experts in an issue and then serve as trusted proxies to other citizens (MacKenzie and Warren, Chapter 5). Robert Dahl (1970) once suggested a third house of the US congress made up of randomly selected citizens, based on the ancient Athenian model of the lot, precisely in order to provide greater citizen input into complex decisions that required more expertise than citizens could usually acquire. Dahl did not expect his third house actually to be created. But now, forty years later, we are seeing a proliferation of groups, ranging in size from six to several hundred, that look much like Dahl's model. They are typically selected through nearly random processes, and provided the time and resources to develop greater expertise on an issue. They can then provide to their fellow citizens a more expert, deliberated, and informed version of what other citizens might think if they too became more expert on the issue. The British Columbia Citizens' Assembly is perhaps the most well known of such groups (Warren and Pearse 2008). This relatively randomly selected body of citizens was charged with choosing an electoral system for the province that would then be put before the citizenry as a whole in a referendum. The Citizens' Assembly required that its citizen members become informal experts on electoral systems over the many weekends that it met in the course of a year. Some provisions in establishing that assembly, such as its screen against members with material or pressure-group interests in the issue, its balanced materials, and its nonpartisan sponsorship, increased citizen trust in this relatively expert proxy group and gave citizens a second-order reason to trust its conclusions when the first-order reasons for and against the different choices required expertise beyond the grasp of most citizens.

---

[7] On the deliberative functions of parties, see White and Ypi (2011).

Certainly, the introduction of such bodies may have other systemic effects. Inserting the Citizens' Assembly into the British Columbia deliberation on electoral processes destabilized the previous deliberative dominance of the political parties, including the Green Party, which had made a particular electoral reform (not chosen by the Citizens' Assembly) one of the major planks in its political platform. A similar partial displacement of existing advocacy groups occurred, as mentioned earlier, when the British government introduced randomized deliberative forums into the health service debate (Parkinson 2006a). Any introduction of randomized deliberative entities, such as citizen juries or deliberative polls, into a deliberative system has the potential for undermining an existing equilibrium by creating new citizen 'experts' and trusted proxies, and thus disadvantaging political parties and advocacy groups that had previously invested considerable political and social capital in creating deliberative trust (Papadopoulos, Chapter 6). Sometimes this displacement is exactly what the system as a whole needs; sometimes it can undermine the epistemic, ethical, and democratic functions of the whole.

Political parties and interest group associations can also make experts to some extent accountable to ordinary citizens by embedding the experts in larger groups whose members share common aims. Experts on the political Right contest the knowledge of experts on the political Left and vice versa. NGOs develop their own expertise and act as intermediaries between partisan and unaffiliated experts and citizens. NGOs can also create channels of input from citizens to experts on the nature of the problems to be solved.

These different ways of connecting experts with citizens can improve the deliberative system in its epistemic function by bringing in more – and more diverse – knowledge, in its ethical function by reducing the lack of respect between experts and citizens, and in its democratic function by including the perspectives and interests of more citizens. They thereby serve to promote the normative legitimacy of the system overall.

Pressure and protest

Jürgen Habermas famously described deliberation as ideally containing only the 'forceless force of the better argument' (Habermas 1975: 108). Very generally, most conceptions of deliberation attempt to distinguish deliberative interaction from other non-deliberative forms of action in which coercion, pressure, or strategic payoffs are the dominant force rather than reason-giving and persuasion on the basis of relevant considerations.[8]

---

[8] For the related practice of bargaining and its role in deliberative democracy, see e.g. Mansbridge et al. (2010) and Gutmann and Thompson (1996: 57–8, 69–75).

Behind all these conceptions is the intuition that being pressured into doing something and being persuaded into it are different. Deliberation is about genuine persuasion, not pressure. A full systemic theory of deliberation would require an elaborated defence of where to draw the line between pressure and persuasion, particularly in light of the standard for democratic deliberation that only the force of the better argument should prevail. Although we do not do that here, we suggest the contours of such a defence.

Non-deliberative pressure comes in many forms. Two of the most difficult for deliberative theory involve money and protest. Both paying people to agree with you and disrupting normal activity until you get your way appear to violate the very core of deliberative persuasion. But money and protest can be effective political tools to advance important social and political causes. A deliberative system approach allows us to step back and ask how this expenditure of money (e.g. in campaign advertisements) or that protest (e.g. an anti-immigrant demonstration or a Greenpeace action) enhances or detracts from the deliberative system.

To illustrate this approach, we will take a closer look at protest. Protest often appears to violate several standards of deliberation. When protest explicitly or implicitly threatens sanctions or imposes costs, it acts as a form of coercion.[9] The slogans protestors use to excite enthusiasm and convey a dramatic message also often undermine epistemic subtlety. Finally, protest sometimes involves levels of disruption and contestation that reduce mutual respect and full inclusion. A forum attempting to engage in the respectful mutual exchange of considerations for or against a policy may, for example, be disrupted by picketers, hecklers, and individuals engaged in shouting down the speakers so that they cannot be heard (Estlund 2001). Could such apparently anti-deliberative behaviours ever enhance the deliberative system? From a systemic perspective, the answer sometimes will be yes. Protest contributes to the deliberative system most clearly as a remedial force introduced to correct or publicize a failure or weakness in fulfilling any or all of its key functions (Fung 2005). Protest can facilitate and promote the circulation of useful information; it can facilitate and promote ethically respectful interactions among citizens;

---

[9] For a definition of coercion as the threat of sanction or the use of force, see Mansbridge *et al.* (2010). However, note that in a systemic perspective what *counts* as coercion may depend on the relation of an individual act to the larger context in which it takes place. For example, a public relations campaign by a corporation to promote anti-union 'right to work' laws may seem or be non-coercive by itself, but may become coercive if it takes place in a context in which other people are engaging in intimidation of union members in other parts of the system. More generally, the normative force of a concept in one part of a system varies depending on what else in happening in other parts of a system.

and it can begin to correct inequalities in access to
more voices and interests into the decision-making

For example, we could imagine using pressure to
marginalized voices or force new reasons, facts, and
lic conversation. In such cases this pressure might
negative, contribution to the ethical function of re
action. These cases pose trade-offs within the system
existing political situation, levels of civility may ha
for levels of inclusion to go up.[10]

Concretely, certain disruptive and only weakly civil Radical Left or
Tea Party protests enhance the deliberative system if they can be reasonably understood as giving voice to a minority opinion long ignored in the
public sphere, or as bringing more and better important information into
the public arena. This is a big if. Figuring out the pros and cons for this
and similar questions is a core undertaking of any deliberative system
analysis.

A systemic analysis must be able to make these judgments and must
have the analytic tools to do so. Without criteria to evaluate when non-
deliberative, weakly deliberative, or even anti-deliberative behaviour
nevertheless enhances the deliberative system, one risks falling into the
blind spot of old style functionalism: everything can be seen as, in one
way or another, contributing to the system. Thus a systemic analysis of
Tea Party protests and disruptions, or of Greenpeace or labour action,
requires a detailed analysis of the possible pluses and minuses with regard
to the deliberative system and a weighing of the results. In regard to certain Tea Party or Radical Left examples, we might in the end want to say
that although these movements brought new voices into public debate,
a move that is system enhancing, these benefits were outweighed by the
partisan and aggressive tenor of many of the public protests and disruptions, a context that creates a toxic atmosphere for deliberation and thus
is not system enhancing over time. In this analysis much would depend
on a combination of empirical and conceptual-analytic findings regarding
the short-run and long-run inequalities redressed by the protesters and the
short-run and long-run chilling effects of their actions upon deliberation.

Political media

Although the political media are a crucial part of the deliberative system in
any modern democracy, they have not played a major role in much recent
deliberative democracy theory. Many innovative deliberative initiatives

---

[10] Sanders (1997), Young (2000), Mansbridge *et al.* (2010).

stitutions are designed to exclude or minimize the role of the media deliberation. 'Face-to-face' means eliminating mediation. A theoretical focus on individual instances of deliberation that involve only face-to-face unmediated communication may implicitly or explicitly impugn the value of the media.

A systemic approach to deliberation sees the media as connecting many parts of the deliberative system. Few citizens in any country read the transcripts of parliamentary and committee debates or even know what other citizens in other parts of the country are saying. Citizen knowledge of debates both in government and in the public sphere comes through the media, along with the framing and perspective-setting in which all media must, by their nature, engage.

The growing proliferation of different types of political media, performing different functions within the system, makes it hard to generalize about the systemic role of the media, let alone any particular form. One source may play different roles at different times or in regard to different issues. The many roles of the media appear in the different roles media professionals craft for themselves in addition to sellers of stories: vigilant watchdogs over power, representatives of citizens and communities, knowledge translators, educators of citizens, and public advocates, among others. A rich and sophisticated literature in media studies tracks and analyses the role of media in democracy. This literature, some of which already takes a relatively systemic approach, can serve as a general guide to the role of the media in a deliberative system. Our account, accordingly, will highlight only the epistemic, ethical, and democratic functions of the media in the deliberative system.

Epistemically, any democracy needs the political media to play the role of transmitter of reliable and useful information, to help citizens interpret facts and make connections between facts, roles, and policies, and to act as watchdogs, critics, and investigators. The epistemic function of the media is strengthened through self-policing as when, for example, one news source exposes the information failures of another. Yet the systemic incentives for media are well known to have their dysfunctional sides for the deliberative system. Efforts in 'civic journalism' to align these incentives more fully with citizen democratic needs have been only partially successful.

Partisan media are the lifeblood of any deliberative system designed along adversarial lines to advance the flow of information and insight through the marketplace of competition in ideas. Theorists from John Stuart Mill to Nancy Rosenblum have made an excellent case for such partisanship.[11] Recently, however, the increase in partisan reporting in the US

---

[11] Rosenblum (2010); also see Muirhead (2006).

has provoked particular concern about the temptation in these media to falsify the facts and disseminate misinformation. Some partisan internet and even television commentators seem more than occasionally to have displayed a reckless disregard for the truth. A systemic approach does not imply that such reckless disregard enhances the overall deliberative system. If a particular individual purveys outright falsehoods, that one individual does not advance the epistemic goals of the deliberative system. But a systemic approach has to go beyond individuals and ask questions such as whether partisan reporting itself increases the likelihood of misinformation and fact bending. The partisan media may contain their own partial corrective for this pathology, as the other side is always looking for the false move of its adversary. Yet, misrepresentations and falsehoods survive even in the atmosphere of heightened scrutiny that often accompanies partisan news battles.

Ethically, the news and other media greatly affect the tone of civility and respect among citizens. Certain kinds of partisan news commentary significantly raise the levels of incivility between citizens, as they did, for example, in the US in the 1900s (Schudson 1978). But it is not clear that partisanship in and of itself is uncivil or involves a lack of respect. Furthermore, at times (as noted in our discussion of protest) shrillness and disrespect may be warranted to raise awareness or get an issue on the agenda. Partisanship in itself is not in principle antithetical to the ethical function of the deliberative system.

Finally, the media play a significant role in democratic political inclusion. The internet holds forth the promise of democratization, but its usage today tracks the usual class patterns (Schlozman *et al.* 2010). To the extent that citizens increasingly get their political information from the internet, the 'digital divide' will continue to undermine the deliberative function of political inclusion. In addition, the tendency of the internet and now the media in general to segregate audiences into like-minded 'niches' prevents citizens from hearing the other side and developing respect for people with whom they disagree. As many have worried, these new technologies may facilitate niche or echo-chamber communication, in which the like-minded talk only with one another (Sunstein 2003).

We should think of any particular deliberative setting as embedded in a deliberative system held together in great part through the media. For example, the British Columbia Citizens' Assembly on electoral reform was designed to function in some isolation from media coverage. Although it had staff responsible for communications during its process of learning and deliberation, it lacked a budget for communicating its recommendation to the broader public (Warren and Pearse 2008). Nevertheless, here, as in a similar Citizens' Assembly in Ontario, the decisions reached in the assemblies were eventually put before the general public for debate and then a referendum. Knowledge of what went on in the assembly, its mode of deliberation, its rationale, and the people who participated in it was communicated to the public primarily by the press (although the government provided brochures). In retrospect, the failure of the government to provide for any deliberative linkage between the minipublic and the broader public was a mistake: by default, it left responsibility for broader public deliberation to the media. There was a marked difference in the tone of the coverage in British Columbia, where the initiative won 58 per cent of the popular vote, and that in Ontario, where it received only 37 per cent. The British Columbia press was generally more favourable to the idea of a citizens' assembly and spent more time (although still not much time) examining how the assembly worked and why it had been chosen to make the agenda-setting decision about the electoral system. The Ontario news media spent less time transmitting relevant information about the deliberation in this institution to the other parts of the deliberative system. Was this a systemic failure? As Parkinson (Chapter 7) points out, the media have few incentives to focus on either the actual workings of any deliberative forum or the arguments and information transmitted therein. Their viewers are not sufficiently interested in these questions for them to be 'news' or even 'human interest'. Yet the media, with their market incentives, serve as the major links to and among the citizenry within any deliberative system. This structure of incentives seems to point to a systemic failure. A systemic approach contributes to this ongoing discussion by situating these questions in the context of the epistemic, ethical, and political functions of a deliberative system in a democracy.

Defects in the deliberative system

The ideal of a deliberative system, then, is a loosely coupled group of institutions and practices that together perform the three functions we have identified – seeking truth, establishing mutual respect, and generating inclusive, egalitarian decision-making. In this section, we describe five pathologies that keep political institutional arrangements from approaching more closely the deliberative ideal in the system as whole: tight-coupling; decoupling; institutional domination; social domination; and entrenched partisanship.

One virtue of a deliberative system is that failures in one institution can be compensated for in another part. When an expert community is too beholden to some conception of disease or risk, for example, citizen organizations or journalists can bring latent experiences and etiologies to their attention (Corburn 2005; Epstein 1996; Brown 1992). But when the parts of a deliberative system are *too tightly coupled* to one another, this self-corrective quality is lost. Think of tight coupling as the problem of group-think writ large, at institutional scale.[12] Perhaps the most familiar experiences of dramatic deliberative system failure from this pathology arise at the nation-state level when some public issue is driven by nationalism or xenophobia and those sentiments begin to drive individuals who inhabit all of the locations in a deliberative system. In the decision of the US Government to intern Japanese-Americans during World War II, for example, what we now believe to be the force of the better argument did not prevail because that argument could find no institutional point of purchase in the deliberative system of that time and place.

A second defect in the deliberative system arises when the parts of the system become *decoupled* from one another in the sense that good reasons arising from one part fail to penetrate the others. Ideally, one would expect the large parts of a deliberative system to converge over time to accept good reasons, at least provisionally, even as each part is open to different considerations in the process of converging. For example, many industrialized democracies now face difficult questions about how best to address their fiscal crises – whether to increase the tax burden, who should suffer that burden, and which public services and social welfare protections to reduce. Proposals and reasons for those proposals emanate from many parts of the deliberative system in these societies – from legislatures, expert commissions, the executive branch, the courts, foundations, universities, public opinion, and even citizen deliberations specifically structured around this topic. In the ideal, through processes of convergence, mutual influence, and mutual adjustment, each of these parts would consider reasons and proposals generated in the other parts.

It may be the case, however, that some parts are particularly resistant to arguments from other parts. Experts, legislative committees, and citizens in the public sphere, for example, may listen to reasons more broadly, while legislators who have not worked on the issue respond primarily to parochial interests – a constituency's pet project or a mobilized but extreme minority opposed to increasing taxes no matter what the costs. Another example of deliberative decoupling is the resistance of some legislators and interest groups in the US to data from the scientific community on global warming.

Third, a deliberative system also fails when one of its parts, whether deliberative or not, dominates all of the others. This problem of *institutional domination* (or in a weaker form, undue influence) appears most starkly in authoritarian societies where a state, party, or leader controls not

---

[12] See Janis (1982) for small group 'group-think'.

only the government but also the media and even civil-society organizations. Even in democratic systems, however, institutional domination can arise, as in Silvio Berlusconi's corporate control of major mass media outlets when he was prime minister.

A fourth and related pathology of the deliberative system is *social domination*. It arises when a particular social interest or social class controls or exerts undue influence over many parts of the deliberative systems. Those who possess and control wealth, for example, exercise disproportionate influence in most, if not all, capitalist democracies. From the perspective of the deliberative system, this situation is especially problematic if the effect of wealth is to shift the balance of reasons for laws and policies at multiple sites in the deliberative system – through, for example, financial support for political campaigns, private ownership of concentrated media, financial backing that tilts the ecology of secondary associations and interest groups (Walzer 2002), and even financing university-based research.

Finally, the deliberative system suffers when citizens, legislators, and administrators are so divided, by ideology, ethnicity, religion, or any other cleavage, that they will not listen to positions other than those emanating from their side. We have made clear above that not every part of the deliberative system need itself be deliberative in this respect. Zealous advocacy, protest, and partisan journalism can all contribute to the quality and depth of deliberation in the system as a whole. These political activities enhance deliberation by offering new reasons or making it more likely that old reasons are considered in an equitable way. But reaping these benefits requires an audience that itself possesses the deliberative disposition to weigh reasons and proposals. That audience might be citizens in the mass public, legislators, bureaucrats, or all three. Yet if these audiences are themselves zealously polarized or otherwise non-deliberative, the arguments fall on deaf ears or reach only the already convinced. Acts of civil disobedience contribute to deliberation by causing an audience (e.g. the public in segregation-era America) to reconsider the justice of its positions (e.g. segregation).[13] If that audience is unreceptive to reasons because it has already made up its mind or has decided not to think more about the question, civil disobedience will not advance public deliberation.

Conclusion

From the beginning deliberative theory has had the ambition to provide a normative and empirical account of the democratic process as a whole.

---

[13] See discussion of civil disobedience in Rawls (1971); Dworkin (1985).

The development of such an account has proceeded incrementally. Much of the work during the first phase focused on developing the ideal of deliberation – its meaning, justification, and responses to theoretical criticisms. Particularly important at this stage was laying out the idea of legitimacy at the core of deliberative democracy. Many theorists formulated the deliberative ideal on the foundational requirement that legitimate decisions be those that 'everyone could accept' or at least 'not reasonably reject'. Above all, any conception of deliberative democracy must be organized around an ideal of political justification requiring free public reasoning of equal citizens (Cohen 1996; Gutmann and Thompson 1996; Habermas 1995). This phase emphasized what might be called ideal proceduralism as a 'regulative' ideal (that is, one that recognizably cannot be achieved fully in practice but sets a standard at which to aim).

A second phase – a 'coming of age' – saw the proliferation of empirical studies and practical applications of the theory (Bohman 1998). Ideal proceduralism had encouraged thinking of the standards for deliberative legitimacy through the image of an ideal deliberative forum. Thus in this second phase, many deliberative democrats started with this image as they tried to think about the ideal in concrete terms and seek approximations in the real world. Activists, theorists, and government officials collaborated on introducing into democratic politics many new varieties of deliberative forums, including citizens' juries, consensus councils, people's parliaments, citizens' assemblies, and other relatively representative 'minipublics' designed to make possible deliberation within some approximation of a microcosm of the citizenry (see e.g. Fung 2003). This practical and empirical turn opened the door for empirical political scientists to study a variety of settings in which deliberative democracy might work well or badly (Thompson 2008a). The empirical studies began to address issues such as the conditions that enable or constrain good deliberative processes.

As we have noted, however, most of these empirical studies addressed discrete instances of deliberation, investigated with little if any attention to their relationship to the system as a whole (Thompson 2008a). This limitation is understandable. The challenges of conducting research on discrete cases is formidable enough without attempting to relate the findings to deliberation in other parts of the political system, let alone to non-deliberative practices in the system. Ultimately, however, none of these deliberative processes can be studied adequately in isolation, apart from their broader, systemic context. Legislative forums, deliberative minipublics, and other communicative venues have unique and sometimes central roles in deliberative systems, but no single institution can meet all of the demands of deliberative democracy at once. It takes a study of deliberation beyond specific arenas, however important they may be, to understand how each venue is influenced by interactions across the various parts of the deliberative system as a whole.

The literature has now reached a point that makes it possible and desirable to begin a third phase, and to try to make good on the original promise of a comprehensive account. Deliberative theory is ultimately concerned with the democratic process as a whole, and therefore with the relationships of its parts to the whole. Deliberative democracy is more than a sum of deliberative moments.

We have proposed here a systemic approach that is intended to guide the progress in this third phase of work on deliberative democracy. We have shown how an analysis of deliberative functions – epistemic, ethical, and democratic, each contributing in different ways to the legitimacy of the system – can illuminate not only the more familiar and obviously deliberative practices in a system, but also the value or disvalue of non-deliberative practices that have often been considered antithetical to deliberative democracy.

We have considered only a few of those practices as illustrations, and have not attempted at all to examine empirically the conditions under which they may promote or impede the goals of the deliberative system as a whole. Nor have we explored in detail the ways in which the various deliberative functions may interact with one another. But we have shown how the systemic approach can serve as a framework for a wide-ranging and fruitful normative and empirical study of the democratic process from a deliberative perspective.

2

Rational deliberation among experts and citizens

THOMAS CHRISTIANO

The point of democratic deliberation

The primary purposes of democratic discussion and deliberation are to enhance our understanding of the interests of all the members of society and of how to advance those interests in a just and equitable way. It does this with an eye to making collective decisions, which have as their aim the equal advancement of the interests of the members of society. So the purpose of democratic discussion is epistemic and practical, it is to uncover facts about interests and equality and how best to pursue them for the purpose of making good collective decisions.

The contents of democratic deliberation concern first, the interests of persons; second, the just way of accommodating the interests of persons; third, the means for advancing the interests of persons; and fourth, the consequences of these activities. Broadly speaking, then, democratic deliberation concerns the aims the society ought to pursue and the means and consequences of pursuing those aims.

But democratic discussion pursues the goal of enhanced understanding in a particular way; it is constrained by a principle of justice, which asserts that this process of discovery must be pursued in an egalitarian way. It must be pursued in such a way that all have the opportunity to participate in influencing the process of discussion and the interests of all are properly taken into account. But most of all, it must be pursued in such a way that the distinct views and interests of every person are given a fair hearing in the process.

It is only one part of the overall democratic process, which includes organization, mobilization, bargaining, compromise, and voting as essential constituents. These latter are essential because, for the most part, disagreement remains after substantial discussion on the merits of different views and the process of collective decision-making must proceed in that context. But disagreement is not only inevitable; it is normally quite fruitful in that it challenges the assumptions and dogmas of fallible human beings. Still, deliberation and discussion are an essential part of the democratic process because without the improvement of understanding they bring, the activities of mobilization and bargaining have limited worth.[1]

To the extent that the production of understanding is the central aim of democratic deliberation and the object of understanding is immensely complicated, the process of deliberation requires a division of labour if it is to be even moderately successful. This is particularly true in large-scale democracies. But the division of labour has traditionally been a problem for democracy and a problem for an egalitarian society. The question for us, then, is how can we enjoy the advantages of the division of labour in politics while treating each other as equals?

The division of labour

One of the most important features of deliberation in a modern democratic state is that it is differentiated. That is, discussion on matters of policy and law, with the ultimate intention of influencing the making of law and policy, takes place in very different settings. These different settings are evaluated normally by different standards but they are meant to fit together as a whole because they are meant to make contributions to a process of collective decision-making. One reason for this differentiation is an intellectual division of labour with respect to matters of discussion of policy. The evaluation of policy includes many different elements such as expert knowledge in the sciences, expertise in the current state of play in law and policy, expertise in how to achieve the compromises necessary to make legislation, the local knowledge of those who are especially affected by legislation and the participation of ordinary citizens in the choice of the aims of policy. All of this takes place within the context of substantial and reasonable disagreement in all of these areas.[2]

---

[1] This general conception of democratic deliberation is defended in my book *The Constitution of Equality* (Christiano 2008). There I criticize a major alternative, that of Joshua Cohen, as well as in Christiano (2009).

[2] This division of labour occurs in many different settings including the operation of minipublics and citizen juries in which experts are called in to explain the science and policy backgrounds of possible policies and ordinary citizens are meant to discuss policy alternatives against the background of these briefings by experts. The operation not

The major normative/social scientific questions about this differen-tiation of democratic discussion concern how the parts fit together and whether the division of labour can be made compatible with the kind of equality that is thought to be the basis of democratic rule.

In this chapter I will focus on the division of labour between experts and ordinary citizens in the process of discussion in a democratic soci-ety. My concern will be with whether such a division of labour is possible as a democratic and integrated whole. In particular I am concerned with the question of whether a democratic society can adequately utilize the intellectual resources a division of labour provides in a way that is compat-ible with the idea of rational discussion among citizens about policy and law. First, I will outline a critique of rational discussion at a society-wide level from a Downsian perspective. Second, I will articulate a conception of the democratic process that attempts to reconcile the division of labour with democratic equality. Third, I will discuss the problems of expertise in a democratic society. I will attempt to show how discussion including expertise can work well and what the limits of rational discussion are in this context. I will argue that it is possible to have a reasonably well func-tioning democratic division of labour including expertise and I will char-acterize some main conditions of that deliberative structure as I see it.

The Downsian critique

At first glance, one might think that the parts cannot fit together at all as a genuine division of labour. On Anthony Downs's conception of the operation of a large democratic society, citizens are rationally ignorant of the facts of the society and of the knowledge necessary to make reasonable policy, while politicians do have some knowledge (Downs 1957). Citizens are rationally ignorant because they have so little expected impact on the outcomes of elections that they have no incentive to do the hard work of collecting information necessary to decide which the best candidates are. Since the expected benefit of voting the right way is so small and the cost of becoming informed is fairly large, the citizen has no self-interested reason to become informed to make a good decision.

Downs qualifies this vision of the rational ignorance of citizens. Some citizens are well informed about certain policy areas as by-products of their particular activities in the society. Public interest lawyers are well informed

only uses a mini division of labour in the process but presupposes the larger intellectual division of labour of the society as a whole. For a discussion of minipublics and deliber-ation, see Robert Goodin (2008: chs. 2–3). See also Parkinson (2006a) for a careful and empirically informed discussion of the claims of minipublics.

about aspects of the law. Tax lawyers are well informed about parts of the tax code. Social scientists are well informed about parts of the political system and/or the social and economic structure of the society. Another qualification Downs allows is that citizens can make use of cognitive shortcuts to knowledge about how to advance their interests. In particular they can use party affiliation and opinion leaders as proxies for determining how their interests and concerns can be advanced. They needn't always be highly informed for the purpose of making good decisions.[3]

A more complex picture of the division of labour

The first thing to notice about the version of the Downsian model above is that it is a vastly oversimplified picture of the kind of discussion that goes on in a democratic society with an eye to the making of policy. There are only two kinds of agents in this system: citizens and politicians. There are no interest group associations, no political parties, no newspapers, no media, no universities, no think tanks, no web logs and so on. In short, there are none of the many institutions and groupings that are distinctive of democratic societies. Indeed, what is characteristic of democratic societies is that there are many of each of these kinds of organizations and activities, each one promoting its own point of view and participating in discussion and debate with many others. And many of these groups are devoted to political issues. This distinguishes democratic societies from non-democratic societies in which there are very few such entities, which tend not to have much in the way of opposition.

Presumably, at least one important reason why there are so many groups of these sorts devoted to politics in modern democratic societies is that they make some sort of difference to the politics of that society. The groups exist with the purpose of influencing policy in one way or another and their continued existence depends on there being some real such influence.

We need not accept the self-interest model in the strong form that Downs and others seem to accept to see that this division of labour poses problems for democratic societies. The deep insight in the Downsian way of thinking about politics is that any large-scale society is organized as a division of labour. Each has tasks to perform that require specialization and an investment of a great deal of time and effort. Few have the time and energy for putting a great deal of effort into political discussion and reflection. The intricacies of law and policy and the empirical research necessary to justify

---

[3] In one recent discussion of the Downsian argument, these last complications are ignored. Pincione and Teson (2006) use the Downsian argument and some psychological theses to argue that rational deliberation at the level of the nation state is profoundly unlikely.

policy as well as the reflection necessary to put together packages of law and policy are significantly too complex and extensive for most citizens to have a good grasp of them. This is not for lack of native talent but simply because each citizen has a job of their own to do and these latter activities are themselves full-time jobs. Furthermore, once a person has completed their job, and made their contribution to the household, they have some entitlement to some time off from hard work. And politics and political issues are hard work. So there is little time left over for politics and politically important issues.[4] Even someone who is morally committed to good politics would experience serious limits to their capacity to read up on and reflect on the many difficult and complex issues that arise in a democratic society.[5] Downs thinks that the kind of division of labour I have described is incompatible with the ideal of political equality.

Truth sensitivity

Some recent Downsian approaches assert that contemporary democracies are subject to massive discourse failure. Discourse failure involves discourse that produces political positions that are traceable to truth insensitive processes. A truth insensitive process is one that disregards the best available reasons, understood as those that define the *status quaestionis* in the relevant reliable scholarly disciplines (Pincione and Teson 2006: 17).

The problem of truth insensitivity is important because it identifies one of the chief challenges for democratic deliberation. The question is: how does one integrate the specialized knowledge of the sciences into democratic deliberation when it is clearly relevant to good decision-making? The worry is that we cannot take democratic deliberation seriously if ordinary citizens generally ignore relevant specialized scientific knowledge when they are deliberating on issues that require such knowledge. Indeed, we might want to look for other non-democratic means for making decisions in that case. By way of illustration, Pincione and Teson focus their attention on the fact that majorities of US citizens are in favour of minimum wage legislation and trade protectionism, which they claim to be shown to be very suboptimal by the findings of contemporary economics. They argue that most citizens are somehow unable to see that minimum wage legislation and protectionism are harmful to the US economy and thus to citizens. They assert that citizens are systematically biased against economic explanations since these are essentially opaque and counterintuitive. Citizens elect politicians who offer these policies in their platforms and so

---

[4] See Hardin (2009) for an attempt to characterize this worry in a more nuanced way.
[5] See Jacobs *et al.* (2009) for a discussion of the extent of current participation.

both citizens and politicians ignore the consensus opinion among economists regarding the effects of the minimum wage and trade protectionism. Thus they ignore the best available knowledge on these questions. From this, Pincione and Teson (2006) infer that the political process exhibits discourse failure and is a truth insensitive process.[6]

I conceive of the problem of truth sensitivity as a problem concerning the division of labour. The question is, are the different parts of the division of labour integrated in such a way that each part is genuinely doing the work that enables the other parts to do their work properly? The thesis of discourse failure and truth insensitivity asserts in this case that the parts of the division of labour that are concerned with arriving at sophisticated and well developed understandings of the social world are not properly integrated with the parts that are concerned with decision-making. The parts of the system that make decisions do not make those decisions on the basis of adequate understandings of how the objects of decision-making work. For example, Pincione and Teson (2006) argue that the work of economists does not have sufficient impact on economic policy-making. This makes decisions concerning the economy essentially blind to the mechanics of the object.[7] They think deeply unwise policy-making is the consequence.[8]

I think that this conclusion is premature and likely to be quite overstated. But it poses a very useful challenge to the conception of rational deliberation in a democracy that I favour, which is centrally focused on making law and policy depend on the best available understanding of the social and political system. In this chapter I want to bring together some ideas that may serve as the beginning of an answer to this kind of challenge. I will argue that Pincione and Teson's conception of how the division of labour is supposed to work is deeply flawed. I will also argue that they miss the fact that it might actually be working by their own standards.

[6] There are a lot of difficulties with the Pincione and Teson discussion. One of them is that there is a lot of debate among economists about the efficacy and consequences of minimum wage legislation and there is serious economic debate about the consequences of at least some elements of protectionist legislation such as protection of infant industries and capital controls.

[7] The disconnect need not cut the society off from economic knowledge. One could advocate a system in which citizens are disconnected from the division of labour but where they have little input beyond voting and experts inform the politicians directly about wise policy. Caplan (2008) argues for giving economists a great deal more power over policy-making. This is close to the solution of Schumpeter (1962). I want to suggest towards the end of this chapter why this may not be a good solution.

[8] Pincione and Teson (2006) do not advocate reform of the political system in order to integrate these parts in a more effective way. Their aim is to argue against the large modern state altogether.

A normative account of the division of labour

Here I attempt to articulate a conception of the division of labour that is realistic and that is compatible with political equality. In it I assign roles to citizens, politicians, experts, and others so that they are compatible with the idea that citizens are essentially in the driver's seat with regard to the society and equals in the process of driving the society. I will briefly sketch what I take to be a just division of labour and then I will sketch an outline of what I take to be a just and feasible system of discussion between citizens and experts in particular. My claim here is not that the division of labour always works in this way but that it can work this way and that if it does, the ideals of political equality can be satisfied. Social science is necessary to confirming the first possibility claim and political philosophy helps with the second.

The basic picture that I want to draw here is that citizens are essentially in the driver's seat in the society as long as they choose the basic aims the society is to pursue. By 'basic aims', I mean all the non-instrumental values and the trade-offs between those values. The non-instrumental values can include side constraints on state action as well as goals to be pursued. As I understand it, citizens disagree on basic values and the trade-offs among those values and their basic function is to choose these. In a democratic society, citizens choose among packages of aims by choosing representatives who advance these packages of aims in the legislature by a process of negotiation and majority rule.

The rest of the political system has a number of complementary functions. One function is to elaborate an adequately wide array of different packages of basic aims from which citizens can make their choices. Political parties are plausibly the primary element in the system for carrying out this task but some interest groups and activist groups also attempt to put together packages of basic aims from which the citizens make their choices. Parties and opinion leaders attempt to persuade citizens respectively that the set of aims they favour is desirable. And interest groups and specialized opinion leaders attempt to persuade citizens of the legitimacy of more particular aims. Citizen deliberation about aims takes place through these processes over many years and culminates in elections in which citizens choose candidates or parties that represent the packages of aims they want the political system to pursue.

Another task of the political system is to negotiate these different packages of aims. Even after extensive discussion, citizens disagree on the basic aims and so the legislature of a democratic society will have representatives of different packages of aims. Legislators, who specialize in negotiation and compromise, strike bargains among themselves so as to form workable majorities in the legislature. The last phase of compromise coincides with the beginning phase of another process, which is the crafting of legislation and policy that can actually achieve the ends a majority of citizens have chosen. But it is only the beginning of efforts to realize the aims.

Legislation is usually very abstract and requires a great deal of effort to implement in actual policy. This is what the function of the executive and administrative parts of government is.

The rationale for this division of labour is that expertise is not as fundamental to the choice of aims as it is to the development of legislation and policy. Citizens are capable in their everyday lives of understanding and cultivating deep understandings of values and of their interests. This is a kind of understanding they can have that is a by product in large part of their everyday lives. Furthermore, if they genuinely do have control over the choice of aims of the society (which assumes that the rest of the system is properly performing its function), they are in large part in control of the society. And finally, though different social scientific theories and approaches can reflect the backgrounds and interests of particular sectors of society, they are significantly less likely to do so than the choice of aims and so persons have a far greater interest in being counted when the choice of aims is made than when scientific theories are debated.

That being said, I will argue below that citizens must have some indirect role in the evaluation of whether the political system is pursuing the aims they have chosen, and an important role in the generation and evaluation of the scientific theories by which the public policy-making process is informed. Those roles do not require anything like one-person one-vote but they do require that the qualitatively distinctive interests of persons in different parts of society are properly studied in research in the social sciences. We will see, therefore, towards the end of this chapter, that there is some reason to expand the role of ordinary citizens in the democratic process.

The principal–agent problem

The key to the proper functioning of this division of labour is that the legislative and administrative parts of the system faithfully implement the basic aims of citizens. They must use their special expertise to determine how to implement the aims. The idea is that if these other parts of the system faithfully pursue the aims of citizens, the citizens are in the driver's seat with regard to the society. Certainly, this is a very big if. It gives us a principal–agent problem of large proportions. It is important to remember here that the following discussion is intended not to give a general description of how the principal–agent problem is always solved, but of how it can be solved. The characterization of a political system I give here is of how a political system can work so that it is compatible with democratic ideals. Social science is necessary to confirm the possibility. I provide some pieces of evidence below for the idea that this is possible, but so far the evidence is incomplete.[9]

The problem of truth sensitivity

But there is another big problem in the political division of labour. The problem is that the major decision-makers, citizens, politicians, and administrators are themselves not experts in most of the areas of science that are relevant to the evaluation of public policy. There is one more important piece to this division of labour. This is the network of intellectual labourers that spans the universities, political parties, political staffers, interest group associations, and parts of the administration. These are experts in economics, sociology, law, political science, and the natural sciences. They influence the making and evaluation of policy, but they also monitor the processes and outcomes of policy-making and can broadcast their opinions on these matters.

It is here that we can see the process of differentiated deliberation. The discussion that goes on among experts, policy-makers, and administrators as well as interest group associations is essential to the proper functioning of democracy. These groups discuss the extent to which the various aims of citizens can be met and what kinds of trade-offs are necessary and how to achieve the aims. Furthermore, they discuss whether and to what extent the legislation and policy in place and in prospect are likely to further the aims of citizens. And this deliberation is itself highly differentiated between those levels of discussion involving scientific expertise and those involving combinations of policy expertise and political acumen.

The subjects of these kinds of deliberations are distinct from the central subject of citizen deliberations. They concern primarily the questions of means to ends and the consequences of legislation or questions concerning what trade-offs are actually imposed on policy-makers. For instance, some of the issues concerning the minimum wage would fall here. Does an increase in the minimum wage increase unemployment, and if so by how much, or what other downsides are there to this policy and what are the benefits? These deliberations are much more subject to specialized standards of scientific evaluation than citizen deliberation. The basic kinds of deliberation here I call instrumental and consequential deliberation.

[9] I have articulated this idea in great detail in Christiano (1996: chs. 5–6). In this chapter I expand the role of citizenship beyond that articulated in my book.

The difficult question here is how does all this sophisticated expert knowledge influence the process of decision-making when the decision-makers themselves are not experts? To put the issue in the terms above, how can the process of decision-making be truth sensitive? The legislators in the system must not only be faithful agents of citizens, their decisions must be truth sensitive as well, or democratic decision-making will fail to advance the aims that are supposed to animate the system.[10]

In what follows, I will lay out a number of mechanisms and institutions which can help solve both the principal–agent problem and the problem of truth sensitivity in a way that is broadly compatible with democratic principles. My focus is on the problem of truth sensitivity but I think that the institutions and mechanisms that help solve the latter problem also help solve the former. The basic process of influence has to be essentially a kind of filter that separates out theories that have some substantial support within the expert community from those that do not. Beyond this the expert community seems to permit a wide variety of theoretical approaches to be used by politicians and ordinary citizens.

I will also suggest that citizens in a democratic society can make important contributions that enhance the activities of the community of experts and therefore that democracy can actually enhance truth sensitivity. They identify issues to be discussed and problems to be solved and can be the source of anomalies for social scientific theories. Furthermore, when the institutions of civil society are sufficiently diverse to represent the wide variety of interests and perspectives in society, they can ensure that the expert community has the kind of robust debate and discussion that enables it to avoid domination by one particular group.

Ordinary citizens perform their roles as the driving element in society on this picture. The first role is as choosers of the aims of the society. The second is as sources of different and competing research programmes in the various expert domains. The third is as evaluators of the pursuit of aims to whom the rest of society is accountable.

Expertise

I shall follow Alvin Goldman (2001) in understanding an expert in an area to be someone who has (1) an amount of true beliefs that is significantly greater than ordinary people have and that meets a threshold with respect

---

[10] Here we can see that the relationship between legislators and citizens is more complex than is normally envisioned in the debate about whether legislators are delegates or trustees of citizens. The picture I am suggesting assumes that they must play both roles in a democratically constituted division of labour.

to: (i) the subject matter in a domain; and (ii) the ideas and arguments within the community of persons who have a lot of true primary beliefs concerning the subject matter in the domain; and (2) a set of skills that enable them to test the ideas and arguments as well as extend the ideas and arguments of the community to new problems and objects within the domain.

So experts have a lot of true beliefs and they are also capable of appreciating the relations of support between many different sets of beliefs with regard to a particular subject matter. I will use the term 'esoteric' to refer to those statements within the area of expertise whose truth value is very difficult if not impossible for someone outside the community of experts to ascertain. Sometimes the statements are difficult to understand and sometimes it is very difficult to appreciate the relation between the evidence and the statements the evidence is meant to support. 'Exoteric' statements are ones that can be grasped and whose truth can be ascertained without the relevant expertise (Goldman 2001: 91–2, 94).

There is a great deal of disagreement among experts on which a substantial amount of democratically made policy depends. But even among those who disagree about which theories are the best ones or about the proper relations of support among statements, there is considerable agreement on a number of statements. And of course experts in the sciences have a great deal of knowledge of the different theories in play and the evidence that does and does not support them.

Mechanisms

Here I want to lay out some of the mechanisms which, when working well, are likely to enhance the democratic character of the division of labour. They solve two main problems of a division of labour in a democratic society: the principal–agent problem and the problem of truth sensitivity in a society in which decision-makers are not scientists. These mechanisms complement each other and some mechanisms can make up for failures in other mechanisms. The four mechanisms I have in mind are solidarity, overlapping understanding, competition, and sanctions. These mechanisms operate in the context of a plurality of political parties and interest group associations. I will lay them out and then I will explain the roles they play in enhancing the democratic character of a division of labour.

Solidarity

By solidarity I mean a mechanism by which two persons may be motivated to advance each other's aims. This might happen in two ways: similarity of backgrounds and like-mindedness. The first may arise from shared ethnic backgrounds or from a shared background of a history of injustice. It can also arise from shared nationality and also shared humanity. But there will be more particular kinds of solidarity such as that between those who have been victims of AIDS. They may share a sense of being victims of this disease as well as a sense of social injustice. These shared background facts can generate mutual sympathies and concern and a more general willingness to participate in pursuing each other's aims as they are related to the shared condition.

People are like-minded when they share political and moral aims and have some broadly common sense of how to achieve these aims. Members of political parties and interest group associations can have this kind of like-mindedness, at least when they are doing what they claim to be doing. Political parties and interest group associations are designed to create communities of persons who are like-minded and thus who have a certain degree of solidarity with each other. When people share this like-mindedness they can trust each other to pursue the common aims even when their opportunities and capacities for monitoring each other are relatively limited. This could be particularly important when some do not fully understand what the others are thinking.

Political parties or parts of them can degenerate into mere systems of patronage, clientelism, or systems for acquiring power. So this is not meant to be a general description of how all political parties operate. In these cases, the mechanism of solidarity will be consequently weakened and the relations of trust will also break down.

Overlapping understanding

By overlapping understanding I mean the state of affairs in which two or more people share some expertise and do not share other expertise. So for instance, suppose P knows about intellectual disciplines a, b, and c, and Q knows about disciplines b, c, and d. Their knowledge overlaps at b and c. This overlap allows Q to understand some of a because P can translate the ideas of a into b and c. Now, suppose that R has expertise c, d, and e, and S has d, e, and f. R and P overlap at c and S and P do not overlap at all, even though in a crucial respect they are about the same object. Despite this, S's knowledge may constrain P and P's knowledge may constrain S through the intermediaries Q and R.

For example, an economist may have highly technical expertise concerning the domain of economics while a public policy analyst may have a lot of expertise in this domain but not nearly as technical. The policy analyst does not have a grasp of some of the most esoteric considerations. The policy expert may have a less deep understanding of these arguments coupled with a deeper understanding of the history and political circumstances under which economic policy is made. These enable him to translate the theoretical considerations of the economist into the language of the legislator or administrator in a way that makes it relevant to the issues they face.

The activity of translation involved here will often omit elements of the argument or model under discussion so the person who understands the translated version of the model or the argument will not have a full grasp of the arguments and ideas under discussion. Some of the argument and ideas are, at least for practical purposes, intractably esoteric. But a lot of content can be translated.

How significant these losses are will depend on the level of sophistication of the different theories and models as well as the methods by which the theories are assessed in the expert community. The efforts to explain contemporary physics, and the empirical basis for it, to ordinary laypersons will lose a great deal of content in the process. The efforts to explain the arguments of international relations theory will lose significant content but not nearly as much. And economics stands somewhere in between, though probably closer to the international relations theory than to physics.

The kind of loss of content that is peculiarly relevant here is the loss of content that is important to discriminate evaluatively between theories or models. Here the receiver may receive a lot of content about the theory and its support but does not receive enough content to make a reasoned choice between different theories. For example, theories that use complex statistical methods may prove to be hard to discriminate for the layperson.

To repeat here, none of this assumes differences in native talent. Every expert will be at a disadvantage with regard to other forms of expertise that are far from their own. A physicist will have difficulty absorbing the fine grain of an economic theory. An economist will have difficulty absorbing a complex historical account of the origins of a war. Experts are ordinary citizens with respect to the expertise that is remote from their own. And ordinary citizens have day jobs and families to attend to.

I want to bring out two features of this phenomenon of overlapping understanding. First, it enables the complex and remote theorizing of the expert in a special science to communicate with persons who are not at all experts. The economist can explain much of what they understand to the policy analyst. The analyst can explain what they understand of this, coupled with a knowledge of the legal and political background, to the politician or staffer or perhaps to relatively sophisticated journalists. The journalists and politicians can explain what they understand to ordinary citizens. These chains of overlapping intelligibility enable politicians and citizens to have some appreciation of the reasons for and against particular policies.

Overlapping understanding enables politicians to make legislation that takes into account the best theorizing available in the society even if they do not themselves fully understand the theories. And it enables politicians and citizens to see to some extent how and to what extent the aims they have chosen are actually realized in policy or not. Second, it helps keep the theorists honest. To the extent that there are many persons who have partial understandings of what the theorists are doing as well as an understanding of the context in which the theoretical knowledge is to be applied, there are ways of monitoring the theorizing that can be made intelligible to the non-experts. This helps make the theorists accountable to ordinary citizens.

As we will see, both of these functions are greatly enhanced when there is solidarity among the participants. And they can also be enhanced when there are the alternative mechanisms of sanctioning theorists and competition among different groups of experts.

Here again, political parties and interest group associations are designed to be communities of like-minded persons in which the persons have a lot of overlapping expertise. They are composed of policy experts, ordinary citizen activists, experts in various disciplines whose subject matter coincides with the interest group's concerns as well as those of politically knowledgeable persons who are charged with the tasks of figuring out how to advance the concerns in the larger society, politicians. Of course political parties attempt to advance a whole variety of aims while interest group associations are more narrowly focused.

Competition

Another mechanism that tends to make politicians craft legislation in a way that is consistent with the best social science is competition within and between political parties. Presumably the system includes many people with overlapping expertise of very different political viewpoints, which means with different conceptions of the ends that should be achieved in politics. They also belong to different political parties or factions within political parties and are attempting to advance different aims. They have interests in making sure that the party of which they are a part and the politicians of their party advance the aims properly. But they also have interests in calling attention to the fact that the opposing parties and the politicians who are members are acting in ways that are not consistent with the best social science. There is thus a set of incentives that are common to adversarial systems that play a role here. Each set of overlapping experts can call into play the various sanctions I describe below to ensure that the members of their own party and of those of the other actually act in accordance with the best theories.

Sanctions

Political parties and interest group associations do not depend only on the conscientious pursuit of common aims. In part, the system imposes a variety of sanctions on those who fail to pursue the aims faithfully and competently. One set of sanctions involves the networks of scientists who supply the principal expertise on which the implementation of aims is based. If a significant number of economists argue that a certain policy does not bring about the aims that it is supposed to bring about, one effect may be to shame those economists who have played a role in making the policy into forsaking the policy. Academic life and intellectual life generally works heavily on the basis of the desire of every person to maintain a good reputation in the field. So if a substantial number of economists point out the clear error in another's work, the other is likely to retract it. And to the extent that each political party and interest group association with its associated aims includes experts in these areas, there will be expert critics representing a broad spectrum of views. And so this particular set of sanctions should benefit all the different groups in the society.[11]

A second kind of sanction can be imposed when a lot of experts see the error of a particular expert so that a legislator may come to regard the expert as no longer trustworthy and cease the direct or indirect consultations with them. Of course both these sanctions depend on the existence of significant competition among experts.

One major complication with all this is that there is a great deal of disagreement among economists on what good policy is. Even Pincione and Teson's favourite cases of minimum wage legislation and restrictions on free trade have been the subjects of a great deal of disagreement among economists of late. Still, we can see here that the making of policy and legislation must ultimately pass through a kind of filter that is set up by the relevant experts in the area of policy. Even if the expert discipline does not produce consensus on a set of evaluations of policy, it does help filter out those policies that are too much at variance with the prevailing views in the areas.

A third set of sanctions can be those imposed by the party faithful who are reasonably well informed of those who fail to pursue the aims for which they were elected. This kind of sanction could be one of shaming but it may also be to strip a person of political power by withdrawing the support of the party for the particular individual. Here too, expertise plays a role. For the views of the party faithful will be partly dependent on the views of

[11] See Goodin (2008: 180–4) for a discussion of similar sanctions among non-profits, which I take to have some similarity to the intellectual community.

the experts on the particular area in discussion. Political parties are complex organizations with their own internal divisions of labour including activists, lawyers, experts on policy, politicians, and so on. A fourth kind of sanction is imposed within the government. Politicians committed to the achievement of certain aims, once they acquire political power, can remove officials who are recalcitrant or remove staffers and so on. A fifth kind of sanction is imposed by the electorate itself. Here they may throw a party out of office on the grounds that that group does not advance the aims they wish to be advanced.

All of these sanctions are imposed on the basis of knowledge that is derived from the chain of overlapping expertise combined with solidarity among like-minded persons and competition from others.

The connections between ordinary citizens and specialized deliberation: from experts to citizens

Let us put together these mechanisms to see how they can constrain the making of legislation. Expertise plays a dual role in democratic deliberation. On the one hand, there are highly sophisticated deliberations among experts concerning what the best theories are for crafting policy. On the other hand, expertise acts as a kind of external filter on the deliberations of other parts of the division of labour such as politicians and ordinary citizens. It rules out certain theories as possible bases of policy-making and permits choice among a certain small subset of theories for policy-making.

In the model that I have laid out, ordinary citizens are normally charged with the task of deciding the aims the society is to pursue, and the more specialized activities of deliberation are concerned with the means and consequences of achieving those aims. Here the citizen is not expected to have an understanding of the specialized knowledge the other persons have. But the process of decision-making is nevertheless truth sensitive because the specialized deliberators do have an impact on decision-making and they are connected with specialized knowledge. That specialized knowledge imposes constraints on what means to the achievement of ends are selected and on how the consequences of the achievement of ends are assessed. Here the expertise serves as a kind of filter on what kinds of theories can actually go into the process of policy-making.

The question is, how does the monitoring of politicians' activities and administrators occur and how does it make the activities truth sensitive? Recall that the definition of truth sensitivity involves not ignoring the best social science in the making of the legislation. Since there is substantial disagreement on what the best theories are in any particular social science, this will usually involve acting in a way that is consistent with one or another

of the best theories in the relevant social science regarding the means chosen to pursue aims and the consequences of the policies. So legislation and
policy will be crafted in a way that uses one or another of the best available
theories in designing the means to the ends, and that uses one or more of
the best available theories in determining the extent to which the pursuit of
the aims is compatible with the pursuit of other aims.

How can this happen? Let us consider some key ways in which it might
happen. Suppose a group of politicians is crafting legislation that ignores
the relevant social science in an area. Within that group's political party,
expert social scientists will see that this is happening. They will be able to
do two things. One, they will be able to shame the staffers who are helping
make this legislation and who are at least partly experts. They will also be
able to inform, either directly or through those who are more capable of
articulating the problems to laypersons, the ordinary citizens of the party
of the problematic nature of the legislation, explaining what the probable
consequences of the legislation will be. The alerted citizen activists can
then put pressure on the politicians to take the relevant social science into
account or face sanctions from within the party. All of this works within a
political party because of the shared aims of most of the participants, the
kinds of sanctions that can be imposed within a political party on members, and the overlapping expertise of social scientists, policy experts, and
politicians.

This calling attention to bad policy-making appeals to those in the parties and interest group associations and thereby engages all the incentives
above. But it also appeals to ordinary citizens in efforts to get them to
switch parties or votes.

We see these kinds of debates being carried out concerning the crafting of policy all the time. Certainly, they are not the only determinants of
policy-making, but they do seem to make a significant difference. Simply
the enormous amount of effort expended time and again in these kinds of
debates suggests that the participants do think that the debates matter.

But this phenomenon does not take place only within parties. There are
many experts and partial experts throughout the society associated with
different parties and diverse interest group associations. And at least some
of them will be watching some of the time and will set off alarms if there is
a serious error in the calculations of the legislators who are crafting policy
or in the deliberations of administrators crafting rules.

The deliberative connection between experts and politicians who are
ultimately responsible for making decisions is complex. In some cases,
politicians have a full grasp of the considerations that favour a particular
policy over another. Expertise is required to discover these considerations,
but once they are discovered, anyone can understand them fully.

But often politicians and non-experts generally cannot have a full grasp of the considerations that favour one policy over another. This is because they do not have a full grasp of the expert knowledge that is necessary fully to see all the considerations. The expert knowledge may partly consist of complex mathematical equations or statistical methods, which require a great deal of knowledge. There are two kinds of cases I want to discuss here: the case in which the politician does not have a good grasp of why the theory they are using is superior to those that the expert community does not accept, and the case in which the politician does not have a grasp of the reasons which favour the view they are applying over other views that are also acceptable to the expert community.

The first case implies that decision-makers do not always choose the theory they act on, on the basis of the best evidence available to the community. They choose it because some significant subset of the expert community favours the view, for reasons the decision-maker does not entirely understand. In this respect the best available evidence is external to the policy-makers' activities. But it may nevertheless influence the policy-maker given the fact that the larger community of experts is monitoring the activities, there is some trust placed in the larger community of experts and they are connected to like-minded citizens in parties and interest group associations. So the process of decision-making can be truth sensitive in the sense that it is highly responsive to the best social science. But the connection between the best social science and the decision-maker is an external connection such that the decision-maker is merely influenced by the community of experts but does not have a grasp of the theories or much of the evidence for the theories. Here the community of experts is simply filtering out theories they do not accept and policy-makers simply make policy within the constraints set by these filters. They may not know in some cases why some theories are filtered out and why some aren't but they respect the constraints by choosing only among those that are not filtered out. When the mechanisms I described are working well, the external connection between the social science and the policy-maker can be a reliable one for producing reasonably good decisions.

Furthermore, the policy-maker may be making a decision on the basis of one theory rather than another (and all of which are acceptable to the expert community) even though the policy-maker does not have good reason to prefer one theory over the other. This follows from the fact that policy-makers often do not grasp all the considerations in favour of one theory over another. Sometimes this will imply that they do not grasp the essential considerations. I think, nevertheless, that the policy-maker's decision can be legitimate here to the extent that they are acting on the basis of a theory that has substantial support within the expert community. Here the expert community sets up a domain of acceptable theories from which it is permissible to choose even if one does not choose for good reasons.

There is a lot of disagreement on the best theories as well as on the implications of the best theories in social science. And there is a lot of disagreement on how to apply the best theories to the social phenomena they apply to. And there is disagreement about the empirical support for these theories. These disagreements make for a great deal of complexity in the application of social science to policy. And they create indeterminacy.

The indeterminacy is interesting because it suggests a limit to the idea that a process of decision-making is truth sensitive. Presumably there is a best theory and a best application at any given time. But there is much disagreement among experts as to what that best theory and application is. The community of experts cannot settle the disputes. Each expert has their own opinion on what views are the best, but it cannot be said that the community has one. This implies that it is indeterminate from the standpoint of the community which view is the best view and whether a political decision-making process is really using the best means to its ends when applying one theory rather than another.

These observations suggest an interpretation of the idea of truth sensitivity that may not be obvious upon looking at the definition. There a process is said to be truth sensitive when it does not disregard the best available science. The question is what does 'disregard' mean? If we are thinking just of the content of the decision-makers' thoughts in making policy, it may be that the decision-maker disregards the best available science. If, however, we think of a process of policy-making as truth sensitive when the policy-makers make decisions that accord externally with one or another of the best available theories (even though they do not understand them and they cannot give reasons for preferring the one they do over others) then the process is truth sensitive. All that is necessary is an external connection between a theory being among the best available ones and its adoption by a policy-maker. So the policy-maker's decision may be truth sensitive in an external sense and there may be a large amount of arbitrariness in the choice of policy.

The policy-maker's decision is not completely unjustified because they have reason to think that the theory on which they are operating is well thought of in the expert community. The endorsement of a number of experts gives them confidence that the theory is a good one though they do not see the reasons directly.[12] One way to think about this process is in

[12] I do not address the question of whether a majority of experts on one side of a debate is legitimate evidence for a layperson in favour of that side. I think in the absence of an overwhelming majority (where almost everyone agrees) the layperson cannot be

terms of the analysis of low information rationality in cognitive science. The policy-makers act on the basis of information shortcuts when they take the assent of experts as defining the boundaries of acceptable science. But for these shortcuts to work to produce good decisions, they have to be used in the right kind of environment. The environment must be one in which the assent of experts is a reliable guide to what are good means to achieving outcomes. But that reliability, I contend, cannot be established without the phenomena of solidarity, overlapping understanding, sanctions, and competition being present at least to some significant degree. If the experts do not particularly care about the aims of the policy-maker or have little incentive to produce the best analysis possible of the means to the aims, their assent to particular pieces of policy may not be trustworthy.[13]

A similar, though more tenuous, connection can hold between experts and citizens. Presumably citizens can have access to experts' views on what constitutes a reasonable theory on which to base a policy. These views are expressed all the time in all the major media by experts of very different stripes. There is a great deal of disagreement among experts but there are usually some limits to that disagreement that define what is acceptable as a basis for policy. Citizens can employ very general theories that have the assent of experts in evaluating policy-makers to some degree. They will normally only have a very partial appreciation of the theories and of the evidence available for them but they can employ them in discriminating between well crafted policy and badly made policy. Here the whole political system acts as a kind of filter on the ideas that citizens use as theories. Political parties generally will attempt to make their general platforms consistent with one or another of the best theories. This is because of the presence of overlapping expertise and the fact that lots of people are looking at the creation of these platforms. Experts will express their views in newspapers and other media in a way that presents the ideas in fairly easily digestible form. And all of these players are constrained by the fact that others with similar and overlapping expertise are looking over their shoulders ready to impose one or another of the sanctions I described above.

I have been discussing an extreme kind of case, though one that is becoming more and more prominent as a result of the prestige of economics, medical science, environmental science, and complex statistical reasoning in policy-making circles. But we see here a highly differentiated

---

justified in choosing one side over the other. See the contrasting arguments for this same conclusion of Goldman (2001) and Coady (2006).

[13] Lupia and McCubbins (1998) marshal a significant body of evidence that the mechanisms of solidarity (or common interests) and sanctions are means by which information shortcuts can help citizens and legislators make good decisions.

deliberative process, with experts deliberating about theories and policies and non-experts deliberating in a very different way.

Non-experts who favour one policy over another on the basis of a theory they cannot entirely defend, either against non-respectable theories or against the theories of their opponents, are in an interesting position from the standpoint of rational deliberation. In the case of policies consistent with one or another acceptable theory, they are promoting policies on the basis of theories they cannot defend against their adversaries in the policy-making world. In the case of policies based on theories that are acceptable as against those that are not, their confidence is often just based on the fact that some subset of the expert community agrees.

From citizens to expert knowledge

Here I want to develop another aspect of the relation between citizen and expert that needs development and that may seem to be incompatible with the idea of the division of labour. I will describe it and suggest why it is not incompatible with the division of labour.

In a democratic society, citizens are presumed to have an impact on expert knowledge. The relationship is interactive, as Bohman (2000) puts it, and not merely from experts to citizens. I want to sketch a number of ways in which this can occur while remaining faithful to the idea that we want the system to be truth sensitive.

There are three ways I have in mind here: (1) citizens can play some important role in determining what the aims of scientific research are; (2) different parts of the society can be the sources of different theoretical approaches to expert knowledge; and (3) citizens can do some checking on the defensibility of expert knowledge.

A democratic society supports a variety of political parties and interest group associations that are grounded in the variety of sectors in the society. The different political parties and interest group associations should reflect the different interests in society. To the extent that these groups provide support for and attract experts in different fields of study, they can play a role in determining the agenda for research. In the first place, political parties highlight the importance of certain interests and aims for the society. And interest group associations highlight the importance of the interests of the group as well as considerations of justice and the common good that favour the group's interests. But the consequence of this should be that the experts that are members of these associations will focus some of their expert knowledge on how to advance the interests of the particular group and how the advancing of the interests of that group are connected with the interests of other members of society. Of course, given the group's connections to particular sectors of society, the conceptions of interests that are in play will be quite fine-grained. They will reflect the input of a diversity of members within that group. To the extent that research questions can be defined in terms of how these interests, adequately understood, can be advanced and accommodated within the society, the research of the experts in this group should define a distinctive research agenda that can play an important role in generating knowledge.

Furthermore, to the extent that each grouping in society has particular local insight into special problems faced by the members of that group, the participation in a particular interest group association can enable the expert researcher to see particular structures of issues that are not apparent from other sectors of society. The experience of members of the group can suggest distinct hypotheses to articulate and test to expert members of the group.[14] Finally, the citizens can sometimes point out anomalies in theories on the basis of long experience with certain kinds of social structures.

In these ways the community of specialized knowledge will have points of view that reflect in part the different sectors of society that forestall movement towards a social science dominated by one class or grouping. If each group can sustain some specialized knowledge and can sustain the kind of overlapping expertise that sophisticated groups have, then to some extent the specialized knowledge cultivated within that group will serve as a check on the domination of the production of specialized knowledge by a particular group. And this can preserve a kind of diversity of viewpoints and approaches within the knowledge community. It simultaneously helps avoid domination by a particular group and it permits the fruitful effects of diversity on the production of knowledge.[15]

We need to say some more about truth sensitivity here. We have understood truth sensitivity to mean that the decision process does not ignore the best available science. But this cannot be the whole story. This account of truth sensitivity is geared to what societies can do to achieve knowledge. The division of labour is a rational solution to the problem of knowledge creation and a truth sensitive process takes advantage of this. But what if this part of the division of labour is dominated by special interests? What if the positions of the specialized community of knowledge merely reflect the interests of a ruling class? Or what if the dominant trends within the community of knowledge reflect this so that others exist but are ineffective?

---

[14] See Anderson (2006: 17–21) for a wonderful discussion of a case study of women whose interests and insight into a local problem have been ignored by an otherwise democratic process and as a consequence the community suffered as well as the women.

[15] See Page (2008) for an argument for the fruitful effects of diversity of perspectives on the production of knowledge. See also Sunstein (2002).

Obviously we need to have a conception of truth sensitivity that includes a method for assessing the community of knowledge itself. And this cannot be the conception that evaluates that community in terms of the best available science.

It seems to me that one principal source of domination of and parochialism in science is domination by class or ethnic interests. The reason for this is based in the simple facts of cognitive bias. Those facts suggest that beliefs and science can easily come to reflect the narrow backgrounds and interests of those who produce them. So if science and expertise are funded by one particular group in the society there is a significant danger that that expertise will reflect the interests and backgrounds of those persons. This will be more of a problem in the case of the social sciences where there is a great deal more uncertainty and where guesswork and intuition play a much larger role in theory construction and defence than in the natural sciences.

More generally the community of experts on which a democratic society depends can be truth sensitive only when there is robust debate among a variety of different kinds of theories, each of which is taken seriously by the others so that stronger and less biased theories emerge from the debates. Without this kind of robust debate, parochialism, group-think, and cognitive bias will distort the process of the production of knowledge in ways that defeat its truth sensitivity. And it seems to me that democracy can make a very important contribution to this by broadening the bases from which the expert community derives.

In this respect we can turn the observation of Pincione and Teson on its head. Instead of democracy failing to be truth sensitive, it turns out that democracy is a necessary condition for the truth sensitivity of the community of experts that makes up social science. It is because of the wide variety of points of view that are grounded in the diverse sectors of society in a democracy that the community of experts in a democracy can go through the kind of vigorous debate that is necessary for the truth sensitivity of the social sciences. Democracy is necessary for this because it is only when all the different sectors of society have the means of articulating their diverse points of view that social science can generate a process of knowledge production that is sensitive to the conditions of all the different parts of society. Under these conditions social science can generate a competitive struggle of ideas that can ensure that the process of social science is responsive to a lot of different sources of evidence.

So I have expanded the input of ordinary citizens into the democratic system beyond merely being choosers of aims. They make contributions by helping to set the research agendas of expert researchers. The problems of ordinary citizens can also help set the agenda to the extent that these problems pose anomalies for the theories of social science. But this contribution, as long as there is a vibrant system of interest group associations and political parties reflecting the diverse interests of persons throughout the society, need not involve all ordinary citizens in the task of contributing to social science. As long as there are a wide variety of associations, the activist parts of these associations can communicate the issues of ordinary citizens to the policy experts, who in turn can communicate them to the social science experts.[16]

This preserves the division of labour in policy-making. It is important that not all citizens be required for this process of generating research agendas and anomalies. Otherwise ordinary citizens will be asked to do too much. But one might ask why it is the case that citizens must participate individually in the choice of ends but not in the process of elaborating and testing theories. My answer to that is that though theories do, to some degree, reflect biases towards particular interests in society, this effect is not nearly as great as in the case of the choice of aims. Social scientific theories have a much more impersonal character, especially when there is significant contestation. As a consequence, we do not need to vote for the theories. But we do need to make sure that there are mechanisms that track all the relevantly different interests in society.

All of this depends on the idealization I have used so far that assumes that members of interest group associations and parties are like-minded and share aims. The four mechanisms work well when political parties and interest group associations are genuine about pursuing their aims and ensuring the devotion of the party and interest group members. But the mechanisms also suggest ways in which the parties have incentives to maintain strong party solidarity among members. For the parties to act as reliable cues for citizens as well as for legislators, they must cultivate fairly strong brand names that communicate the pursuit of the aims in a way that can be trusted by citizens (Lupia and McCubbins 1998: 207).

One final concern is that my approach to political parties and interest group associations assumes that it is possible somehow to make sure that the whole set of these associations is adequately representative of all the different sectors of society. This is not an easy thing to achieve. It seems pretty clear to me that it is not achieved in the society in which we live. How to go about achieving it is a difficult matter and I cannot discuss it here.

---

[16] It should be clear from these remarks that my proposal is very far from the kind of 'vulgar democracy' criticized by Kitcher (2001: 117). Indeed, I think I am articulating a decentralized method for achieving significant democratic input into the creation of science.

Concluding remarks

We have then a complex picture of the discursive relations between experts and ordinary citizens. In the account of the democratic division of labour I have sketched, citizens rule over the society by choosing the aims of the society and experts, along with the rest of the system, are charged with the tasks of implementing these aims with the help of their specialized knowledge. Democratic deliberation proceeds through citizens' discussion concerning the aims and the various legitimate trade-offs among the aims and then through the deliberations of experts and policy-makers in crafting legislation designed to achieve those aims. The deliberations are started by one group and then completed by another. The second stage is complex since experts discuss the merits of the various theories that help them design the means, and then policy-makers craft legislation in a way that is consistent with the theories that remain acceptable to the expert community. In this way democratic legislation can be highly sensitive to the best social science without the crafters always knowing how to discriminate in favour of the best social science.

But expert knowledge itself has, at least in a democratic society, some of its main roots in the discussions of ordinary citizens. They provide the basic research questions for much of social science. Their concerns pick out what is important for a social science to study, and the problems they experience in living their lives are the bases of research agendas. And the experience of ordinary citizens, when it is clearly and significantly at odds with the conclusions of social science, is an anomaly that can prompt the revision of social science.

3

Deliberation and mass democracy

SIMONE CHAMBERS

This chapter investigates deliberative democracy as a form of mass democracy. In particular I ask two questions: in what sense does the mass public engage in deliberation, and how can we understand the outcomes of that deliberation as a form of democratic decision-making? I argue that only a broad systemic approach to deliberative democracy can operate at the scale of mass democracy. This, however, requires that we rethink some standard definitions of deliberation and deliberative democracy. Finally I argue that one of the most fruitful ways of understanding the impact of mass deliberation on democratic decision-making is through the influence of public opinion on political decisions. I end the chapter with an assessment of three models of public opinion, ultimately endorsing an idea of considered public opinions borrowed from Jürgen Habermas's systemic approach to deliberative democracy.

Deliberative democracy, representative democracy, and mass democracy

Deliberative democracy, representative democracy, and mass democracy are not, of course, three competing models of democracy. The real competitions go something like this: deliberative democracy competes with aggregative models of democracy over the place to look for legitimacy (notice, however, that deliberation does not replace aggregation as a decision rule, rather it shifts the focus of the observer/reformer); representative democracy competes with direct democracy over who legislates (and sometimes who deliberates); and mass democracy competes with restricted or elite democracy over who participates. Democratic deliberation, representation, and mass participation are all, in some form, present and central in modern liberal democracies. The essential question is really one of balance and mix. How these three dimensions of our democratic system work together (or, sometimes, against each other) or ought to work together is very complicated and highly disputed. Let me try to make a few preliminary observations about the possible models of interaction that can be found in the deliberative democracy literature.

As I have noted, most people agree that deliberative democracy is not an alternative to representative democracy. Instead it offers, on the one hand, a theoretical perspective from which to study and evaluate representative democracy and, on the other hand, a way to supplement and augment representative democracy. As a theoretical perspective it invites scholars to shift the study of democratic regimes from a voting-centric research agenda to a deliberative- or talk-centric research agenda. Deliberation is part of any democratic order. The question is really about what weight and significance, both theoretical and practical, one gives to deliberation. The normative agenda tied to this research agenda involves promoting more, better, and more empowered deliberation throughout the system. Although almost all deliberative democrats see the deliberative model of democracy as fitting into representative democracy, there is a great deal of variety regarding the details of this fit. I am only going to talk about three possible ways to understand this fit among many.

One approach focuses on the design, proliferation, and empowerment of deliberative initiatives that either feed into the policy process or create new sites of governance that supplement traditional representative institutions. This approach focuses on such things as middle democracy (Gutmann and Thompson 1996) or participatory governance (Fung 2004), mini-publics (Goodin and Dryzek 2006), or deliberative polls (Fishkin 1997). Here the relationship between deliberative democracy and representative democracy is often one in which institutions of deliberative democracy supplement (and sometimes supplant) the large-scale traditional institutions of representative democracy by which I mean parties, elections, and legislatures. Instances of deliberative democracy, for example citizens' assemblies, spring up as innovations in the system intended to enrich the democratic and deliberative pedigree of policy proposals. In this approach, deliberative democracy does not refer to the overall system, as in, 'we live in a deliberative democracy', but rather to instances of a species, as in, 'the Ontario Citizens' Assembly is an example of deliberative democracy, national elections are not'.

A second approach focuses on the central and mass institutions of representative democracy, which is to say, parties, elections, and legislatures, and seeks to find, analyse, and often enhance their deliberative character.

One avenue of research, for example, looks at parliaments and legislatures and evaluates them along deliberative lines (Bessette 1994; Steiner *et al.* 2004). Another looks at ordinary citizens and studies their deliberative encounters (Jacobs *et al.* 2009). From a normative point of view, this approach often does not seek to supplement representative democracy with innovative deliberative initiatives so much as to augment or improve the legitimacy and accountability of pre-existing representative institutions.

A third way of approaching the relationship between deliberative democracy and representative democracy integrates the first two but sees deliberative democracy in systemic terms. Rather than focusing on single instances, institutions, or even spheres, this approach looks at the connections between instances, institutions, and spheres. This volume is a contribution to such a systemic approach. Prominent examples of this approach can be found in Habermas's centre/periphery analysis of democracy, Dryzek's 'overlapping discourses', Hendriks's 'integrated' view, and Parkinson's deliberative system (Mansbridge 1999; Dryzek 2000; Habermas 1996; Hendriks 2006a; Parkinson 2006a).

How does mass democracy fit into this picture? While there are many ways to approach issues of mass democracy from a deliberative point of view, a central and defining question is: to what extent or in what sense does the mass public deliberate? Does deliberation, as a real political process, impose structural, spatial, or numerical limits on participation? The three branches of deliberative theory described above tend to divide along this question. In the first approach above, the institutional innovations that bring more and better deliberation into the system are not usually open to mass participation. They often involve face-to-face encounters of self-selected, randomly selected, or stakeholder participants. More often than not, then, 'genuine deliberation', undertaken in manageable and designed settings, is itself representative of a broader public (Goodin and Dryzek 2006; Warren 2008). This can be contrasted to studies that see deliberation as a mass phenomenon. With the exception of proposals like a national deliberation day (Ackerman and Fishkin 2004), democratic deliberation as a mass phenomenon is not usually understood as mass deliberation in the sense of millions of people engaging in deliberation at the same time, about the same things, and within the same institutional format. Instead, studying deliberation as a mass phenomenon means talking about phenomena, that is, generalizing about multiple, plural, and overlapping forms of political talk over time and place. This approach often requires some broad theoretical framework to articulate the connections and relationships between the multiple parts including the relationship of all the talk to formal institutions (both deliberative and non-deliberative) of representative democracy. For this reason it is only the second and primarily the third systemic approach to deliberative democracy that can see deliberative democracy as a tool in analysing and reforming mass democracy.

In what follows I ask two questions. In what sense does the mass public deliberate, and in what sense is this deliberation a form of democracy? In investigating both questions I appeal to recent studies in public opinion research. Empirical studies have shown that citizens regularly engage in political discussion. But is this genuine deliberation? This question leads to an analysis of underlying definitions of deliberation. I argue that a systems approach must embrace a capacious rather than narrow definition of deliberation in order to include the mass public (as opposed to the constituted publics of minipublics). The second question – in what sense is mass deliberation a form of democracy? – seeks a connection between two sorts of outcomes of deliberation: public opinion formation and democratic decision-making. Even if we did want to say that the demos deliberates, we need to know how such deliberations or more importantly how the conclusions of such deliberations get translated into authoritative decisions. One way, of course, would be through elections and votes. But in this chapter I argue that in understanding a democratic system as a deliberative democracy we must investigate and attempt to enhance alternative avenues of transmission (Dryzek 2010a).

Measuring mass deliberation

In the book *Talking Together: Public Deliberation and Political Participation in America*, Lawrence Jacobs, Fay Lomax Cook, and Michael X. Delli Carpini set out to assess how much, how often, how well, and where Americans deliberate (Jacobs *et al.* 2009). While most empirical studies of deliberation focus on a contained deliberative event or single case study, this is one of the very few that looks at and measures deliberation as a mass phenomenon.

In *Talking Together*, Jacobs *et al.* (2009) describe their study as 'one of the first comprehensive studies of a critical component of democratic citizenship: the process of citizens talking, discussing, and deliberating with each other on public issues that affect the communities in which they live – from one-on-one conversations to email exchanges to more formal meetings' (2009: 3). The researchers set out to map 'deliberation in practice. Whether, how, and to what effect citizens discuss matters of community concern in public' (2009: 4). While the study is a direct contribution to deliberative democracy studies, the authors see deliberative democracy studies as a continuation of a long-standing debate (at least since Plato) about citizenship. This debate centres on the capabilities and

competencies of citizens and therefore the feasibility of democracy. Are
citizens in a position to make informed judgments? How do they come to
their preferences and opinions? Thus the focus is squarely on the conditions of democratic citizenship broadly understood. Jacobs *et al.* (2009)
see deliberation as a form of political participation just as important as,
if not sometimes more important than, voting. Deliberation is studied as
a mass phenomenon.

The analysis in *Talking Together* is based on a national telephone survey
undertaken in the US over a six-week period in 2003, consisting of a random sample of 1,001 respondents and an over-sample of 500 of what the
investigators called 'face-to-face deliberators'.

> The survey asked Americans about six different types of public deliberation
> that they might engage in – one-to-one talking about public issues; one-to-one
> discussions on the Internet via email; Internet communications that involved
> chat rooms, message boards, or other on-line discussion groups; participa-
> tion in more collective conversations (i.e. participation in a formal or infor-
> mal meeting organized by the individual, by someone else who is a personal
> acquaintance, or by a religious, social, civic, governmental, or political group);
> attempts to persuade another person about a particular stance on a public
> issue; and attempts to persuade another person about whom to vote for.
> (Jacobs *et al.* 2009: 35)

The authors consider all six forms of engagement as 'distinct types of public deliberation', although they acknowledge that face-to-face deliberation
of an organized group comes closest to the ideal of deliberation and as
such they pay special attention to this group in the study (Jacobs *et al.*
2009: 25).

At the most general level Jacobs *et al.* report that 'two-thirds of our
respondents reported that they had informal conversations about public issues at least several times a month ... One-quarter of Americans
reported engaging in the most difficult and time-consuming type of discursive participation – attending a formal or informal meeting in the past
year to discuss a local, national, or international issue' (Jacobs *et al.* 2009:
37). Even more interesting and indeed startling are the findings regarding
who deliberates. The data appears to show a different pattern of participation than voting, with age, income, and education having much less of
a role to play in the correlations (Jacobs *et al.* 2009: 43–63). The study is
very rich and suggestive with a great deal of empirical material for normative theorists to work with and mull over. For now I want to stay with
some basic questions of definition, however. Are Jacobs *et al.* really measuring deliberation? In what sense are their 1,001 respondents engaged in
deliberative democracy?

What counts as democratic deliberation?

Not all forms of talk are deliberative and not all forms of deliberation are an exercise in deliberative democracy. Investigating whether the talk that Jacobs *et al.* measure is deliberative will expose competing definitions of deliberation and deliberative democracy. One such definition, often associated with an institutional approach to deliberative democracy, insists that binding decisions be the outcome of deliberative democracy. The second, more capacious view of deliberative democracy insists only that the deliberation be systemically connected to authoritative democratic decisions. Joshua Cohen offers an example of the first sort of definition and indeed he has questioned whether studies like the one undertaken by Jacobs *et al.* are measuring deliberation at all. Cohen's work is foundational, offering as it does one of the first and most influential articulations of the principles and ideals of deliberative democracy (Cohen 1989). Indeed, his definition of deliberative democracy is the standard definition cited and employed widely in the literature. While his core insights about legitimacy and democracy are unassailable, it is worth taking a moment to highlight aspects of his definition of deliberative democracy that fit uncomfortably with a systemic approach. We need a systemic approach to be able to think about mass democracy in terms of deliberative democracy.

In 2007, Cook, Delli Carpini and Jacobs published some preliminary findings from their study in an essay to which Joshua Cohen was asked to respond (Cohen 2007; Cook *et al.* 2007).[1] Cohen took that occasion to clarify what he takes to be the central defining feature of deliberative democracy: 'The *point* of deliberative democracy is not for people to reflect on their preferences, but to decide, in light of reasons, what to do' (Cohen 2007: 222). Reflecting on preferences and coming to well informed opinions will enhance the process of 'deciding in light of reasons' but they are not themselves essentially deliberative activities. Beginning from the conviction that deliberative democracy is about 'reasoning as distinct from other forms of communication and participation', Cohen looks at a number of empirical studies, including Jacobs *et al.*'s, and wonders if they are really about deliberative democracy at all.

---

[1] While Cohen's response is to an essay that preceded publication of *Talking Together*, I will continue to refer to the book throughout. There is no substantive difference in the findings and argument between the two, although there is additional evidence offered in the book. Although I use Joshua Cohen's argument as the focal point of my objections to a restrictive definition of deliberative democracy, I would like to add that (1) he is not alone in this position; and (2) my objections to his excluding political discussion from the idea of deliberation in no way detract from what I think is his seminal and important contribution to deliberative democracy theory.

In response to Jacobs *et al.*'s conclusion that there is a lot more deliberation going on in America than we might have thought, Cohen notes
that 'while the findings about discursive participation are hopeful and
important, I am uncertain about their bearing on deliberative democracy.
Participation, even discursive participation, is not the same thing as deliberation. So we need to know whether discursive participants are reasoning and whether that reasoning has any impact on the exercise of power'
(Cohen 2007: 223). Cohen is sceptical that either of these two things (reasoning and impact) is present in the talk that Jacobs *et al.* set out to map
and measure. I want to take a closer look at both these ideas. I agree with
Cohen that reasoning and impact are defining features of the exercise of
deliberative democracy. What I wish to investigate further is what counts
as reasoning and impact. What do we mean by reasoning and how do we
know if it is present in talk? What counts as impact and how do we measure it?

Reason-giving

In ordinary language, deliberation usually means something like careful
consideration before a decision. Scholarly opinion starts with a similar
idea. For example, Cohen defines it this way: deliberation 'is about weighing the reasons relevant to a decision with a view to making a decision on
the basis of that weighing' (Cohen 2007: 219). I endorse this definition. I
agree that not all talk is deliberation. Deliberation is essentially practical.
So, for example, contemplating the beauty of the universe is not a form of
deliberation, even if it involves a stimulating discussion with other con-
templative types. It is not a form of deliberation because there is no practical question of the type 'what ought to be done?' on the table. Thus an
essential difference between conversation and deliberation is that deliberation has a practical orientation and involves giving, assessing, and evaluating reasons for and against courses of action. Another, perhaps more
Aristotelian way to put this, is to say that if the purpose of deliberation is
to decide what to do, then contributions to this purpose must be understandable as reasons for or against some practical option. I begin then, as
do most theories of deliberative democracy, with an idea of deliberation as
essentially practical and involving reason-giving

How would we track reason-giving? If we wanted to know how much
reason-giving was going on, how would we measure it? As it turns out,
Jacobs *et al.* did track reason-giving of a sort. Jacobs *et al.* (2009) measure deliberation along five dimensions: they ask how universal, inclusive,
agreement-oriented, politically significant, and reason-based are the discursive practices of Americans. I cannot go into all their findings here so

I will confine myself to a discussion of their definition of 'reason-based'. Public talk is reason-based for Jacobs *et al.* when it 'relies on logic and facts' (Jacobs *et al.* 2009: 19). This definition seems narrow.

Most people working within deliberative democracy theory today have come to accept that reason-giving comes in many forms and may involve multiple methods of communication. It is not possible to distinguish mere conversation from deliberation on rhetorical grounds, for example, with the argument that the former allows all manner of communicative styles to enter while the latter is restricted to factual claims presented logically. Reasons can come in many packages. Often they are straightforward empirical claims about the consequences of a proposed course of action. But they can also come in the form of storytelling or even iambic pentameter. We can sometimes miss the message embedded in forms of communication, failing to see how it stands as a reason for or against some proposed course of action. And these misunderstandings can often be traced back to cultural differences. So there is lots of room here for misunderstanding within deliberation about the way in which contributions work as reasons. But this is not the same thing as stipulating in advance that, say, expressing how one feels about something can never be a reason in practical deliberation. Sometimes it is a reason and sometimes it is not a reason. It is not the form that determines whether something is a reason but rather the function or purpose it serves in a discourse.

We need lots of information about discursive encounters to know whether reason-giving is going on. While Jacobs *et al.* have a somewhat narrow and rationalist view of ideal reason-giving, they have the right idea about what the opposite of reason-giving might look like. It is not chat, aimless conversation, or preference clarification that stands opposed to reason-giving; rather, it is manipulation and coercion. This seems a more promising contrast and one that could be operationalized in an empirical way. I am just not sure how one would actually try and find out if a conversation was mere preference clarification (what do I really think about health care reform?) versus deliberation (what should we do about health care reform?). Thus identifying some talk as mere conversation about public issues and other talk as deliberation about what we should be doing about public issues cannot rely on the rhetorical style of the speech. And indeed, most people who embrace an institutional definition of deliberation usually do not try to construct a rhetorical definition of reason-giving. Instead, reason-giving is folded into a broader idea of democratic decision-making. On this view, then, Jacobs *et al.*'s respondents were not engaged in democratic deliberation not because they were not talking about important political matters in a serious way, but because they were not taking a democratic decision that had authoritative impact. On the institutional model, whether an utterance functions as a reason or not is determined by the institutional context in which the utterance was made. Mentioning to your neighbour over coffee that tax cuts will be disastrous because they will sink the country further into debt is not a form of deliberative reason-giving, but standing up in a legislative body and making the same argument is a form of such reason-giving. This way of thinking about deliberative reason-giving tends to exclude from the get go informal public debates and mass forms of deliberative participation.

Binding decisions and democratic power

There is nothing particularly democratic about deliberation. A solitary individual, an oligarchy, or a despot can deliberate. So what makes deliberation democratic? Deliberation is democratic when it is undertaken by a group of equals faced with a collective decision. So the question is how do – or ought – a group of equals reason together? Another way to put this is that democratic deliberation contains a model of collective democratic practical reasoning. On this view, democratic deliberation is not itself a decision procedure. It is compatible with a number of decision procedures from consensus to majority voting. Therefore, although deliberation is decision-oriented in that it is about the grounds on which we decide as a group what to do, it is not strictly speaking a way to make a decision, although it is clearly incompatible with some decision rules. When Cohen says that 'democracy is a way of making binding, collective decisions that connects those decisions to the interest and judgments of those whose conduct is regulated by the decisions' (Cohen 2007: 219) he cannot be referring to any particular decision rule but to a generic idea of deciding collectively as equals. For Cohen, what is important when one adds democratic to deliberation is that the term becomes political in a specific sense and implies the idea of 'binding collective decision' (Cohen 2007: 220). Dennis Thompson also appears to endorse this view and says of democratic deliberation that 'its essential aim is to reach a binding decision', although he uses the weaker phrase 'decision-oriented' on occasion as well (Thompson 2008a).

Why is a binding decision part of the definition of democratic deliberation? And what does binding mean exactly? One rationale to include binding decisions in the definition of democratic deliberation appears to be based on a psychological assumption about the conditions of reason-giving (Fung 2007; Thompson 2008a). Something has to be at stake, so the argument goes, if participants are going to engage in real deliberation, which is to say, collective problem-solving. That something has to be at stake makes sense but what is not clear is why a binding decision needs to be in the offing in order for something to be at stake.[2] For example, asking your class to choose a set of policies for a hypothetical colony on a distant planet is different from asking citizens to discuss the best way to reform health care, even if neither group has been authorized to make this decision. The passion that can often be seen in consultative town hall meetings is evidence that citizens often act as if something very important is at stake, even when they are not in a position to make a binding decision. The issue of motivation does raise some questions about experimental research that draws conclusions from hypothetical scenarios, but it is not clear why reason-giving cannot or will not happen if there is no proximate and binding decision as long as participants see themselves as affected by or responsible for the outcome.

Furthermore, what counts as a decision is often left unclear by those who insist that binding decisions are a defining feature of democratic deliberation. During the last round of Canadian constitutional talks, for example, there were a series of stakeholder and citizen conferences that took place across the country (Chambers 2001). These were intended to bring together individuals and groups with serious differences of opinion to see if some agreement could be reached on constitutional principles. Each conference ended in a joint statement articulating points of agreement. Although the conferences were high profile with lots of media coverage and attention from elites, they had no actual mandate of any kind. The participants signed the statement at the end. This was one of the high points of constitutional deliberation as the conferences were excellent examples of democratic reasoning in action. Did participants take a binding decision? I am not sure. I am sure they all felt bound to stand by the document they signed but that document itself did not bind the nation or legislature or courts in any way. This was no hypothetical debate, however. Participants knew that they had the attention of the media and indeed the country. Thus the psychological argument while perhaps pointing, in a general way, to some empirical conditions conducive to deliberation, does not seem strong enough to warrant binding decision being part of the definition of deliberative democracy.

There is a second, stronger reason, for including binding decisions in the definition of deliberative democracy, however. Democracy involves a set of institutions and practices through which the people rule. Therefore deliberative democracy or democratic deliberation is about how people rule themselves. This leads many to conclude that real or authentic democratic deliberation must be about the exercise of power: 'It [deliberative

---

[2] Binding decisions may have other psychological effects on participants, for example making them more likely to bargain as the pressure of decision time nears.

democracy] is about making collective decisions and exercising power in ways that trace to the reasoning of equals who are subject to the decision' (Cohen 2007: 220). The Jacobs *et al.* study is not about the exercise of power in any direct sense. Some of the deliberation is in formal settings, for example school board meetings and community action groups, but a lot of it is not. A lot of the talk is informal and, although decision-oriented in the sense that 'what is to be done?' is the *topic* of conversation, not directly tied to the exercise of power. In the next section I argue that a systemic approach can show how informal talk has an important impact on power. Right now I want to argue that the institutional definition of deliberative democracy narrows what is to count as deliberative democracy in such a way as to tie it too tightly to the *status quo* power structure.

Let's say we wanted to know how much democratic deliberation is going on in America today using the institutional definition of deliberative democracy favoured by Cohen and others. The answer would have to be found not by counting voices but by counting institutions – and a very particular type of institution. The institution in question would have to have two characteristics: (1) it would have to have rules and procedures that promoted democratic reason-giving; and (2) it would have to exercise power or be tied to the exercise of power in some direct way. But in what sort of way? I think a lot hangs on this question. How formally empowered must the deliberation be for it to be an exercise in deliberative democratic decision-making? How temporally and spatially proximate to deliberation must the exercise of power be and in what way ought we to understand 'impact'? The frequent reference to binding decisions as a defining feature of deliberative democracy implies that deliberative *democracy* is only being *exercised* when deliberative bodies are formally empowered or at least recognized by the state. The risk, then, is that only state-sponsored or generated initiatives come into view. There seems little room to study the potential of bottom-up models of impact and influence. In contrast, a broader, more capacious view of deliberation offers a critical framework within which to ask how strong, weak, or non-existent is the impact of this or that political talk on the exercise of power. To put this in social science terms, the institutional definition of deliberative democracy risks sampling on its dependent variable. Sometimes the very question at issue is what impact do the informal deliberations of the general public have on the exercise of power? Narrow definitions of deliberative democracy pre-empt this sort of investigation by definitional fiat.

Impact through participation

I have argued that respondents in the Jacobs *et al.* study were deliberating in the sense that they were talking about political matters in a practical (as opposed to a theoretical) way. Their talk was decision-oriented in the sense that they were talking as democratic citizens commissioned to make judgments about collective matters. But what relation does this talk have to the exercise of power? Or, more broadly, what relation does this talk have to the exercise of democratic self-rule? In this and the next section, I explore a number of ways of conceptualizing, tracing, and identifying the impact of mass deliberation on authoritative decision-making.

Jacobs *et al.* acknowledge that 'in terms of mass public, deliberation is often derided as amounting to little more than idle talk that is disconnected from actual decision making' (Jacobs *et al.* 2009: 117). To be able to think about mass democracy within the framework of deliberative democracy we must be able to show not only that the mass public deliberates but also that that deliberation can and does have an impact on democratic decision-making. Jacobs *et al.* identify two types of effects that deliberation may have on the exercise of power. The first is indirect, behavioural, and focuses on the way deliberation appears to influence or at least correlate with citizenship practices. The second involves a more direct effect on policy outcomes. It is only the first that Jacobs *et al.* are able to measure as their study is confined to measuring practices (e.g. 'do you talk about politics?', 'have you ever written to your congressman?') and not opinions (e.g. 'do you support gay marriage?') and their impact. The central question they investigate via survey interviews is the relationship between discursive participation and civic and political engagement. This engagement in turn then has an impact on the exercise of power. Are the people who are attending town hall meetings and engaging in face-to-face political discussions also the people who are writing letters to their congressmen or getting out and voting? These are important and interesting questions if we want to build an empirical picture of the patterns and levels and political talk on a mass scale. Jacobs *et al.* do in fact find significant correlations between face-to-face deliberation and civic participation, electoral participation, and elite contacting (writing letters to congressmen, etc.).[3]

---

[3] Jacobs *et al.* (2009: 116). These findings offer an interesting counterweight to Diana Mutz's work (e.g. Mutz 2006). She has argued, using impressive public opinion research, that the citizens who are open to deliberation and listening to others are not very keen on jumping into the fray of politics and so shun active participation. The startling conclusion of her research is that deliberation and participation seem to be on a sliding scale. Jacobs *et al.* use a different (and I would argue more useful) definition of participation. While Mutz has activists at the top of her participatory scale, Jacobs *et al.* look at everyday types of participation. Activists, it turns out, tend not to be very deliberative and are often disinterested in hearing the other side. But Jacobs *et al.*'s findings indicate that those who engage in political talk regularly are also more engaged in the political system and more likely to exercise other participatory behaviour connected to democratic citizenship.

Jacobs *et al*.'s findings regarding the impact of deliberation on civic engagement, while interesting and helpful in building a picture of mass deliberation, do not go to the heart of the issue, however. Deliberation is about weighing reasons and considerations with a view to taking a practical decision about what to do. Democratic deliberation is about engaging in this sort of exercise in concert with fellow citizens and seeking out reasons that reflect the interests, concerns, and claims of citizens at large. From this point of view, if we wish to think about deliberation as a mass phenomenon then we need to think about the ways the outcomes of that deliberation impact law-making. What are the outcomes of mass deliberation? The mass public deliberates in a decentred, plural complex set of overlapping conversations taking place in multiple and divergent settings. The outcomes are political opinions about what is to be done. From a systemic point of view such opinions are connected to power in a number of ways, which I outline below.

Impact through votes

First, public opinion translates into law via elections. As all theorists of deliberative democracy acknowledge, deliberation rarely ends in a consensus and, as the group of those participating increases, the likelihood of consensus becomes more and more remote. Deliberation almost always ends in a vote. Majority rule is the most common decision rule. In formal deliberative bodies like legislatures or citizens' assemblies, the relationship between deliberation and voting is often direct and transparent. As Robert Goodin reminds us, 'first talk, then vote' is a central tenet of modern democracy (perhaps all democracy) that has been given new depth and significance through theories of deliberative democracy (Goodin 2008) but was not invented by theories of deliberative democracy. From a deliberative perspective on democracy, the seat of legitimacy moves away from the isolated act of voting, that is away from will separated from reason, and towards the talk, reasoning, and justification that precedes voting. A classic formulation of this can be found in Bernard Manin's work. He argues that it is not the general will or the will of the people that legitimates outcomes of voting, but the general deliberation that precedes the vote. Majorities must have reasons not just votes for what they do, and these reasons must be made public, discussed, and weighed carefully (Manin 1987). Good reasons are those that justify law in terms that all can accept or that speak to the interests of citizens generally. Particularly important for Manin are the reasons that a winning majority might give a losing minority for the public policy. These reasons cannot be simply that we were stronger and have more votes. That is a causal explanation for the outcome but not a reason or justification of the policy. The closer the connection one can make between talking and voting the stronger (potentially anyway) can be the claim to legitimacy of the outcome. Parliamentary debates in the ideal, where reasons are directly tied to votes, are a paradigmatic case (Bessette 1994). But the quality of the talk is only one factor in questions of democratic legitimacy. Inclusion is also important. And while the quality of democratic talk can be measured by the inclusiveness of the interests and concerns discussed, actual not only virtual inclusion is an essential component of legitimacy. In a democracy citizens at large are asked to cast decisive votes during election times.

What about the relationship between the unstructured political talk of both elites and private citizens during election campaigns and the votes taken to elect representatives? Can we see an analogous relationship between talking and voting? The obvious first point to note is that the calibre, structure, tenor, and substance of election campaign talk hardly lives up to ideals of deliberation. We might then be tempted to say that this is not real or authentic deliberative democracy. The scale is too big, the quality of talk too low. From a systemic approach, however, the low quality of the talk does not necessarily disqualify it from analysis as part of a deliberative system. The bottom line is that the standard of democratic legitimacy is the same for general elections as it is for votes in the House of Commons: first talk, then vote. And if the talk is bad so much more reason to take a good long look at the talk from within a deliberative framework to see the most obvious weaknesses and perhaps find some ways to improve the talk. I reject a full division of labour in which one part of the system, say representative institutions or minipublics, performs an epistemic function based in high quality deliberation, while another part of the system, say elections, performs a democratic function of mass participation. This would be dysfunctional it seems to me. Although some division of labour is to be expected and desired, a healthy deliberative system requires some level of deliberative engagement by the general public.

In any event talk, even bad talk, shapes opinions and influences preferences to some extent. 'To what extent?' is an interesting question for empirical theories investigating opinion formation. There is a large sector of public opinion research that focuses on precisely this question. A growing number of these researchers start from a deliberative democracy framework (Druckman 2004). In evaluating mass political conversation we need to know a few things. We need to know how free and open the debate that precedes voting is. We need to know what sorts of reasons (if any) are being exchanged by citizens and elites and used to justify choices to be able to assess the legitimacy of the outcome. We need to know from where citizens are getting their information and how reliable that information is. We need to know with whom they are talking. Probably most important in mass democracy is that we need to know the role played by the media in these conversations. From a systemic approach, then, demographic indicators through which social scientists predict votes (e.g. income and religion) recede from the research agenda and questions of the conditions and circumstances of opinion formation become more important to the agenda. For example, framing studies that evaluate the biases through which citizens gain information become important in evaluating the deliberation that precedes the vote (Druckman and Nelson 2003).

Voting for a representative involves a decision. We would hope that citizens would deliberate carefully, or as carefully as circumstances allow, about those decisions. And further we would hope that they would deliberate carefully in concert with others. But do they? Large-N studies can tell us something about the quality and quantity of mass deliberation. If it turns out that the quality and quantity is low, which is to say there is not enough good talk going on in the general public, then one strategy is to try to minimize the impact of a minimally deliberative mass public by, among other things, replacing it with deliberative minipublics when possible. But such a strategy holds both pragmatic and normative risks. Pragmatically, the mass public still holds determinate power at election times. Minipublics are embedded in large-scale mass democracy and are circumscribed by decisions accountable to the mass public. Normatively, bypassing the mass public as much as possible because of the weak quality of mass deliberation appears democratically suspect.

Impact as responsiveness

Democracy means being systematically responsive to citizens' needs and interests (Goodin 2008). Elections are a core mechanism of accountability. When elites fail to be responsive, they are voted out of office. How do citizens communicate their needs and interests to elites? How do citizens themselves know what their needs and interests are? Of course voting is itself a form of communication, often sending a clear message. But in addition and perhaps more importantly, ongoing channels of communication and information must be open between elite decision-makers and the general public if representation is to work in a responsive and democratic way. Here we are looking at the more general relationship between the opinions, concerns, and interests of the general public and the policy output of governments and elected institutions. A key question from the point of view of the deliberative system is how deliberatively accountable (or responsive) are elites to citizens? Can we measure and evaluate how much elites actually listen to citizens, for example? Can we draw a systemic picture of the impact of public opinion on policy formation and decision-making? Finally, what normative standards do we want to place on the democratic interplay between mass public opinion and policy output? For example, if the general public is ill-informed or perhaps even misled, do we want elites to listen closely and follow the public's wishes?

In what follows I move through three models of public opinion that contain corresponding ideas of responsiveness. The first two see responsiveness as an input/output model: strong responsiveness means that policy output reflects opinion input. In the third model, drawn from Habermas's work on the public sphere, responsiveness is understood not in causal terms but in deliberative terms. To be responsive to public opinion is to engage public opinion deliberatively, talk about it, and publicly and collectively assess its epistemic and democratic value. The question, 'is public opinion well informed and does it adequately reflect the concerns and interests of all affected?' is a topic of public debate and not the sole purview of expert analysis by social science observers.

In survey research, responsiveness is measured by correlating citizen preferences and elite choices (Page 1994). If the correlation is weak then one may suspect that something other than the opinions of citizens and constituents is driving public policy. These studies can and do tell us something interesting about democracy and they flag problematic patterns in elite choices that might lead us to question – if not the legitimacy of the choices – at least the elites' ability to justify the choices in terms that speak to the interests, needs, and values of citizens.

A study by Jacobs and Page, for example, shows that 'public opinion – the aggregate foreign policy preferences of ordinary citizens – was repeatedly estimated by our Models 1–3 to have little or no significant effect on government officials' (Jacobs and Page 2005: 121). One might want to say that foreign policy is about national interest and perhaps elites should not be blown around by the whims of a fickle electorate, but the authors conclude that the 'evidence suggests that business may exert the most consistent influence on government officials' (Jacobs and Page 2005: 121). Such studies can alert us to problems within the system but they do not contain a satisfactory model of responsiveness. In the first place they are studies in statistical correlation and as such leave many questions open as to what actual mechanisms are in place that are influencing and shaping public policy. Second, at a normative level this model of responsiveness seems thin. While the Jacobs and Page results should give us pause as democrats, from there we should not conclude that if only there had been a higher correlation between citizens' preferences and public policy then democracy is alive and well. We want elites to listen to and respond to the needs of citizens. But aggregated survey data is only one snapshot of those needs and itself requires interpretation. Furthermore, we would want to know how and under what conditions those preferences were formed. Did respondents have all the information? So, we should worry if studies show that representatives are listening to business more than citizens, but we should also worry if representatives are simply channelling uninformed or perhaps biased preferences of citizens as well. For this and other reasons, James Fishkin has developed an idea of responsiveness that appeals to deliberated public opinion rather than raw (Fishkin 1997; Fishkin and Luskin 2005).

Deliberative polls bring a relatively small number of randomly selected individuals together for an intense weekend of deliberation about important and pressing problems of public policy. The opinions that are surveyed at the end of the weekend almost always vary to some degree from what individuals claimed was their position or opinion at the beginning. Thus they come in with 'raw' opinions but leave with deliberated opinions. Fishkin argues that elites should draw on these deliberated opinions in designing and choosing public policy because they 'represent what the public would think about the issue if it were motivated to become more informed and to consider competing arguments' (Fishkin and Laslett 2003: 128).[4] These opinions then are intended to help elites make decisions that have deliberative legitimacy.

Deliberative opinion polls return us to the question at the beginning of this chapter: can the demos deliberate? Deliberative opinion polls assume that the mass public cannot deliberate and so set up representative minipublics to speak on behalf of the larger public. While I do not doubt that many of the outcomes of deliberative opinion polls represent opinions that the general public might have come to if they were given the same opportunity, it is not clear what weight we should give this opinion in policy formation. From the point of view of democracy, it seems problematic to give precedence to deliberated opinion over the raw opinion of actual citizens. Furthermore, proliferation of and reliance on deliberative opinion polls sets the epistemic dimension and democratic dimension of deliberative democracy at odds (cf. Mansbridge et al., Chapter 1, this volume). While the system will inevitably have a division of labour between epistemically high quality deliberation (often found in small sometimes expert fora closed to the public) and inclusive deliberation (found in the general public), deliberative opinion polls propose *substituting* for or replacing inclusive

---

[4] The results of deliberative opinion polls 'have prescriptive force because they are the voice of the people under special conditions where the people have had a chance to think about the issues and hence should have a voice worth listening to' (Fishkin 1991: 4).

deliberation. Rather than a division of labour, then, this model appears to seek the eclipse of raw opinion.

If representatives should be cautious about both raw as well as deliberated opinion, what source can they rely on when framing public policy that speaks to citizens and their concerns? I turn now to Habermas's model of considered public opinion. In his model, 'considered public opinions set the frame for the range of what the public of citizens would accept as legitimate decisions in a given case' (Habermas 2006: 418). Although opinions worked up in the informal public sphere are detached from decisions taken in the formal halls of power, they still influence those decisions and indeed ought to be seen as facilitating the 'deliberative legitimation process' (Habermas 2006: 415). What are considered opinions? They are made up of, on the one hand, published opinions communicated through the mass media, and, on the other hand, polled opinions that measure aggregate preferences of ordinary citizens. The role of considered public opinions in the system is primarily to 'prepare the agenda for political institutions' (Habermas 2006: 416). If the system is working well then that agenda will reflect authentic concerns and interests of citizens as well as their judgments regarding the controversial issues of the day: 'Public opinions make manifest what large but conflicting sectors of the population consider in the light of available information to be the most plausible interpretations of each of the controversial issues at hand' (Habermas 2006: 418). What makes them considered?

Habermas's idea of what makes for epistemically and normatively sound public opinion differs from both the standard view found in most public opinion research (POR) as well as Fishkin's idea of deliberated opinion. For both POR and Fishkin the question of the quality of opinion (whether it is well informed, thoughtful, has taken other people's opinions into consideration, etc.) is evaluated at the individual level. Quality opinion within POR is often measured by contrasting the aggregate of individual opinions on a subject to some objective standard of fact. For those inclined to question the competency of citizens there are many studies that show Americans have poor knowledge of the content of the constitution, are unable to name their congressional representative, and are generally poorly informed about important questions of public policy (Caplan 2008). On the other side of the aisle are POR scholars who reject a model that expects citizen to live up to an epistemic standard of experts and instead trace information shortcuts and heuristics that allow citizens to come to reasonable conclusions despite a shortage of high quality information (Page and Shapiro 1992). My intent here is not to assess this literature. Instead, it is simply to highlight that the debate is about individual level opinion and the reasoning process undertaken by individuals to come to their opinions.

Like POR, Fishkin is also interested in individual-level data. Deliberated opinion, while the product of a collective process of deliberation by a group, is measured by evaluating what happens when an individual gets more information and is offered the opportunity to discuss that information with people who disagree in an atmosphere of cooperation. The stress is on individual reflection and learning.

By contrast, Habermas's idea of considered opinion involves a public rather than private process. In a healthy democracy we, of course, want thoughtful consideration to take place at an individual level. On the individualist model, the picture is of individuals thinking about what they as individuals want or need or care about. But in the public model, reflection on needs and concerns is mediated through a reflection on what the public appears to need and want. Public opinion itself, as opposed to my opinion, becomes the object of reflection. Opinions become considered, then, when they pass through a reflexive process where they become the subject of public debate and scrutiny: 'That both elected governments and voters can take an affirmative, a negative, or an indifferent attitude toward public opinion highlights the most important trait of the public sphere, namely its reflexive character. All participants can revisit perceived public opinions and respond to them after reconsideration. These responses, from above as well as from below, provide a double test as to how effective political communication in the public sphere functions as a filtering mechanism. If it works, only considered public opinions pass through' (Habermas 2006: 418).

This seems to me to be a fruitful way to think about the impact of mass opinion formation on political decisions within a systemic view of deliberative democracy. The system is working well when there are high quality public debates about what citizens want, need, or care about that inform the legislative process. Aggregative survey data – whether raw or deliberated – becomes the topic of public conversation and not the simple inputs in policy formation. Public rhetoric in most liberal democracies already reflects, albeit often in very shallow and sometimes manipulative ways, an imperative to respond to mass public opinion. We hear endless appeals to what Americans want or what the Australian people demand or what French citizens cannot do without. These appeals to mass opinion are used as justifications for public policy. In a healthy deliberative system the conversation goes deeper and asks questions like 'how do you know that is what Americans want?'. In this picture, survey data are used to hold up a mirror or rather multiple mirrors to society. We would encourage elites and the media to reflectively engage survey data rather than simply use it selectively to make their case.

For example there have been a number of studies recently in the US that show that Americans in general embrace relatively egalitarian values while at the same time preferring economic policies that often favour markets over equality (Bartels 2008; Page and Jacobs 2009). This research questions the argument that Europeans tend to have larger welfare states and more egalitarian economic policies than Americans because they have more egalitarian values and culture. But in addition, this data can be introduced into debates about, for example, health care reform as a check when weighing various policy options, and as a way to reflect upon the shared values that ought to guide democratic decisions.

Conclusion

It is possible to think about mass deliberative democracy in a fruitful way. Much of this thinking is an updated take on the old question of the 'rational public'. The update involves placing questions of citizen competency and the impact of mass opinion in a deliberative systems framework. This cannot be studied without public opinion data and aggregative survey data. It is difficult to get a handle on what citizens do, whom they talk to, what they talk about, and how does that talk affect democratic decisions, without recourse to aggregated public opinion. But it is possible to pry that data loose from impact studies that assume fixed preferences determining public policy in an unreflective way.

Democratic deliberation is about reasoning and impact. If we want to understand deliberative democracy as a form of mass democracy then we need to know in what sense and to what degree the masses engage in practical reasoning. Studies like *Talking Together* can help answer this question. We also need to know in what sense and to what degree the political choices made in those deliberations can be tied to the exercise of power. Responsiveness studies can help answer that question. But if we take the epistemic dimension of deliberation seriously then we need to be somewhat suspicious of raw opinion. We should not dismiss raw opinion altogether, however. This is for two reasons: first, because studies like *Talking Together* suggest that there is a large continuum between the opinion of an uninformed citizen insulated from epistemically helpful debate and the opinion of participants in minipublics; and second, because raw opinion may be reflective of what citizens actually think, believe, and care about. Democracy deviates from this for the sake of epistemic quality at its peril (Walzer 1981). Rather than dismiss raw opinion, we should thematize it in public political debate. In a democracy, the bent of public opinion is in itself a reason for public action. In a deliberative democracy we talk about and evaluate our reasons for public action including, perhaps especially, the reason that the people want this public action.

4

Representation in the deliberative system

JAMES BOHMAN

Democracy has historically taken many different forms. The recognition that there are limits on the scope of democracy as an organizational principle has been equally variable. For the purposes of this discussion, I will take democracy in its most minimal sense to be some ideal of *self rule*, whatever institutional form it takes. Given the wide variety of circumstances of politics, this form can be quite variable, from Greek assemblies to modern nation states and contemporary transnational polities. We cannot simply assume that there is some single best conception of democracy for all the different types of polities and political units, nor can we assume for that matter that there is some particular feature common to all democracies, such as territoriality or a unified demos, or that the subjects of the laws are also its authors. Indeed, new, plural forms of democratic self rule have emerged, including the European Union (EU), which, in Weiler's (1999: 268) terms, is 'a People of others', so that there is a lack of fit between much of traditional democratic theory based on nation states and new kinds of entities such as the EU. Once we abandon the idea that a polity is a democracy only if it accords with some single democratic principle or set of such principles, we must also change how we regard many of the familiar features of democratic institutions, many of which have undergone fundamental transformations in recent years.

When concerned about improving democratic practice, deliberative democrats have focused on the idea of an ideal deliberative forum and thus sought to improve deliberation and overall legitimacy based on such an ideal. No single forum, however ideally constituted, could possess sufficient deliberative capacity to legitimate various decisions and policies. A different approach would be more institutional. Instead of focusing on ideal

72

conditions, it would be better to look at deliberative, democratic practices as a whole with interacting and interdependent parts. Here I do not wish to engage in discussing the idea of a deliberative system itself, but rather use such a conception normatively to evaluate one of the more important institutions in democratic practice that is undergoing significant transformation: the democratic practice of representation. Recent criticisms of representative democracy might be thought to suggest that new emerging forms cannot be understood on the common electoral model, such as when they argue for descriptive forms of representation they are concerned not so much with the lack of meaningful participation, but with exclusion due to a lack of a basic political status. Representation is not just a necessity imposed by the size of modern polities, but is rather an important means by which the legitimacy of the demos can be expressed, challenged, and transformed. As Urbinati and Warren (2008: 402) put it, representation is not desirable as some second best, practical alternative but 'an intrinsically modern way of intertwining participation, political judgment' and, most importantly, 'the constitution of *demoi* capable of self rule'. How these tasks are to be fulfilled no longer depends on either electoral forms of representation, or the normative significance of a single legislature that is the authoritative voice of the People, where representation depends on a pre-existing and bounded demos.

This analysis will not pursue these more standard forms of analysis, but rather show how representation does indeed constitute 'an intrinsically modern way of intertwining participation and political judgment'. But it does so because it plays an important role in modern deliberative systems. A system designates a relation among interdependent parts. As a part of a deliberative system, it is important to see representation as promoting deliberation in both general and particular settings. Deliberation is not usually located in only one institution or forum, but involves many different feasible institutions and forums. My purpose here is to show how a systems approach makes it possible to see the range of different institutional roles that representation plays in a deliberative system (which could be either national or transnational). Indeed, the idea of a system captures the complex interrelationships among various institutions in any complex modern polity and as such it is a powerful tool for the normative appraisal of institutional norms and practice. But it also suggests a constructive principle for improving democratic practice without looking for some optimal design or blueprint. The focus on representation in modern democracies, both national and transnational, allows us to engage in both types of analysis of deliberative systems. While the first half of my argument is primarily evaluative of practices of representation, the second and more practical half employs the conception of the deliberative system in order to construct and improve democratic deliberative systems.

My discussion of the role of representations in modern deliberative systems has three steps. First, I discuss the importance of the idea of a deliberative system as a way of understanding profound changes in the current organization of democratic institutions and use the idea of a deliberative system to test the capacities of such forms of democracy. Using an example of debates about health care reform in the UK, I want to show that the resolution that was reached can best be illuminated by a deliberative system approach. With this account in mind, I turn to the functional role of representation within this and other deliberative systems: that is, to how representation makes the emergence of communicative freedom and communicative power possible through practices of inclusion. Third, I want to show that under conditions of wide pluralism, electoral and other common forms of representation fail to fulfil this role by themselves. However, it is still possible for communicative power to be distributed throughout the deliberative system as a whole and across its various levels.

With this discussion the use of the idea of a deliberative system can be made more practical. But the accompanying distributed conception of communicative power requires considerable innovation: new forms of representation, new sorts of deliberative institutions, and new ways in which citizens act as representatives for other citizens. Here, too, the standard accounts fail to see the interaction among representatives and the represented within various institutions and publics. Rather than employing standard models of these relations between representatives and the represented, a multilevel modern polity develops new locations in which representation can be distributed. In order to convert communicative freedom into communicative power successfully, citizen bodies and assemblies must begin to act as intermediaries within the deliberative system. These include different types of citizen representatives who convert communicative freedom into communicative power in two distinct forms: indirectly in minipublics and directly in minidemoi. Thus, a deliberative system approach shows the need for a variety of forms of citizen representation, if the system is to intertwine judgment and participation in a distinctly modern way at a variety of levels of scale.

Democracy and deliberative systems

Given that changes in the global order mean that long-held assumptions about democracy and representation can no longer be taken for granted, we must find an alternative to one of the most common solutions to the problem of identifying what is distinctively democratic. As Bruce Ackerman

(1991: 181) puts it, it is tempting to resort to a 'naïve synecdoche' that identifies some part, such as the legislature or parliament, for the whole. Instead, it is only because each part together with all the others makes up a democratic system that legislatures have their functions and roles. This potential can be shown when they are thought of in terms of their contribution to the whole, even with their weaknesses taken singly. Thus, on the deliberative systems approach representation can more clearly show that some of the functions of representation are no longer tied to the standard legislative model, particularly in the wider public role in opinion formation and in creating the access to political influence against powerful interests. Every deliberative system at whatever scale must find a variety of ways to fulfil this functional role and to secure the two great achievements of modern democracy: it must link free and open communication in the public sphere to empowered participation by citizens in decision-making. Every deliberative system must be able to generate communicative power out of the different spaces for communicative freedom opened by the deliberative system as a whole. Of course, this function is not achieved by representation alone. In this way, a deliberative system ought to be structured so as to promote political interaction across various levels and types of institutions so as to achieve the possibility for self rule.

An example of employing representation in a deliberative system in use may be helpful. John Parkinson has analysed a case of deliberative public involvement in health policies in the UK through a citizens' jury, an issue which he describes as 'a tough testing ground of the ability of any deliberative process to handle legitimacy deficits' (Parkinson 2006a: 44). He argues that focusing on the citizens' jury as a single deliberative forum is misleading, since the deliberative process involved a complex deliberative system with interacting parts. In the case of health care policy, a whole set of actors and institutions contributed to the achievement of a deliberatively legitimate public policy, including public hearings, activism, expert testimony, administrative consultation, designed forums, the media, referendums, and more. Not only that, the issue could only be resolved if the solution takes into account the myriad ways in which such problems cut across a variety of levels, from the local and regional to the national. Parkinson shows that it matters a great deal which groups commission various 'micro-deliberative' forums; it also matters a great deal at what level of the hierarchy the different deliberative procedures are used. Citizen representatives and other such experimental forums 'tend to be used lower down in the hierarchy because their legitimation needs are stronger and because of the pressure on them to be responsive' (Parkinson 2006a: 64). In a deliberative system, the differentiation among actors at various levels opens up the possibility that citizens' forums are not necessarily the best way to organize health care reform. As Parkinson notes, we have to understand interactions and interconnections among the parts of the system: 'the citizens' jury was not the entire deliberative process, but just its focal point' (Parkinson 2006a: 177). In taking a deliberative system approach, the analysis sees the citizens' jury in relation to the various networks and the larger deliberative system that allows us to see its democratic weaknesses.

There is a clear sense in which any deliberative system cannot do without appropriate claims to representativeness. In any particular deliberation, it is impossible for all to deliberate and hence those who do so are acting as representatives for those who are not participating. In general, the experience of people in deliberation in which some deliberate for others (such as the British Columbia Citizens' Assembly) is that these citizens are competent and representative, acting on behalf of everyone else. Thus, given the limits on number of participants, real-world deliberation is inherently representative. At the normative level, one central role of representation in most of its modern forms is to provide a means by which actors are able to introduce communicative freedom into the deliberative system; as such, it has to also be a location in which issues of political exclusion are thematized and worked out. If it can do so, then the system possesses sufficient deliberative capacity to be consequential and thus able to transform communicative freedom into communicative power. Dryzek (2010a: 10–11) offers three important features that must be present in a deliberative system. Such a system possesses deliberative capacity 'to the degree that its structures are able to accommodate deliberation that is authentic, inclusive and consequential'. But it can do so only if the system's deliberative capacity is able to generate communicative freedom and communicative power (Urbinati and Warren 2008: 403–4). However, when thinking of representation as part of a deliberative system, it is, as van Gunsteren (1998: 34) argues, important to see that in both of these respects 'a definition of plurality only in terms of social groups will omit a great many phenomena for which we do not yet have an established conceptual category'. In these contexts inclusivity is a function of spaces for the exercise of communicative freedom. The role of representation in parliamentary contexts is primarily deliberative and decisional; the laws are made for the people by the representatives that they authorize and empower to act on their behalf; but it is in generating communicative power that such a system is consequential. This role of representation is in the first instance to generate decision-making authority; but even in the parliamentary element of the deliberative system, representation is often also clearly deliberative; even if it does not aim at an authoritative decision, it is nonetheless often democratizing by the achievement of communicative power that can receive uptake at other modes and locations within the system.

With this deliberative context in mind, the second task is to determine which among the many possibilities is to be represented within various formal and informal deliberative bodies: groups, interests, opinions, discourse, and so on. Discourses fail to be authentic, primarily because they are constructed prior to deliberation. Discourses also fail to realize communicative freedom to the extent that such freedom requires a continual openness to new perspectives. While this approach is a feasible alternative to electoral representation at the global level, just how discourses are selected to be part of 'the Chamber of Discourses' (Dryzek and Niemeyer 2008) is also insufficiently democratic, since selection seems to be left to social scientists. Thus for the purposes of determining the deliberative purpose of representation it seems that perspectives are fundamental to the possibility of achieving new policies or institutions. For this reason, such a political form is 'multiperspectival' precisely because it does not seek to transform 'citizens' heterogeneity into an assembled People' (Ruggie 2000: 186), but rather seeks to transform heterogeneity into creative new possibilities through the exercise of communicative freedom. While Ruggie is here discussing transnational democratic forms, the same applies within porous, contemporary states. Such an account embraces institutional pluralism, especially when it is put in the context of a deliberative system that would include a variety of modes of representation. It may be difficult to tell in advance why one part of the system may be more responsive to public opinion and function to be better able to represent certain interests and perspectives within political judgment. Indeed, as Dryzek himself points out, the greater the differentiation among actors and forums the more the system as a whole is able to engage in good deliberation and achieve overall legitimacy (Dryzek 2010a: 8).

While representatives do not mirror their constituents, it is still the case that deliberation can function formally and informally to assemble the People. Using the EU as a model, two sorts of institutions are crucial for the functioning of the deliberative system as modes of distributing representation in discursive interaction and formal decision-making, which I call minipublics and minidemoi (Bohman 2007). These particular institutions are not only important features of the deliberative system; they are also locations for the generation of communicative power. While minipublics play an important deliberative role, minidemoi offer a form of representation in which deliberative decision-making is sufficient to transform communicative freedom into communicative power, to the extent that they become authorized to make binding decisions. With these distinctions in mind, the deliberative systems approach can help determine what role non-elective representation plays in the generation of communicative power.

From communicative freedom to communicative power

In the modern state, a self-ruling people consists of all those and *only* those who are both authors *and* subjects of the law. In this sense, the People are a supreme sovereign, as it is often expressed in constitutions. But this standard view neglects the fundamental tensions between universality and particularity built into the constitutions of most democratic states, especially those aspects that concern universal human political rights on the one hand and the rights of citizens on the other. As Habermas (2001: 63) puts it, the form of natural law theory espoused by most founders of modern constitutional orders requires that the political community as a whole (and not just its electoral jurisdictions) must consist of *a determinate group of persons,* 'united by the decision to grant to each other precisely those rights that are necessary for the legitimate ordering of their collective existence by means of positive law'. Thus, the fundamental distinction is between the status of being a citizen *within* a political community and the often negative status of being merely a non-citizen bearer of human rights with claims *against* the political community. The body of citizens cannot really directly decide what is to be done, and for this reason Thomas Christiano (Chapter 2, this volume) sees the citizens as only determining the ends of the polity and not its means, where public officials may act as their trustees. Thus, there is an unavoidable gap between the ideal of self rule and the requirements of representation, so that, in their role as citizens at least, the people do not actually transform communicative freedom into communicative power. Discursive forms of representation in fact gain their appeal through the lack of a well defined people at certain levels of complexity and scale.

At the very least this suggests that having only one form of representation, electoral or otherwise, is insufficient for the task of self rule under conditions of large scale and wide diversity. A variety of devices must be used to connect delegates and agents to their principals, and representatives to their constituents. These ties may become more tenuous as the community grows larger and multilevelled, and generally the legitimacy of international institutions is often thought to come entirely through the executive function of national governments, over which citizens have little democratic control. Such institutions have in fact developed to the point that they are neither deliberative nor easily influenced by electoral control except in the long run, so that they may often be sources of domination. Are there forms of representation that might preserve the possibility of self rule in a large-scale and plural form of democracy? From a deliberative systems perspective, other institutions may take over some of the functions of representation, as when a vibrant public sphere transmits citizens' claims and successfully mediates between the free and open public sphere and the decision makers, often without being concerned with issues of constituency. This signals the importance of communicative freedom in a deliberative system.

Habermas's (1996) idea of the public sphere as a 'transmission belt' leads to new possibilities of public rather than political representation. Electoral representation can fail to capture the relevant dimensions of the diverse public, and it may also lack the institutional capability to exercise communicative power through various forms of accountability. For this very reason, Dahl (1999) and others are sceptical of the idea of any form of democracy in which the chains of delegation expand, because the accountability of officials to citizens becomes more difficult to achieve. Rather than thinking of assemblies and legislatures as deliberative in the usual sense, there may also be cases in which citizens act as representatives for others, either formally or informally, in various kinds of minipublics, so that communicative freedom and communicative power emerge through a subset of the people who act as representatives of others. In multilevel polities, parliaments or legislatures must transfer their decision-making powers to some other subset of citizens who are better able to make some particular authoritative decision. Thus, we might say that legislatures are themselves minipublics; constructed out of the public at large, they act in such a way as to use their deliberation to acquire some testable and public decisional authority through the common exercise of communicative freedom. Indeed, as Saward has pointed out, elections can undermine communicative freedom by restricting the nature and range of representative perspectives and voices (Saward 2010: ch. 1).

Nonetheless, it is important to recognize that *any* such group of citizens acting to represent others, however constituted, may always fall short descriptively and normatively and fail to be inclusive and consequential. How might representation nonetheless be legitimate? Here we might think of what a jury does when it acts as a fully empowered public capable of deciding guilt or innocence of the accused under the appropriate legal constraints. This empowerment of the public fits the description of what we have been looking for: a form of representation in an institution that transforms the communicative freedom of citizens into communicative power (subject to the revisions by other citizens doing the same). What is distinctive is that they do so not by directly consulting the opinions of their fellow citizens, but rather, in Mark Warren's (2008) apt phrase, by acting as 'citizen representatives', and thus to that extent citizens in these contexts represent themselves in their role as citizens. At the same time, they are citizens who represent other citizens, in which a few actively deliberate and decide for the sake of all other citizens. The important difference is, then, that citizens not only represent other citizens, but that the decision-making power of the body of citizens is no longer only tied to a single form and mechanism for representation. This has in fact been the role of various kinds of minipublics.

Whatever the role that officials play in making and executing proposals, the difference is that citizens deliberate by handing over their powers of citizenship to other citizens who act independently and on their behalf. But because they are citizen representatives, they cannot claim that they form a demos, even as they may claim to represent many demoi. In the deliberative system, properly selected citizen representatives can for particular issues represent other citizens precisely because their decision-making can be justified in deliberative terms. Given that this use of representation is open to being scaled up, representation is primarily a matter of inclusion and thus can be distributed across institutional levels. As part of a deliberative system, the state has important problem-solving functions that make it difficult to see how citizen representation could function without this or some similar capacity to help in resisting the domination of powerful private actors. Thus far, no other institutions have such capacity, even if it is now expected to be exercised more broadly in a multilevel deliberative system, even as states are now finding their problem-solving capacities diminished in the face of transnational issues.

Citizenship as a multilevel status: perspectives or opinions?

In existing democracies, citizenship and representation are statuses tied to territory in a variety of ways. Once an institution that generalized statuses beyond locales, territorial citizenship has now become a status that cannot assure that all those affected will be able to have a say on issues and problems that affect them. In current conditions, many non-citizens should be counted among those affected by many issues within the territorially delimited community. The EU has established rights of local participation that are based on residence alone. Even so, interdependence extends affectedness to many of those who are outside of the delimited community, and the same is true of even large territorially defined political communities. If citizenship and representation are so delimited, then they may not be sufficient for the purpose of avoiding domination even by democratic polities themselves. One goal of democratic representation should be precisely to avoid both of these forms of domination internal to the practice of democracy itself. Under such circumstances, the tasks of representation are at the very least twofold: to secure self rule and freedom from domination. Many constitutional democracies identify universal statuses, including the rights of citizens to *habeas corpus* and other minimal conditions of justice (Bohman 2009). Dennis Thompson (1999) has argued for a special form of representation for the unrepresented within legislative deliberative bodies, so that at the very least the generalizable claims of those outside the polity (and of future generations) could be heard. Thus, he argues for a 'tribune' whose task it is to monitor the effects of policies upon the interests of such unrepresented groups and exercise a veto in cases when their interests are ignored. The *desiderata* of good representation could also help identify at least counterfactually the range of concerns that result from the exclusion of those who lack standing on territorial grounds or access to influence over decision-making because they are dominated. Various institutional and non-institutional locations for such pre-emptive and inclusive deliberation have been proposed and debated, as has their feasibility.[1] It is important that any such mechanism cannot be based directly upon electoral mechanisms.

Properly generalized to include statuses, Thompson's (1999) solution has the advantage of organizing deliberation so that people outside the polity will be less likely to be dominated or have costs externalized to them. The issue is indeed one of expanding deliberation by rethinking the role of representation in transnational issues. We might think that such a possibility functions as an ideal, on the basis of which all such arrangements are subject to revision. Addams's (1902: 11–12) idea that the legislature 'should be an exact portrait, in miniature, of the people at large' offers a fully extended descriptive account of representation or what that might mean. Nonetheless, it provides no guidance as to the relevant features of inclusion. Stratified sampling appears to be successful in making even small groups statistically representative, thus achieving Addams's aim of a portrait in miniature according to some specific criteria, whatever they are. Here deliberative accounts could serve to narrow the range of considerations, since in any particular case the criteria cannot achieve some perfectly proportioned miniature. Richardson (2002), for example, shows that deliberative approaches reject preference- or interest-based accounts, since these would presuppose an independent fixity of individuals' positions. Thus, it is not these qualities of citizens that ought to be fairly represented, but rather 'their political views' (Richardson 2002: 23). Hence, proportional representation through voting, for example, wrongly distributes communicative power according to just such considerations. However, by Richardson's own criteria, this unduly makes citizens' views rather than perspectives the basis for representation. Opinions seem too fluid to be the basis of representation, even if they may be the marker of something else more fundamental. These issues become salient when deliberation

---

[1] For discussions of the varieties of theories of deliberative democracy, see, among others, Bohman (1998); Chambers (2003); and from a Rawlsian perspective, Freeman (2000).

operates through the selection of citizens in a minipublic that must in some sense be a 'public in miniature' to achieve legitimacy sufficient for the exercise of communicative power.

The aspects of diversity among citizens can be defined along cultural, social, and epistemic axes. Furthermore, each aspect of diversity can be measured along various deliberative dimensions: in terms of values, opinions, and perspectives. These roughly correspond to the main aspects of diversity, and thus provide the basis for thinking about what it is that should be represented. They can all be taken into consideration, even if they are often at cross purposes. In order to avoid such conflicts, those who see the importance of diversity favour one aspect over others. Like Richardson, Mill (1975) and others celebrate diversity of opinion as important to deliberation. This is certainly true so long as deliberators can isolate disagreements along this dimension, and difficulties arise when issues include not just basic beliefs, but also beliefs about the way in which beliefs are justified. Values in this sense include basic moral norms, various cultural conceptions of the good, religion, and important political norms (including conceptions of the common good). The complexity and pluralism across multiple criteria create many different social positions, whose differences in perspective primarily emerge from the range and type of experience.[2]

Instead of the selection process, one alternative to deal with possible error is to impose *ex ante* limits on possible reasons or *ex post* constraints on outcomes. This way of constructing empowered minipublics points in the right direction. However, such policies on their own fail to promote sufficient diversity to avoid bias and other cognitive errors. Goodin argues that representative inclusion is limited by the conditions of effective participation in a deliberative forum, since it 'proves to be impossible to represent the particulars of diversity within the assembly'.[3] Goodin argues that there are strict limits on 'presence' and thus that there is no viable solution to 'the sheer fact of diversity'. Alternatively, we might, with David Estlund, adopt a policy that it would be best to maximize the quantity of available reasons, since judgments of quality might suggest 'individious comparisons' that adversely affect the chances of the least influential to participate effectively in deliberation.[4] There are, however, many possible versions of this

---

[2] For a fuller development of the argument for toleration aimed at perspectives, see Bohman (2003).

[3] See Goodin (2008: 247). Instead of seeking maximal, but impossible, inclusion, Goodin believes that it is possible for representatives to act in such a way as to deliberate without the pretension of maximal inclusion and thus internalize their fundamental fallibility in overcoming the 'sheer fact of diversity'.

[4] On 'the epistemic value of quantity', see Estlund (2000: 144); this leads to his 'epistemic difference principle' as formulated to emphasize quantity (Estlund 2000: 147). However,

'epistemic difference principle', to use Estlund's term. Any such difference principle must identify the appropriate *maximandum* that would achieve this end. Otherwise, the policy suggested by a difference principle might be self-defeating. Maximizing all possible inputs, for example, may also increase opportunities for manipulation. But within a deliberative system maximization at every level is not necessarily desirable, and looking at representation in terms of specific deliberative mechanisms rather than as a system leads to a mistaken focus of the epistemic difference principle on reasons rather than perspectives.

Goodin (2008: 11–38) and Estlund (2002: 78) point to limitations in linking the use of minipublics to the ideal of descriptive representation. Goodin comes close to a feasible version of such deliberation when he recognizes that in any political order deliberation cannot be concentrated in a few institutions, but rather must be 'distributed'. However, he fails to see that inclusion via representation is also a distributed property of the *deliberative system* as a whole, whatever criteria of selection or deliberative norms we use in order to maximize the pool of available reasons. The epistemic motivation for selecting a particular formulation of the difference principle is better served by looking at the use of various kinds of representative publics. In light of the democratic aims of the deliberative system as a whole, any deliberative system should not seek to optimize the outcomes of each and every deliberative institution as much as seek to avoid bad ones. This is because the relevant aspect of diversity that is necessary for improving the process of deliberation is not the pool of *reasons* as such but the availability of the *perspectives* that inform these reasons and give them their cogency. Mill (1975: 188) argued that the 'workingman's view' was excluded from deliberation. Richardson (2002: 201–2) argues that in certain contexts perspectives are significant because they 'orient the ways in which political views would be articulated and adapted to face new challenges' and thus 'deserve independent attention'. These arguments, however, do not go far enough, even as they suggest that the inclusion of perspectives is an important corrective. Given the variety of topics of deliberation, it is not possible to decide in advance which among the potential candidate perspectives ought to be included, as Young (2000: ch. 3) does when she argues that it is social perspectives defined by 'objective structural positions' in a society that are

---

maximizing input is not intrinsically valuable from the participants' perspective unless it increases the possibility of each perspective being heard. Increasing input could be democratically justified to the worst off only if it increases the number of perspectives in discussion. In order that the worst off (here the least effective in deliberation) may accept the epistemic difference principle, the relevant value is the diversity of perspectives rather than quantity of input.

worthy of inclusion for their distinctive contribution to the reduction of bias overall. Thus, a systems approach suggests that the reduction of bias overall is the proper goal for the system as a whole, and this is best achieved by inclusion of perspectives.

But the benefits of such inclusion in avoiding bad outcomes are quite real and depend on previously excluded groups acquiring representative status. For example, Argarwal (2001) has studied the effects of the exclusion of the perspective of women from deliberation on community forestry groups in India and Nepal. Because women had primary responsibility for wood gathering in their search for cooking fuel, they possessed greater knowledge of what sort of gathering was sustainable and about where trees were that needed protection. Mixed groups of participants were in this case much more effective in achieving the goals of enforcement. In such cases, the improvement of practices depended upon achievement of representative status, by which women's available reasons came to have the decisional authority that they previously lacked. This is not just the status needed to be heard in deliberation, but the status to have one's perspective become representative of the group as a whole. The difference is not simply in having one's interests considered by others, but that such interests are now the interests of the group and thus inform one of the perspectives in terms of which a decision may be framed. In these cases, communicative freedom can be transformed into communicative power, from discussion and persuasion to playing a part in self rule. It is also important to see that institutions that generate the joint exercise of communicative freedom and power create the deliberative capacity to address domination within and across borders. Deliberation, representation, and non-domination are key features of democratization. In the next sections, I use the deliberative system approach constructively to improve practices of representation with various forms of deliberation.

From minipublics to minidemoi

Democratization has two main dimensions: first, it requires institutions, publics, and associations in which communicative freedom is realized; and second, that this communicative freedom also be exercised in institutions that link such freedom to the exercise of normatively generated communicative power. As I have argued, communicative freedom is the exercise of a *communicative status*, the status of being recognized as a member of a public. It is a societal and thus a universal property, which can be attained for each only if all have it. But communicative freedom is transformed into communicative power only when it is incorporated into institutionalized processes of decision-making. Communicative power is thus exercised by those who possess a *decisional status* within an institution in which one's perspective is taken to be representative of those who exercise communicative freedom. Under these conditions, the communicative freedom to initiate deliberation becomes the communicative power to place an item on an institutional agenda and then further to have the status to influence decisions made about items on that agenda. But whatever else characterizes these forms of decision-making, these bodies will inevitably consist of some subset of participants and citizens taken as a whole. For this reason, such bodies must be able to plausibly claim that they are representing others at one or many different levels.

This description focuses on the process of democratization as a whole. An adequate account must capture complex interrelationships of civil society, the public sphere, and formal democratic institutions, all of which are required as conditions for democratization as I have described it. As the deliberative systems approach suggests, rather than look for a single axis on which to connect emerging publics to decision-making processes to various institutions, it will be more useful to consider how a variety of connections can be made between communicative status and decisional status. In considering possible institutional designs that enhance and democratize deliberation, it is necessary to see that different institutional arrangements can function best at different levels and scales, and distribute decisional authority across the local, the national, the regional, and the transnational levels.

This systems approach will require different forms of representation at various levels, with different modes of constituency and legitimacy. Such an account checks the tendency to see only one sort of representative body as distinctively democratic or closer to some particular democratic ideal. Or, as Dryzek (2010a) argues, we might see interactive effects, where weaknesses in one part of the deliberative system are compensated for by developments in another part, say the informal public sphere compensating for poor deliberation in formal bodies such as legislatures. These interactive effects of the deliberative system might at times lead to bad consequences, as when the presence of well functioning deliberative institutions like a constitutional court could permit the legislature to propose bad laws simply to appeal to voters, expecting them to be struck down. Currently, different forms of democracy are often discussed, such as corporatist or consociational democracy, and we might see such variety within deliberative systems. This suggests that we do not need to idealize deliberation in each dimension (or that a particular part must be maximally deliberative according to its type), but rather test the deliberative system as a whole and how it functions overall according to a basic list of democratic functions, including representation.

Here we might think of the EU as an example of a deliberative system in which certain functions are weak or even missing, such as a transnational public sphere for the EU as a whole. The EU decision-making practices claim to be deliberative, and some organize empowered deliberation across various levels in practices such as the open method of coordination. A clear advantage of a deliberative system is that it permits not just various interacting and interconnected sites for deliberation, but also relations across various levels and types of deliberation. Here I want to focus on the different ways in which deliberative representation becomes as significant as non-electoral forms. In keeping with the distinction between communicative freedom and communicative power, I want to look at two distinct types of deliberative institutions: minipublics and minidemoi. Minipublics take many forms from citizen juries, to deliberative polls, to citizens' assemblies that are authorized to supplement rather than replace other forms of representation. Random selection provides a kind of legitimacy to their deliberation, not because they will somehow mirror the public as a whole, but because they promote political equality and better deliberation (Parkinson 2006a: 74ff). A reason to adopt such innovations in the transnational context is that the relatively small groups of deliberators that make up minipublics can lay claim to various kinds of representativeness. They also may have various claims to legitimacy, often tied to the procedures of selection (such as random selection) or to the forms of non-partisan deliberation they engage in (Fung 2003). However participants are selected and whatever the norms governing their deliberation, the members of minipublics act as representatives in two ways: first, as mutually recognized members of a public stand-in for the deliberation of the many (whose agreement is revocable); and second, in their deliberative standing they may have some kind of decisional power, however weak. In the case of the British Columbia Citizens' Assembly, the task of the minipublic was to deliberate about and propose electoral reforms to be voted upon by all citizens. The use of this procedure was clearly motivated by having the decision about electoral reform exhibit 'representativeness', that is, the randomness of the selection procedure was supplemented with broader recruitment of citizens, so that the decision was made by 'citizens like us'. Even so, the Citizens' Assembly only made recommendations to be approved (or not as in this case) by a referendum.

Such representative publics then fall between weak and strong publics. Unlike weak publics, they do not merely spontaneously engage in discourses within the broader public sphere, thereby introducing arguments that may flow in various ways into the formal political system, as when environmental groups introduce a discourse of sustainability. At the same time they are also not strong publics in the full sense, since many such publics lack full decisional authority. Rather, whatever decisional power they have, they have in virtue of being authorized by some body or authority within the formal political system, usually by legislatures of various kinds. But this is not sufficient; while minipublics may improve deliberation and even political equality, they need not improve democracy. What is needed here is a combination of both: a public with the representativeness of minipublics and the decisional authority of existing democratic institutions. However complex the deliberative system becomes, it is possible for constructed publics to achieve decisional status, often on the background of the absence of effective territorial institutions for dealing with pressing problems of international society. The lack of effective and empowered global deliberation has meant that crosscutting issues of common concern, such as climate change, have not been easily made subject to binding deliberative agreement.

Minipublics are different from many other representative bodies to the extent that their selection procedures are constructed precisely to validate their claim to be representative for the citizenry as a whole, at least sufficiently to raise the legitimacy conferred by political equality. In terms of the representation of interests, minipublics are often more diverse than most empowered institutions such as legislative bodies. But the importance of inclusion becomes most pressing in the case of deliberation that aims at an authoritative decision. When, in addition to their shared communicative status, such strong but small-scale publics also possess a decisional status, their members have ceased to be minipublics and have become minidemoi. As a minidemos, citizens have all the structural features of an inclusive public, but so as to provide opportunities for the exercise of communicative power through participating in deliberation aimed at making a determinate decision, where groups of citizens, rather than experts or office holders, have the communicative freedom to deliberate and form opinions as well as the communicative power to make recommendations or actual decisions (as they do on juries who decide the facts of law and citizen juries who often make recommendations). The deliberative advantage is that such minidemoi are able to deliberate within specific institutional, functional, and temporal constraints in ways that the public at large cannot (except over the long term, as in the case of the abolition of the slave trade). Rather than being simply a form of consultation or of recommendation, this form of deliberation would require that institutions jointly transfer some of their authority to the minidemos whose deliberation they empower, opening up a directly deliberative process within the institution which includes as many perspectives as possible. The use of randomly selected citizens for empowered deliberation is useful not only for democratization at the transnational level, but it can also serve to enhance the quality of deliberation. Such empowered publics with decision-making powers for particular issues or sets of issues would likely be authorized by the wider set of institutions in which communicative power is exercised; and while the minidemos is concerned with making some decision, this issue and process would still be debated and tested in the relevant public spheres. Decision-making competence can thus be distributed among various types of publics, which then become minidemoi to the extent that they are formed to make authoritative decisions. As minidemoi, publics are empowered to decide as strong publics; their use is of course rare within states, given their monopoly powers. Even so, officials of the World Trade Organization (WTO) represent state interests with powers transferred to authorized experts that act as their agents. A strong minidemos would not act as an agent to some principal; instead it would be an instance of an empowered form of citizen representation, where citizens are empowered to deliberate in the place of other citizens in a more direct form of deliberation, analogous to the strong decisional power of juries rather than weaker consultative bodies.

The advantage of this form of deliberative representation is that it can develop different forms of representation across various overlapping demoi. The fundamental justification here is republican: democracy at any level is better served by overall institutional pluralism, in which there is a variety of overlapping and mutually checking procedures, each formulated according to its contribution to the division of decision-making and epistemic labour within the deliberative system as a whole. Thus, given the variety of forums and decision-making bodies, inclusive representation does not limit empowered decision-making to territorial bodies alone. Indeed, territorial bodies oversimplify the task of representativeness, and in doing so cannot take available perspectives into account. Unlike other, more broadly distributed, forms of representation they are more likely to be able to ensure non-domination. A robust public sphere may often be more effective in ensuring non-domination due to its capacities to mobilize and contest dominating forms of decision-making whose constituencies are fixed too narrowly or are too restrictive in identifying available perspectives.

According to this approach, constituencies are variable depending on a diagnostic use of the all affected principle. Even if constituencies remain variable, it would be possible for citizen members of a minidemos to develop forms of citizen involvement and accountability that can also be exercised within the wider deliberative system and compensate for the lack of strong publics and consequential forms of representation. Experts will sometimes exert some influence over such decisions and improve their epistemic quality, particularly when certain types of issues are at stake. The normative basis of the legitimacy of these representatives can thus develop over time and in interaction with citizens whom they represent. New forms of representation are particularly important when the deliberative system expands and is in need of greater legitimacy in the use of communicative power.

This lack of democratic legitimacy has been an important impetus for change in emerging and incompletely multiperspectival polities, such as the EU, in which the deliberative system still lacks capacity for deliberation to be sufficiently diverse, inclusive, and consequential (Dryzek 2010a: 10). In making such judgments about such a deliberative system, it is important to distinguish between the deliberative capacities distributed throughout all the macro-level institutions in the system as a whole from the capacities of any particular micro-level deliberation in a given public or demos. Institutionalization at the macro-level is important to democratization to the extent that interacting with such institutions helps to shape the diversity of perspectives according to the goals that they have and the means of representation that they make available. In this way, institutions can bring out latent perspectives, perhaps even bring them about in terms of the various sorts of legitimate decision-making powers that they have. Given that institutions play an important role in shaping how perspectives get taken up in deliberation, no single institution such as parliaments or legislatures could fully express the decision-making capacities of the various demoi. When perspectives are integrated into the deliberative system, empowered minidemoi and not merely authorized minipublics can emerge. In a multiperspectival, transnational polity, minidemoi of empowered and diverse citizens can shape deliberative outcomes so as to incorporate the overlapping perspectives of citizens, who in constituting themselves as a representative minidemos transform their communicative freedom into communicative power. While the concept of a strong public is the more typical way of discussing this kind of institutional possibility, it is misleading to the extent that any strong public is so only in virtue of its having become a demos. In this way, democratization aims at transforming publics into demoi through deliberation. The exercise conception of representation through demoi makes democracy the achievement of self rule through the deliberative system as a whole. This achievement is that citizens can represent other citizens not in their beliefs or any other descriptive features, but in their active capacity *qua* citizens.

Representing transnational demoi: citizen representation and the EU

Addams's well-known portrait conception of representation (see Pitkin 1967: 60–8) has plausibility only if we presuppose that there is a determinate and delimited demos to be portrayed, with the goal of complete representation within a legislative assembly. When structured by the assumption that democracy is such because it entails such a demos, citizen representation may not go far enough for cases in which many different possible demoi exist so that the difficulties of any mirror conception of representation proliferate. But what sort of representation could there be when it is not the constituent parts of the demos that is to be represented? In this respect, Cohen and Sabel (1998) are correct that there is both a certain directness and diversity involved in a 'directly deliberative polyarchy'. Nonetheless, such a polyarchy that is also deliberative involves some form of representation or another. A polyarchy is in the first instance direct only in the sense that the representatives are *citizens*, acting in their representative capacity. Thus, we might think of direct citizen representation in terms of an 'exercise conception' of deliberative representation (Maliks 2009). Citizens represent other citizens in their active capacity within an institutional division of deliberative labour, so that a polyarchy of demoi gain political agency and exercise their political freedom through their representatives exercising their same powers. The exercise conception thus serves to emphasize the agency of both the represented and the representative in the deliberative process, precisely because communicative power is generated from communicative freedom in the deliberative system as a whole. Minidemoi represent via specific achievements, such as the emergence of an overlapping consensus on specific recurring issues, rather than a once and for all comprehensive constitutional settlement.

Given size, scale, and complexity, citizens cannot have influence if they only act for themselves in deliberation, but rather become influential by distributing the decisional status through representation to others. Thus, citizen representatives are such only by having such powers distributed into a variety of roles and institutions, rather than by having some more unitary conception of self rule in a collective assembly. When acting in a variety of ways through others, we make manifest that the minidemoi are plural, that we do not, to paraphrase Rousseau (1987: 116), obey only ourselves when we act through the decisional status of others. Even if Habermas (1996: 327) is correct that publics as such do not rule, they act through their representatives who participate in empowered processes of deliberation that are so empowered by other citizens, not simply by some legal mechanism or other. Thus, having the role of representative even as one is represented is rather open ended, since it does not necessarily map on to other, non-deliberative aspects of citizenship. An undocumented worker could act in a representative capacity so long as they are able to jointly realize communicative freedom and communicative power in some recognized deliberative process and thus act in a representative capacity for citizens and non-citizens. Here representatives are performing a complex function of bringing together distributed participation and inclusive deliberation, and in so doing constitute demoi capable of self rule, as Urbinati and Warren (2008) have put it. It is time to consider how transnational representation might be possible as a special case of deliberative representation.

For citizen representatives in a deliberative system, this way of exercising representation does not necessarily depend on electoral authorization. Were citizen representatives to depend on this form of authorization, they would simply represent other representatives and thus form another parliamentary body. But in this case, they cease to be citizens who are acting as the representatives of other citizens. This problem is manageable once we see that there is no single source of such authorization. Instead, the authority to empower citizens to represent other citizens must be distributed across many different institutional locations from the informal to the executive, judicial, and legislative branches, each of which is able to distribute the tasks of citizen representatives, often when the formal and official structures suffer from democratic deficits. If the EU were based on citizen representation, its authorization as a minipublic or minidemos would often best be done by a representative European Parliament, whose function would be to act as an intermediary and to set procedures and monitor the democratic character of the deliberations and outcomes. We might think that one central function of the EU parliament is to act as a kind of Ministry of Minipublics and Minidemoi, when its authorization includes not only procedural specifications such as selection criteria, but also the basic task about which citizens are supposed to act as representatives. Here we have to go beyond current EU practices, although perhaps some, such as the much discussed open method of coordination, provide structural analogues to the representation of demoi. One might think that in contrast to a minipublic, a minidemos would be self authorizing, to the extent that it realizes both by exercising jointly held communicative freedom and communicative power. Even such directly deliberative and polyarchical processes cannot do without some institutional intermediaries at both the deliberative and the implementation phase.

Besides the epistemic benefits that representation across different groups would bring, inclusive decision-making of this sort also promotes democracy through the joint exercise of self rule. Such a process can also benefit from informal intermediaries that seek to transform a weak public into a strong public. In this regard, the history of the Women's International League for Peace and Freedom (WILPF) illustrates how communicative status can be transformed into decisional status at the international level (Cochran 2008). The WILPF saw their task as two-fold: they sought not only to form public opinion by bringing women's perspectives to bear, but also attempted to shape the decision of extant international institutions, the League of Nations in particular. Their communicative freedom was effectively transformed in a campaign to influence the League of Nations to do something about the many state-less women and children who continued to be held in Turkey after World War I. It was a self-consciously formed public that sought to legitimate its influence on such decisional processes as representatives of women and humanity as a whole. The WILPF did not just influence specific decisions but interacted with the League of Nations so as to reshape and direct this institution away from its initial orientation that gave priority to member states and towards emerging strong international publics who were at the time concerned about creating the conditions for peace through publicity.

The example of the WILPF also shows that transnational representation does not always require explicit and formal authorization. Given how dispersed global governance institutions are, it is not surprising that this role is occupied by a wide variety of organizations and groups, many of which attempt to influence a particular domain or policy issue. Apart from the sort of structure found in the EU, current transnational publics are weak, in the sense that they exert influence only through changing discourses and general public opinion without the benefits of institution-alized deliberation. We might consider such non-authorized forms of representation as primarily discursive, as when Dryzek insists that 'delib-erative and democratic global politics can most fruitfully be sought in the more informal realm of international public spheres'.[5] As in the case of the abolition of the slave trade in the early nineteenth century through trans-national networks of advocates, such discourses can influence important informal norms, and may become representative without any formal elect-oral or institutional authorization. Global publics and social movements have contributed not only towards instituting conditions of communi-cative freedom, but also attempt to achieve what Dryzek calls discursive representation so that international institutions are not dominated by one kind of perspective, as has been the case with neoliberalism in global

---

[5] Dryzek (2006: vii). In *Foundations and Frontiers of Deliberative Governance* (Dryzek 2010a), Dryzek has now changed his view, allowing not only for discursive representa-tion but also for ways in which deliberative decision-making is distributed and secured in a transnational deliberative system. This view is similar to the one I endorse here and in Bohman (2007: ch. 1).

economic institutions. We might think of these forms of representation as generative of new and potentially decisional publics that seek to influence various decisional publics or networks. Here we have a different kind of democratic deficit, one that can only be corrected by changing the discursive basis of many different sorts of practices, economic as well as political. These publics are not yet minidemoi, but may construct the possibility of the emergence of such a demoi by opening up various previously closed arenas for deliberation to form new minidemoi, such as would focus efforts to find binding solutions to climate change.

Conclusion: democracy, representation, and non-domination

I have used intentionally broad terms in describing citizen representation in deliberation; it is both a means to achieve greater democratic legitimacy, but also for democratization, as the union of communicative freedom and communicative power, of the communicative and decisional status of publics. It is also broad because there does not seem to be a royal road to democracy, and democratization has to be possible even without fully democratic institutions. Many democratically minded cosmopolitans have turned to the informal realm of civil society and social movement in order to talk about discursive democracy or democracy from below. However important transnational associations and movements have been to many social struggles, they provide only one dimension of the processes of democratization. As political communities become more transnational, pluralistic, and complex, democratization requires both various formal and informal intermediaries, emerging publics to generate communicative power across borders, and transnational institutions in which publics can elaborate constituencies with decisional statuses.

These same considerations of size and complexity also suggest that informal democratization works best with formal democratization, when the communicative freedom of publics becomes linked to decisional status within a larger deliberative system. In this context, representation of some sort is not only inevitable for reasons of scale and complexity, but also promotes democratization. I have argued for a conception of citizen representation in deliberation in which citizens *qua* representative have some sort of decisional status, however weak or strong that might be. In this case, it is not only possible to represent demoi, but also to form them so as to enable the exercise of a distributed form of self rule across an inclusive deliberative system aimed at distributing decisions and statuses to all those affected. The mark of the achievement of such a deliberative system would be the prevalence of the exercise of communicative power, especially through the authorization of a variety of minipublics and minidemoi. The absence of an effective deliberative system that is genuinely representative at the international level is an obstacle to important achievements of political equality in the international system (including the recognition of increased global inclusion), resulting in the recognition of the costs of problems with highly uneven consequences, such as global climate change.

5

Two trust-based uses of minipublics in democratic systems

MICHAEL K. MACKENZIE AND MARK E. WARREN

Introduction

An important success of deliberative democratic theory and practice over the last two decades has been to show that ordinary citizens are capable of sophisticated and democratically legitimate political judgments, if they represent the constituencies relevant to an issue and participate in focused, deliberative processes. Among the most interesting of these processes are *minipublics*. A minipublic is a deliberative forum typically consisting of 20–500 participants, focused on a particular issue, selected as a reasonably representative sample of the public affected by the issue, and convened for a period of time sufficient for participants to form considered opinions and judgments. Examples of minipublics include deliberative polling, citizen juries, planning cells, consensus conferences, and citizens' assemblies. Experience with these processes suggests that, on average, participants develop thoughtful, well-founded judgments that can crystallize latent public opinion, complement expert judgments, and formulate politically viable policy options (e.g. Blais *et al.* 2008; Crosby 1995; Dienel and Renn 1995; Fishkin 1997).

While the basic structure of these processes is already well developed, the question of what functions minipublics can and should perform within a democratic political system is less well understood. The purpose of one of the best-developed forms of minipublic – James Fishkin's deliberative poll – is to provide an alternative to conventional public opinion polling techniques. Rather than providing a reflective snapshot of public opinion, Fishkin has claimed that deliberative polling helps us understand what public opinion would be like on a given issue *if* the public were well informed, *and* had subjected their beliefs to deliberative scrutiny (Fishkin 1997, 2009; Fishkin and Luskin 2005). Other kinds of minipublic have been justified as ways of providing advice to decision-makers that represent considered public opinion. Minipublics have also been justified in very generic terms, as devices to increase citizen participation in public decision-making. The most complete surveys list the potential functions of minipublics within the political systems that encompass them. These include contributions to the development of citizens' civic dispositions and capacities, inclusion, representation, popular control of political agendas, informed decision-making, accountability, effectiveness and efficiency, and legitimacy (Bohman 2007; Fung 2003; Gastil 2008; Goodin and Dryzek 2006; Smith 2009; Warren 2008; cf. Chambers 2009).

Here we examine a different class of potential functions: those having to do with trust. We suggest that minipublics can serve two important trust-based roles defined by trust issues that are distinctive to legislative and executive domains of politics. Within the legislative domain, although *mistrust* is the norm (usually appropriately so, since interests diverge), citizens must still place their trust in representative agents such as elected representatives, political parties, or advocacy groups that actually engage in political conflict, negotiation, deliberation, and decision-making. The executive domain brings other trust issues, not the least of which is that executive agencies often (and increasingly) deal with political issues through policy development and rule-making, sometimes because legislatures lack the capacity, sometimes because they simply transfer political issues to agencies, and sometimes because potentially political issues are created by the very acts of policy-making. In all such cases, citizens may become actively engaged, but it is more likely that they will make judgments to trust political representatives or administrative agencies, sometimes on good grounds, but more often simply by default. In complex political systems, citizens must make a variety of trust judgments, simply because no one can participate in all the collective decisions that affect them; a *democracy* should enable citizens to make *good* trust judgments, such that their trust is not misplaced or abused.

We argue that minipublics can help address the two trust trouble spots that arise in legislative and executive domains in ways that strengthen democratic systems. In the legislative domain, minipublics can serve as *trusted information proxies* to guide citizens' political judgments in situations characterized by limited information. In the executive domain, minipublics can serve as *anticipatory publics* to guide policy-makers in rapidly developing policy areas that may become contentious in the future but which do not (yet) have public opinion attached to them. In the first case, the primary trust relationship is between citizens and minipublics. In the second case, the trust relationship is between citizens and the executive agencies that might use minipublics to help guide policy-making processes.

In developing these potential functions of minipublics, our framework is that of democratic theory: we are interested in the potential roles of minipublics within the broad institutional ecologies that comprise democratic systems. But our approach departs from the democratic theories that frame received expectations for minipublics in one significant respect. These expectations hold that minipublics contribute to *active citizenship* by enabling better and more effective participation. Although we hold that they can and do perform these functions, here we build on the proposition that citizens' political resources – particularly their time and attention – are *scarce* (Bohman 1999; Warren 1996, 1999). Thus, a key question for democratic systems – one not often addressed by democratic theory – is that of how they allocate or maximize the scarce political resources of citizens.

In the first section, we argue that democracies should design institutions that enable citizens not only to actively engage in the matters that affect their lives, but also enable them to make credible judgments about when and how to remain passive – to trust that others will decide and act in their interests. That is, citizens need to make good decisions about how to best allocate their political resources – particularly their time and attentiveness – between participation and trust. In the second section, we frame the problem of trust in government and look at how democratic systems use trust selectively by organizing distrust into the more political functions of government, while reserving trust for relatively settled areas of consensus. In the third section, we examine the two trust trouble spots that we believe minipublics can help mitigate. In the fourth section, we specify the general conditions under which minipublics might be conceived of as objects of trust. In the fifth section, we build on this conception of minipublics as objects of trust and examine their potential to serve as *information proxies* for issues beset by political and technical complexities where citizens are ordinarily left without the capacities to judge independently but also without trustworthy proxies to judge on their behalf. In the sixth section, we develop the idea that minipublics can serve a second function as *anticipatory publics*, signalling potential problems and indicating solutions to erosions of public trust within the executive domain. Though our purpose is primarily to develop normative democratic theory, we illustrate these two extensions of democratic theory with two examples of minipublics: the British Columbia Citizens' Assembly and a 'deliberative public engagement' on establishing biobanks in British Columbia. We conclude by suggesting that minipublics have, potentially, a uniquely innovative role in enabling citizens to maximize the democratic impact of their political resources by enabling warranted forms of trust.

An economic problem: dividing labours between participation and trust

If we understand the good of active citizenship in very basic terms – as a key dimension of the democratic goods of self-development and self-determination (Young 2000) – we can also say that modern societies support an increasing demand for this good. On average, modern societies enable and emphasize individual self-determination and self-development. But they do so within a context of increasing interdependencies, such that these ideals require collective cooperation and action. Modern societies also provide many of the conditions of these ideals, including a production of wealth sufficient for most people to engage in learning (at least in principle), as well as high degrees of toleration for individual difference and pluralism. In economic terms, we might say that the demand for self-development and self-determination is increasing (Dalton 2008; Inglehart and Welzel 2005).

But many of the same trajectories subject individuals to so many collective interdependencies that no individual can hope to influence more than a small fraction of them. This will be so even in a society that maximizes the democratic 'all-affected principle' by opening *every* collective decision to the influence of those potentially affected (Goodin 2007). Again, casting this situation in economic terms, we might say that the *relative* supply of opportunities for influencing the sum total of effects to which individuals are subject will tend to decrease, *even* as the supply of opportunities for participation increases, as it does in modern democracies (Cain *et al.* 2003; Warren 2002). For each individual, this means that participatory resources are *increasingly scarce* relative to the collective interdependencies that, in theory, constitute the democratic demand for them. So even when individuals are politically attentive and active they are making allocation decisions: they choose to attend to some collective decisions and not to others. As a result, every decision to engage is, by default, also a decision *not* to engage – to remain passive – with respect to the majority of collective decisions to which individuals are subject. Choices for passivity are necessarily dominant owing to political resource scarcity, and they will comprise the vast majority of decisions made by even the most active of citizens.

For the most part, democratic theories that emphasize active citizenship fail to theorize this necessary division of political labour, with the cost that they fail to theorize its better and worse forms. Good democratic institutions should, on average, encourage high quality (effective, deliberative, appropriate, etc.) participation in areas of contention: those areas in which a citizen's interests and/or values are either not held or not considered by decision-makers. But individual choices to remain passive with respect to particular issues can themselves be made on better or worse grounds. So when democratic theories overlook the dominant choices for passivity that most citizens *must* make, focusing instead only upon active citizenship, they also overlook the chance to theorize better and worse (or more and less democratic) forms of passivity. The bad forms of passivity are those that follow from individuals' ignorance, apathy, or disaffection from arenas in which their interests are not congruent with those of decision-makers. In contrast, *good* forms of passivity are *trust-based*. They occur when individuals have good reason to allow others to act on their behalf, and to do so without monitoring and other forms of active engagement. It follows that a good democracy should provide institutions that not only enable individual political activity, but also enable *good passive choices* – that is to say, warranted decisions to trust individuals or institutions to decide and act on their behalf. It also follows that a good democratic system should support good passive modes of citizenship by enabling citizens to make good choices about when to trust rather than participate (Warren 1999).

When decisions to trust are warranted, they constitute a good form of passivity in a specific sense. When an individual makes a decision to trust, he is entrusting a good in which he has an interest to another agent – to an individual, a group, or an institution. In deciding to trust, he is also deciding to forgo any direct judgment about the use or protection of a good. All problems of knowing about the good – how to maintain, protect, further, or develop it – are off-loaded onto the trustee.

In making a trust decision, the truster is, of course, taking a risk: because a trusted agent is entrusted with a *good* – the education of a child, a retirement plan, a means of transport, oversight of nuclear weapons, etc. – the trustee can cause harm to the truster. A child's potential may be retarded, a retirement fund can be lost or embezzled, an aeroplane can crash, or a nuclear weapon could end up in the hands of a terrorist. It is because trust can be abused or betrayed that judgments about whether to trust can be better or worse. At the very least, a truster must decide whether a trustee is (a) motivated to act in his or her interests, and (b) competent to act in his or her interests. So, trust-based judgments are not passive in the sense that disaffection and disengagement are passive. Rather, trust-based judgments are *active choices to remain passive* – to hand over powers of decision to others and to forgo monitoring. Such choices can be made for better or worse reasons. When trust decisions are made for good reasons, they enable the truster to assume a passive relationship to their specific interest, confident that they will be well handled by the trustee.

Here is the challenge for democratic theory: because the vast majority of matters that affect our lives are in the hands of trustees, it would be best if citizens could make judgments about when, where, and who to trust. It would be best if citizens had good grounds for making these judgments. But trust-based judgments are challenging in themselves. All trust judgments are risky: just because trustees are agents, they can decide to abuse the trust placed in them. They can change their minds, engage in deceit, and act in ways contrary to the character they portray. So when individuals decide to trust, they are also making a judgment about a trustee's *trustworthiness*: whether she can be counted upon, in terms of her motivations as well as her competence, to act in her truster's interests. The social baseline for this kind of judgment is interpersonal knowledge about character. Perhaps unsurprisingly, such judgments fail to extend to risky interdependencies in complex societies. Most of the agents who have an effect on citizens' lives are strangers to them, operating at vast distances of space and time. In theory, the very judgments of trust that are most important in complex societies are also the most risky, since most individuals will have little knowledge upon which to base their judgments of character of those who would act on their behalf (Hardin 1999).

It is this challenge that makes the presence of credible institutions so important to enabling citizens to make good choices about when to trust. Individuals can infer trustworthiness from a variety of sources. The most important of these sources in complex societies are institutions. An institution is a set of sanctioned norms which defines roles and purposes of positions and offices. The norms indicate the duties of the office holder, while sanctions provide incentives for office holders to act in accordance with the norms that define the position. The job description of a bank employee entrusted with money includes the norms of honesty, proper accounting, and so on. The institution underwrites this norm by regularly monitoring the employee – requiring balancing the accounts at the end of the day, regular audits, etc. – and enforcing sanctions should he fail in his duties. The bank itself may be subject to the sanctions of a competitive market in trust, the failure of which can destroy the institution itself. Under these conditions, individuals can easily and for good reason infer the trustworthiness of a bank employee from their knowledge of the institution. In short, when they are working properly, institutions enable individuals to make well-founded trust judgments.

Trust in politics and government

But if we were to import this simple concept of institution-based trust into the domain of politics and government without modification, we would have glossed over the complexities of trust judgments that are particular to politics. One of the constitutive features of politics is that it occurs in areas of disagreement that, typically, follow from underlying conflicts of interests or values. So as a general matter, the conditions for trust do not hold in politics: just because politics is marked by conflict, individuals should, on average, distrust those with whom they disagree, and particularly distrust those who hold power (Sztompka 1999; Warren 1999).

Democratic institutions address this problem by organizing distrust in such a way that it does not disable collective decision-making or become corrosive within the larger society (Warren 1999). They do this in three important ways: (1) by reducing the risks of power through distributions of rights and protections; (2) by reducing the risks of conflict by constraining participants to the use of voice and votes; and (3) by organizing conflict into institutions that encourage bargains and consensus. Democratic institutions work best when they align or realign interests and values, enabling issues to move out of overtly political domains and into trust-based organizations and systems.

But because of the risks of trust, individual decisions that enable this kind of productive transformation of conflicts are more complex in political domains than in most other social domains. The ways in which trust is organized into democratic systems is likewise more complex. To illustrate this complexity, we can redescribe the standard theory of the separation of powers among the legislative, executive, and judicial domains of government. Within separated power systems, the most overtly 'political' domain is the legislative one: conflicts of interests and values are to be expected, and so the underlying alignments of interest necessary for trust in legislative institutions should not be expected. Insofar as warranted trust exists in the legislative domain, it can be found in the trust that citizens place in the rules that govern legislative processes and, correspondingly, trust that legislators will follow these rules in the conduct of conflict (Warren 2006). In addition, citizens may also trust their specific representatives. As Mansbridge (2009) has argued, an individual might select representatives based on the judgment that the representative shares his or her values, and can be trusted to act upon them. So rather than monitor and sanction representatives with their votes, in this situation individuals simply trust them to do the right thing. Yet this kind of trust is neither blind nor undemocratic. Elections, for example, provide individuals with opportunities to periodically monitor the conditions of trust and to remove the trustee if the conditions are violated. But on Mansbridge's model, the primary judgment a voter makes is to select a representative in whom they can place trust. They only 'check in' with their representative come election time to ensure that their trust has not been misplaced. Similarly, an individual may judge that an advocacy group embodies his or her values, and that he or she is warranted in trusting this group to insert his or her voice into the political process. Individuals can monitor and sanction the conditions of trust they place in advocacy groups through entrance and exit – choosing, that is, whether or not to retain their membership. Finally, individuals use many kinds of trusted agents – family, friends, networks, and groups – as information proxies to guide their political activities of voting, monitoring, and voice (Lupia and McCubbins 1998). So divisions of labour between participation and trust occur even within the 'political' domain of government, and well-placed trust judgments most certainly support a greater level of citizen influence than could occur on the basis of participation alone.

We should expect trust within executive agencies to follow a different pattern. When legislation is completed, it embodies a majority bargain or consensus. The textbook theory of representative democracy extrapolates from political process an alignment of interests and values. This alignment is expressed in the purposes of the legislation, which is then entrusted to the executive branch to carry out through its agencies. These agencies are, in the textbook theory, proper objects of public trust because their employees are keepers of the public trust with respect to the purposes and duties of their offices (Warren 2006). In the standard theory, the conditions of trust in an executive agency are monitored and sanctioned horizontally through legislative oversight and auditors general. The judicial branches of government are subject to similar expectations of trust, with the exception of those who are party to the conflicts adjudicated by courts.

Two trouble spots for trust-based citizenship

There is something right about the textbook theory. Suitably interpreted, it reveals that existing democracies do much of the work required of them by dividing participation-based relationships from trust-based ones, and then allocating participation (in the forms of voting, advocacy, etc.) to domains which lack conditions of trust. It also reveals that trust-based relationships are accompanied by devices – voting, oversight, auditing, and transparency, for example – that (ideally) ensure that citizens' trust-based judgments remain warranted. In short, when democratic systems are working well, they also provide citizens with the tools that they need to divide their own political labours between active and passive forms of citizenship.

But once we highlight these features of democratic systems, we can also see that there are trouble spots not covered by the textbook theory. Some of these trouble spots revolve around issues of corruption. In these situations, the trust that citizens place in institutions and individual office holders is betrayed. Other trouble spots, however, are not the consequence of malfeasance or conspiracy, but rather, simply, the failures of representative systems to support the judgments citizens must make when dividing their political labours.

A first trouble spot can be found in the political domain where the standard theory would suggest that mistrust is the norm. This trouble spot involves issue areas that combine *technical* and *political* complexity, such as reforming health care in the US or addressing global warming. Such issues are *technically* complex because they require a great deal of expert knowledge in order to formulate an informed opinion or judgment. So, although most individuals can understand the importance of these issues, even the very well educated have little hope of mastering their multiple dimensions. Such issues are *politically* complex because they involve so many interests, protracted conflicts, and overlapping jurisdictions that there are no institutions (nor officials within them) that have the mandates, the capacities, and the incentives to address them. Such issues often combine complex trade-offs in such a way that elected officials have few political incentives to propose agendas or solutions. In the case of health care reform, for example, any one set of proposals tends to mobilize intense interests in opposition that outweigh, politically speaking, the more compelling but diffuse public interest. From the perspective of citizens, the combination of technical and political complexity often means that few have the capacities necessary to relate their interests to policies. We might say that, at least for these kinds of issues, current forms of representative democracy do a poor job of relating decisions to the judgments of affected publics.

For some political issues, an increasingly common response to legislative incapacity will be (for politicians) to put an issue to a referendum, or (for groups) to push their interests through an initiative. In many cases, ballot initiatives put propositions to voters that are too complex for many to judge unaided by information shortcuts, as was apparently the case with the recent electoral system reform proposal in British Columbia (Cain and Miller 2001; Cutler *et al.* 2008; Lupia 2001). In other cases, citizens find themselves simply overwhelmed with the quantity of judgments they must make, as is clearly the case with ballot initiatives in California (Ferejohn 2008).

A second trouble spot exists with respect to the conditions of public trust in the executive agencies. Of course, the textbook model (famously) underplays the extent to which bureaucracies make policy. Much of the recent innovation in democratic theory and practice has revolved around these policy-focused 'governance' processes, which occur within nominally undemocratic domains of government (Hajer and Wagenaar 2003; Richardson 2002; Warren 2002). But there is yet another class of issues that threatens public trust, one for which there has been no democratic solution. These are issues that are not yet politicized and have no meaning-ful public opinion attached to them, but which are driven by governance imperatives – often technological – that might come to undermine public trust. These issues, we might say, combine technical complexity with *temporal complexity*.

Temporally complex issues are those that cannot be dealt with *as* political issues through the standard political institutions simply because they have not yet developed their political dimensions and thus have not (yet) become the subjects of political contestation. But for similar reasons, temporally complex issues are not well suited to be addressed in the executive domain because if public interests have not yet been defined then there can be no alignment of agency goals with politically settled issues.

There are, then, several reasons why temporally complex issues are especially difficult to manage with respect to maintaining the public trust. First, no *public* opinion currently exists and any potential political disagreements have not (yet) been identified let alone discussed. This characteristic of temporally complex issues in turn leaves whatever political guidance might exist vulnerable to the influence of vested interests that *are* organized and articulate, as is often the case in emerging areas of technology. Finally, once policy is set on course, future decisions that are subject to the path dependence of initial decisions will lack the legitimacy of public guidance simply for lack of a public (e.g. Pierson 2004). For these kinds of issues, anticipating future public concerns is essential if trust in public agencies is to be maintained.

An example of a field in which these issues might arise would be genomics-related research, much of which is funded by public agencies. Of particular concern are areas of genomic research that are relatively unfamiliar to the general public but have the potential to generate ethical, moral, economic, or environmental concerns or conflicts of interest which undermine the conditions of public trust. In these cases, the increasingly popular 'public engagement' devices are of little use because there is little public opinion available to guide policy development. Furthermore, 'public engagement' events that rely on self-selection may undermine the present conditions of future public trust by providing a means for well organized and well financed vested interests to influence agendas and policies without the countervailing influences of interests that have yet to organize. Future publics can in this way be organized out of policy processes by the very participatory devices that claim democratic credentials. Even without processes that privilege vested interests in the initial stages of policy development, if elites guess wrongly about the concerns future publics may have with an issue such as biobanking, policies will diverge from public interests, eroding the conditions of public trust.

Minipublics as objects of trust

Could minipublics address these two kinds of trust-related trouble spots? In principle, yes: *if* minipublics can be constructed as objects of public trust in their own right. The conditions are demanding: minipublics can serve trust-based roles if they are representative of affected publics, *and* if they screen against conflicts of interest, *and* if they are deliberative, *and* if they can come to agreement on the issue or set of issues at hand. More specifically, minipublics can meet the conditions of trust if they include the following:

- *Representativeness*, which, when combined with deliberativeness, will enable a minipublic to articulate interests that express those of the public from which it is selected.
- *Screens against conflicts of interest* to provide checks against particularistic motivations that undermine a minipublic's attentiveness to the interests of the public from which it is selected.
- *Deliberativeness* to produce competence within the minipublic, as well as to define interests that may be identified and judged by the broader public.
- *Agreement on the issue* to provide the public with a statement which can be the subject of a trust judgment.

Representativeness

With respect to their representative qualities, most minipublic models follow Robert Dahl's concept of a 'mini-populace', which is a body of citizens selected from a larger population, in such a way that it is a reasonably representative sample of that population (Dahl 1989: 342; Fishkin 1997; Goodin and Dryzek 2006; Smith 2009: ch. 3; cf. Fung 2003). Examples of such minipublic designs include deliberative polling, citizens' assemblies, citizen juries, consensus conferences, and planning cells, and have been used by AmericaSpeaks, the National Issues Forums, GM Nation, the BC, Ontario and Dutch citizens' assemblies, and multiple science-and-technology related consensus conferences around the world.

The justification for representative sampling is that it produces a body that is, literally, a *mini*-public, or a representation of the larger public from which the sample is drawn, including differing kinds of persons, experiences, perspectives, potential arguments, and visions in rough proportion to their (expected) presence in the population. A minipublic should represent 'the diversity of social characteristics and plurality of initial points of view in the larger society' (Goodin and Dryzek 2006: 221).

By way of contrast, the two other common methods of constructing representative bodies, election and self-selection, are unlikely to reflect the larger public. Election is biased in favour of those who have the means to stand for election, and whose characteristics reflect the dominant culture. Elections tend to produce representative bodies that are homogeneous relative to the publics that elect them. Self-selection is biased towards those who are well organized and intensely interested in an issue, and favours vested and well resourced interests. In contrast, representative sampling tends to include interests and perspectives that are unorganized, inarticulate, and latent in proportion to their presence in the larger public.[1] Although representative sampling is often achieved through random sampling, this is only one means of producing a representative minipublic. For smaller minipublics, stratified random sampling may provide better representation than purely random processes, since the smaller the sample, the greater the chances that purely random processes will produce an unrepresentative body.

In addition, the standards of representativeness in minipublics differ from public opinion polls because the objectives are different. Both polling processes and minipublics aim to obtain a representative sample but the standards in the case of the former must be different because the objective is to produce a sample of the population that can be used to make inferential judgments about the opinions of an entire population. In the case of minipublics, random sampling or stratified random sampling helps solve the problem of whom to ask to participate when all those potentially affected cannot be included. The objective in this case is to ensure that a roughly representative range of interests, perspectives, and life-experiences are included in face-to-face deliberations rather than to ensure that views

---

[1] A potentially important self-selection bias is, of course, introduced by the fact that only those who actually agree to participate will be included in a minipublic process. For example, there is evidence that those who participated in the British Columbia Citizens' Assembly (BCCA) on Electoral Reform were 'joiners' such as soccer coaches or Parent–Teacher Association members. Nevertheless, the resulting assembly was much more diverse than the provincial legislature in terms of age, income, gender, and other demographic characteristics (Warren and Pearse 2008). The BCCA was also more diverse than the average town hall meeting in a different but very important way: those who joined the BCCA only agreed to join because they were specifically asked to do so. Some of these members may have been motivated to participate in public meetings on electoral reform but many others would not have. This means that despite the self-selection processes that are inevitably involved in populating public forums of any kind, using random processes to populate minipublics produces assemblies that are more diverse and representative of the demographics, interests, ideas, perspectives, and life-experiences of potentially affected citizens, than self-selected or elected assemblies.

expressed by independent participants will be reflective of public opinion when aggregated.

Of course, the integrity of a representative sample will depend not only on the selection method, but also on initial decisions about the relevant public, which, under democratic principles, would include all who are potentially affected by an issue (Goodin 2007). Sometimes the affected publics are obvious: all users of a public health care system, for example, are potentially affected by health policy decisions. Sometimes the affected public is diffuse or even (necessarily) absent: global warming, for example, affects far-flung publics as well as future generations. In these cases, the representative qualities of minipublics depend upon participants' capacities to represent those who are necessarily absent through deliberatively formed judgments. The initial diversity of views should increase the chances that participants can put themselves in the place of absent others: their children or their children's children, for example.

Screens against conflicts of interest

These are standard in public trust-based offices. The logic here is prophylactic. Because it is difficult for citizens to monitor the motivations of public office holders, offices should be structured in such a way that their occupants are not tempted to act against the public interest. Insofar as minipublics are structured as objects of trust, the same considerations hold: although members of minipublics will have interests in the issues they are considering, they should not have vested interests. As a description of Danish-style consensus conferences on technological issues states, participants are:

> everyday folks who *do not* have a direct stake in the issue being reviewed; however, they have an *indirect* stake in the issue as taxpayers who subsidize R&D [research and development], and as community members and world citizens who live with the good and bad consequences of technological change. Because their interest in the issues is general rather than pecuniary, they are more likely to be objective about specific projects and proposals than the researchers, policy advocates, and private companies that typically promote technological change (Loka Institute 2009).

When screens against direct or vested interests are in place, members of the broader public should have greater confidence that interests within a minipublic are not impeding deliberation or causing its members to harbour ill-will towards those they represent – both of which would be good reasons for distrust.

While vested interests are not, on this model, included in the assembly, they can be included through their representations to the assembly. The model here is much like that of a jury: the body that judges should be selected in such a way that members do not have conflicts of interest – pecuniary, professional, or familial, for example – that would compromise their judgment. Within political systems, the more powerful interests tend to drown out less powerful, unorganized, and latent interests. In the minipublic model, interests of those who have immediate stakes – vested interests – are included in the same way that advocates are included in a jury trial: they make their cases before the jury and judge. In the minipublic design, advocates make their cases to the assembly during learning phases of the process. In this way, intensive and well organized interests are included, but indirectly, so they neither swamp unorganized interests or latent public interests, nor compromise or corrupt the judgment of the assembly. Minipublics replicate, in effect, the well known device for increasing the integrity of judgments under conditions of conflict: judges should be separated from causes.

Deliberativeness

This serves two dimensions of trust in addition to the representative functions suggested above. The first, *competence*, is straightforward: the more minipublic participants learn about an issue, the more competent they are in their judgments, which in turn increases their trustworthiness. The second dimension addresses the alignment of interests and values between truster and trustee necessary for a warranted trust judgment. What we might expect from a minipublic is the emergence of an identifiable public interest, which would then warrant public trust. The emergence of such an interest, of course, is contingent rather than necessary, and will depend upon the nature of the issue as well as the design of the process. So what sampling-based representativeness achieves is an initial alignment between the diversity of interests within the public and their presence within a minipublic. But because interests may be diverse and conflicting in both minipublics and the broader public, sampling-based representation on the input side is not sufficient to generate the conditions of trust. What it does provide are the conditions for finding underlying public interests, which, if then articulated through deliberation on the basis of broad initial inclusiveness, may then produce a necessary condition for trust.

In the case of deliberative polling, for example, the purpose of deliberation is to represent what public opinion *might* look like, if it were the result of information and deliberation (Fishkin 1997; Fishkin and Luskin 2005).

From the perspective of trust, it is precisely this development of opinion within minipublics that can transform it into an appropriate object of trust-based judgments. Deliberation may transform a collection of diverse interests and values into an expression of public interest of a kind that fails to congeal in the broader public, members of which will often lack time, knowledge, proximity, and interests that are pressing enough to override everyday obligations. In principle, minipublics can overcome these constraints to produce an alignment of interests and values with the broader public that would support trust judgments.

Agreement on the issue

If deliberativeness is necessary for a minipublic to identify and express the public interest, what is also needed is an agreement on the issue in order that the minipublic's judgment might become the object of a trust judgment with respect to that issue. The condition implies at least the following.

First, if a minipublic is to come to some kind of agreement on an issue, and produce a position that broader publics can identify with the minipublic, it must make a *decision*. Minipublics whose purpose it is simply to aggregate deliberatively forged individual opinions – as is the case in deliberative polls – do not involve a decision of the kind that can become an object of trust. If trust involves A (the public) trusting B (the minipublic) with respect to X (some good), then the minipublic must identify that good for a trust decision to have an object. Thus, the initial framing of the topic is important: if a topic is too diffuse, then a minipublic is likely to reproduce the diffuse qualities of the broader public and it will fail to issue a decision of the kind that could be the object of trust. But if a topic is well focused, the chances increase that a minipublic will come to conclusions with which the broader public can identify.

Second, judgments to trust will be more warranted the more a decision is a reflection of agreement within the minipublic. Because agreement signals to citizens that the minipublic's judgment is not contentious, citizens will be warranted in their decision to trust the judgment rather than (say) engage in further learning and participation. Of course, when minipublics decide, they often decide by means of a vote, which means that agreement is a matter of degree – from contentious, split decisions to consensus, signalled by the vote itself. So trusting should also be a matter of degree: the closer a minipublic's decision is to consensus, the more it makes sense to trust. The closer a minipublic's decision is to a split decision, the more it makes sense for citizens to learn, deliberate, and participate. Depending upon the issue and the composition of the relevant public, a minipublic might clarify disagreements or solidify underlying cleavages. It would make no sense for citizens to trust a minipublic that evolves in this way because, far from identifying a clear statement of a common interest, split judgments are an indication that unresolved or irresolvable concerns remain. But a divided minipublic may still function as an information proxy, though of a different sort. The information signal is, in this case, that citizens should pay closer attention to the issue: they should participate rather than trust. The value-added is, in this case, a credible signal to citizens as to how they should divide their political labours between trust and participation.

These conditions for trust may seem so restrictive that it might appear that no minipublic could ever hope to satisfy them. But just to the extent that we can identify the conditions of trust, we can also design minipublics that have a greater chance of satisfying them – for example, by tasking a minipublic with a discrete issue, and empowering it to make a specific decision of the kind that can be used as an information proxy by citizens. Moreover, it is also possible for minipublics to satisfy these conditions in practice, as illustrated by two cases we discuss below: the British Columbia Citizens' Assembly on Electoral Reform (BCCA), and a 'deliberative engagement' process about biobanking in British Columbia. There are, as well, other examples where minipublics might become trusted information proxies.

Minipublics as trusted information proxies

Let us assume that minipublics might, in principle, satisfy the conditions necessary to become objects of trust, and that minipublics might be constructed around some non-trivial set of issues. As we argued above, because citizens need to allocate their participatory resources, they also have a need for trust. A good democracy would provide institutions that support warranted trust-based judgments. One way minipublics can underwrite trust is by serving as *trusted information proxies*, particularly in areas where standard trust-ensuring mechanisms fail. What we have been arguing is that democratic systems should enable citizens to make good decisions about when to trust and when to participate. Generally speaking, *political* issues are not good candidates for trust, because the absence of a key condition of trust – convergent interests – is exactly what defines an issue as 'political'. That said, when citizens participate, they can and do manage the complexity and volume of what they need to know by using trusted information proxies. Minipublics can, in principle, serve this kind of function in ways that are consistent with democracy and extend the participatory capacities of citizens.

Such a possibility fits nicely with Lupia and McCubbins's (1998) understanding of how citizens make reasoned judgments about their political agents (both elected officials and unelected delegates). Although citizens' capacities for learning are constrained by the 'twin scourges of scarcity and complexity', they maximize their capacities by relying on third parties such as political parties, friends, media personalities, associations, and trusted politicians for guidance (Lupia and McCubbins 1998: 37). On Lupia and McCubbins's model, individuals learn from third parties when they are persuaded to do so. Persuasion has two key conditions: (1) individuals must perceive that the third party has *interests in common* with their own; and (2) they must believe that this third party has *relevant knowledge* of the issues that concern them.

Recast in the terms we use here, these two conditions of persuasion closely parallel the two kinds of judgments – interests and competence – that warrant trust. On Lupia and McCubbins's model, individuals can infer the existence of these conditions if: (1) there are external sources of verification that the third party holds in view to guard their reputation; (2) there are penalties for lying; and (3) the third party has put 'costly effort' into their judgments (Lupia and McCubbins 1998: 53–4). When these conditions exist, individuals can infer that third-party information is trustworthy, and can credibly use third parties as information proxies.

Can minipublics meet the conditions of trusted information proxies? Well designed minipublics can, in theory, meet not only the four conditions for trust listed above (representativeness, screens against conflict of interest, deliberateness, and agreement on the issue), but Lupia and McCubbins's conditions for trusted information proxies as well. The BCCA provides an example (Warren and Pearse 2008). The Government of British Columbia created the BCCA in 2004 for the purpose of assessing British Columbia's electoral system. If the BCCA decided that the system could be improved, they were empowered to recommend an alternative system to the voters in the form of a referendum question.

The BCCA was composed of 160 citizens who were randomly invited to participate in the process. All those on the voters' list were eligible to participate in the process with the exception of elected or party officials who might have conflicts of interest on this topic. The assembly was given a budget, a staff, and ten months to work, which it divided into three phases: the first devoted to learning about electoral systems, the second to public hearings and submissions, and the third to deliberation and decision-making. The assembly returned a recommendation for a single transferable vote (STV) system. Put to voters in May 2005, the referendum garnered a 57.7 per cent 'yes' vote, which fell short of the legislated supermajority threshold of 60 per cent.

The process through which a minipublic is constituted should function as an initial cue to individuals as to whether the body represents their interests. Random processes combined with screens against vested interests, for example, should signal both that participants should, in aggregate, hold the public interest in view, and that the body is unlikely to include organized factions. Under these conditions, cue-takers would be warranted in concluding that the interests of the body align with the interests of the broader public from which it was selected, even if they do not attend to the substance of its work and recommendations.

For cue-takers that look for further verification of interest alignment, Lupia and McCubbins note the importance of environments that are favourable to transparency, including mechanisms for oversight, competition between information providers, and opportunities to openly challenge statements, claims, or positions. These factors help ensure that cue-takers could, in principle, verify that the basic idea or 'good' of an institution is indeed aligned with their interests. Transparency also allows those who are willing, in principle, to forgo the efficiencies of passive trust, to actively verify whether a minipublic is competent or sufficiently knowledgeable, *and* whether deliberations were substantive and sufficiently well conducted to allow for the emergence of an identifiable expression of public interest.

The BCCA process met these conditions: learning materials were made available on the website, the plenary sessions were open to the public, interested observers were encouraged to send written comments to assembly members, and public meetings were conducted in all areas of the province. The expectation, of course, is that those who might use a minipublic as an information cue will *not* engage in these monitoring activities; but the fact that these verification opportunities exist, and that some citizens make use of them, is a cornerstone condition for maintaining warranted trust in these institutions.

Lupia and McCubbins's *penalties for lying* condition would appear to apply only when there are obvious incentives for actors or speakers to engage in lying to their principal or potential trusters. In the case of the BCCA, these incentives were missing, in part because of the initial screen against vested interests – that is, political officials who had career interests in the outcome. Where screens against conflicts of interest are feasible, the minipublics mitigate concerns about deception. But questions may remain about whether judgments are made in good or bad faith. In the case of minipublics, these concerns are mitigated by the fact that if they have any influence at all, it is influence generated by the advice and recommendations they render. Citizens should be able to infer from this strategic interest that minipublic participants will have an overriding interest in maintaining their credibility.

Lupia and McCubbins's knowledge condition (our deliberativeness condition) is satisfied if cue-takers perceive the minipublic to be collectively competent. Lupia and McCubbins are dismissive of deliberative mechanisms, noting that they often fail to achieve public enlightenment (Lupia and McCubbins 1998: 266–7). True enough. But the claim is easy to make – too easy, as they fail to examine the deliberative models, minipublics among them, designed precisely to generate enlightenment, both among participants and between the minipublic and the broader public. Minipublics that involve intensive learning processes extended over several weeks or even months, and backed up by deliberation, provide grounds for trusting the quality of the information emanating from these processes. Cue-takers may or may not be convinced that final recommendations or outcomes are worthy of trust, but they will have good reasons for believing that they might be, given the signal of 'costly effort' that minipublic members put into participation without the possibility of a direct return. In the case of the BCCA, members dedicated almost a year to a process that involved regular weekend deliberations, reading, some independent research, public meetings, and travel. After the process was complete, many members continued to participate in an 'alumni association' that actively promoted the BCCA's recommendation during the subsequent referendum campaigns. Furthermore, information cues emanating from minipublics might be considered trustworthy *because* these recommendations have been tried, tested, and accepted by informed participants in a discursive arena. Deliberation is what democratic citizens might be *expected* to do when they have the time, energy, interest, and motivation to pay attention to public affairs. Passive citizens can hardly do better than to rely on information proxies that do exhibit these characteristics, especially if there are good reasons to believe that minipublics are (collectively) competent, designed to encourage enlightened discourse, aligned with the public's interest, reasonably transparent, and expending costly efforts.

The BCCA also met our final condition for trust by issuing a clear statement of agreement. The final recommendation for STV was supported by more than 90 per cent of the members of the assembly and it was accepted by all as the final outcome of the process.

While the BCCA meets the conditions for citizens to treat it as a trusted information proxy, did they actually do so? Fortunately, the BCCA has been the most carefully studied minipublic experiment to date. Findings reported by Cutler *et al.* (2008) suggest that a significant proportion of voters in fact treated the BCCA as a trusted information proxy. An overwhelming proportion of voters knew little about the proposed STV electoral system. But rather than vote 'no', they appear to have asked themselves a second question: who is proposing the system? The more voters knew about the proposer – the BCCA – the more likely they were to vote 'yes'. One group of voters that Cutler *et al.* called 'distrustful populists' simply wanted to know if the BCCA consisted of 'people like us' who have the public interest in view. If they could answer yes to this interest-convergence question, they were then more likely to support the proposal. A second, more educated, group asked the same question as the populists when it came to considering interests, but also appeared to ask themselves about the competence of the BCCA. Following the same pattern, the more these voters knew about the BCCA, the more likely they were to answer 'yes' to both questions, which then predicted a 'yes' vote in the referendum. In short, it appears that a significant number of voters used the BCCA as a trusted information proxy.

The impression that the BCCA functioned as a trusted information proxy in May 2005 is reinforced by a rerun of the referendum in May 2009. Whereas in the 2005 referendum the BCCA had a relatively high public profile (Cutler and Fournier 2007), this time the BCCA had almost no presence in the public discourse. Indeed, the issue had little visibility until the final weeks of the campaign. During this period, public discourse was structured in an adversarial style by publicly funded 'yes' and 'no' campaigns. This time, public debates focused on the substance of the choice between the current single-member plurality system and the proposed STV system rather than the information proxies. The 'yes' vote fell to 39 per cent.

One explanation for the large fall-off in 'yes' votes is that inattentive voters – most voters in this case – lacked the trusted information proxy they had in the previous referendum. This suggestion is consistent with survey findings reported by Carty *et al.* (2009). They found that in '2009, the influence of the Citizens' Assembly all but evaporated'. In that referendum, decisions 'were primarily determined by views on the substance of STV' and not on the fact that the new system was proposed by a minipublic made up of 'ordinary folks' who had spent time learning about alternative electoral systems and deliberating their comparative merits. This does not mean that voters learned more about the details of STV during the 2009 campaign. In general, they did not. What it does mean is that voters who did not know much about the system lacked a trusted information proxy to help guide their vote.[2]

---

[2] Of course, the absence of the BCCA was not the only factor that affected the vote in 2009. Carty *et al.* (2009) provide evidence that Liberal Party supporters and undecided voters were simply more supportive of the current system in 2009 than in 2005. They also argue that a change in the wording of the referendum question may have had an impact on the vote. In 2009 the ballot question specifically mentioned the current system in addition to the new system proposed by the BCCA and this might have primed voters to opt for

There are, as well, other examples where minipublics might become trusted information proxies. In Oregon, the Citizens' Initiative Review involved two panels of near-randomly selected citizens who were tasked with reviewing two ballot initiatives (one on legalization of marijuana for medical purposes, the other on mandatory minimum sentencing guidelines) before the 2010 general election. Their job was to review the initiatives and make a recommendation, which then appeared in the Oregon Voter's Pamphlet. The panel examining medical marijuana returned a split decision, whereas the panel examining mandatory minimum sentencing guidelines returned a near-consensus decision. Preliminary survey research suggests that while both panels increased voters' knowledge, the panel returning a near-consensus recommendation not only met our theoretical conditions for functioning as a trusted information proxy but was also used by voters as a trusted information proxy. In contrast, the panel that did not come to an agreement on the issues was not rated as useful or informative when it came to helping voters decide which way to vote on that proposition (Gastil and Knobloch 2011).

The Oregon experience suggests that a similar minipublic design would be useful in California, where ballots are routinely overloaded with multiple measures, some essential to the basic functioning of state government, many others placed on the ballot by advocacy groups and various vested interests. Citizens lack basic information about the choices they make in the ballot box, and most citizens for most items lack trusted information proxies. Similar to the Oregon experiment, one proposal calls for a citizens' assembly process to vet ballot initiatives, which would in effect amount to a trust-based use of a minipublic as an information proxy (Ferejohn 2008). Proposals also exist for a citizens' assembly to recommend reforms to California's increasingly unworkable constitution (New America Foundation 2009).

Of course minipublics are highly artificial constructions, and are themselves costly of time, attention, money, and sometimes political capital for the organizer. Given the many other kinds of information proxies already in existence, we should think of their potential functions in terms of the

---

the *status quo*. This suggestion is consistent with research that shows that in situations of perceived distrust, individuals will make the decisions that require less cognitive complexity – in this case, a vote for the *status quo* (Schul et al. 2004). What is clear is that the proposed system was not rejected because voters learned more about the details of STV and did not like what they saw. It failed because there was more support for the existing system among certain voters and because 'of the disappearance of the positive influence of the Citizens' Assembly' (Carty et al. 2009). These findings are consistent with our argument that, given certain conditions, minipublics can (and do) function as trusted information proxies.

particular niches they might fill within democratic systems. As suggested above, such niches exist in issue areas where no other information proxies meet the conditions of trust: common interests and credible knowledge. Such deficits occur most typically in issue areas that combine high political complexity with high technical complexity, which has the effect of leaving the field of trusted proxies empty and citizens without trusted information resources. The BCCA addressed precisely this kind of politically and technically complex deficit. A similar deficit can also occur when the demands on citizens to make judgments exceed the availability of trusted proxies, as is so clearly the case with California's initiative and referendum process (Garrett and McCubbins 2008; Ferejohn 2008). In cases such as these, minipublics may be able to fill these information proxy vacuums.

Minipublics as anticipatory publics

In the case of minipublics conceived as information proxies, the democratic function is to *mediate* citizens' political judgments by expanding a relatively small amount of information about the credibility of the minipublic into political judgments. In a second class of trust-based uses, however, minipublics might *substitute* for citizen judgments by anticipating concerns in contexts within which public trust is the norm. Substitution within such contexts is already an entrenched feature of the division of labour between participation and trust in the developed democracies. If substitution occurs within domains in which public trust is already the norm – primarily within the many executive agencies that are custodians and beneficiaries of public trust – then it is consistent with democracy. In the standard theory, these kinds of institutions are not themselves democratically organized; their role, rather, is to operationalize the output of the 'political' branches of government. So the baseline expectation is trust rather than democracy.

Of course this sketch needs to be modified by the (well recognized) fact that much of the activity of democracy is shifting into executive agencies. This trend is driven by the fact that executive agencies must engage in a large amount of political work as part of their missions of transforming legislated purposes into actionable agendas (Warren 2009). So although trust in executive or administrative agencies is typically necessary for their effective and legitimate operation, the politicization of these agencies creates the conditions for warranted *mistrust* to develop (Warren 1999). Over the last several decades, legislatures have increasingly recognized these political functions, and have directed agencies to engage affected publics as they develop and implement rules and regulations. Although most of these directives are vague (requiring 'community engagement' and 'public engagement'), there are recent cases of more specific directives. The 21st Century Nanotechnology Research and Development Act of 2003, for example, directed the implementing agencies to develop 'mechanisms such as citizens' panels, consensus conferences, and educational events, as appropriate' (Goodin and Dryzek 2006: 241). In practice, agencies increasingly use advisory committees of interested citizens, activists, and stakeholders to solicit public input and test policies, and do so with increasing sophistication (Brown 2006; National Research Council 2008).

Most such processes, however, are designed for uptake from publics that have already been formed, so their purposes are nominally participatory and democratic. However, agencies increasingly face a class of problems that cannot be covered even by well specified and appropriate democratic processes – those characterized by *temporal complexity*. These are issues that are potentially but not yet 'political': that is, they have not yet generated attentive publics, and any potential political divisions have not yet been drawn or discussed and compromises have not been negotiated. But as these future-oriented issues play out, potential public concerns will become manifest, while the current decisions of agencies create path dependencies that may prove to be very costly in the future.

Temporal complexity exists in most policy arenas, but it is found particularly within areas of rapid scientific, technological, and organizational development that agencies must generate and regulate in order to carry out their public functions. Environmental regulation, use of public lands, transportation planning, regulation of food supplies, public health, innovations in education, and new technologies generate new issues simply as a consequence of their development. The most future-oriented dimensions of these issues are not appropriate for democratic processes in any traditional sense, mostly because the publics that are potentially affected are not yet interested and organized – that is, they do not yet exist *as* publics. In these cases, agencies must *anticipate* responses from *future* publics that will maintain the conditions of public trust, by ensuring that new policies continue to align with the public interest. The temporal challenge is that, if they have an interest in maintaining the trust invested in them, agencies must anticipate the concerns of future publics. The potential political problem is that substantive expertise accumulated within an agency will not, on average, equip it to anticipate future public responses. Left to their own devices office holders can, at best, make educated guesses about the political problems they might avoid by anticipating future public concerns.

The challenges of temporal complexity are even greater in cases in which *partial* interests are attentive and organized, but the broader publics potentially affected by an issue are not. Under these conditions, policy-makers will find that responsiveness to existing publics will tend to undermine the future conditions of public trust, even when decision-makers in administrative agencies genuinely desire to maintain the public trust in their decision-making processes.

For these kinds of issues, minipublics that meet the conditions of trust specified above – representativeness, screens against conflicts of interest, deliberativeness, and agreement on the issue – can function *in the present* to anticipate *future* threats to public trust. In this use, a minipublic simulates publics that are not yet present, initially through selection of a group that is likely to represent a range of potential concerns, and then through processes of learning and deliberation that develop and articulate *potential* public interests and concerns. Insofar as this kind of minipublic guides the decision-making of executive agencies, they might enable agencies to align their decisions with current approximations of future publics. Insofar as they are able to do so, they are better placed to reproduce the conditions of warranted public trust than they would be without credible representations of these future publics.

Unlike the first case where minipublics are used as information proxies and where there is a direct trust relationship between citizens and the minipublics, in this case the trust relationship is between citizens and executive agencies that might use minipublics to guide policy-making. In making this claim, we are assuming that there is a background level of trust between citizens and their executive agencies, and that individual citizens will not necessarily know where or when minipublics are being used to guide public policy. Instead, we argue that agencies that use minipublics are in a better position to make decisions that do not undermine the trust of citizens. In this scenario, trust in executive agencies over the long term will be primarily based on assessments of policy outcomes. This would be the norm. But for anyone who wished to more actively monitor the activities of executive agencies they would find integrity in the process where anticipatory publics were used and could be conceived of as objects of public trust.

The role of minipublics as anticipatory publics within democratic systems is quite different from that of the trusted information proxy. When minipublics are used as information proxies, they will, at most, be supplements to ordinary processes of representative government on a limited number of very big issues such as electoral system reform or constitutional change, vetting ballot initiatives and referendum questions, or perhaps providing broad guidance on contentious but complex policies, such as health care or pension reform. In their function as anticipatory publics, however, minipublics could be used to inform decisions on a much larger number and range of issues – potentially any issue that falls within the mandates of executive agencies. Indeed, because potential issues are, in effect, anticipated by (agency-based) elites who are trustees of public purposes, broad publics may not even know that they are convening minipublics in what are, really, advisory capacities. They would be using minipublics to ensure that they make decisions, particularly in rapidly developing areas of policy (genomics, nanotechnology, intellectual property, etc.) in such a way that conditions of public trust are not eroded. Instead, their trust will be a function of more diffuse processes in which public decisions are judged to be good ones, broadly speaking and over time, only if they reflect credible interpretations of the public interest. Anticipatory minipublics can give decision-makers access to potential public concerns in ways that they would otherwise simply have to imagine.

This kind of anticipatory public was demonstrated in a recent deliberation on the topic of biobanking in British Columbia (O'Doherty and Burgess 2009). Biobanking involves collecting tissues from multiple patients – tissues typically collected during surgeries and biopsies – into a few sites for research purposes. A biobank catalogues tissues and serves as a one-stop-site for permissions to use the tissues in research. The research demand for such a system is driven by advances in genomics that enable researchers to link genetic materials to probabilities of diseases. But because of the low incidence of many gene-linked diseases, researchers require large sample sizes. Current privacy and consent regulations require, however, that permission to use tissues be sought from each tissue donor with each new use. The process is so cumbersome that it effectively stunts 'large-n' genetic disease research. Biobanking not only consolidates and catalogues tissues, it also offers opportunities to simplify permission and consent procedures, thus enabling a new generation of gene-related disease research.

Biobanking is an example of a policy driven internally by the development of a public mission within public agencies. It is also an example of a policy area that, almost literally, has no public opinion attached to it – attentive publics are not, or at least have not yet, developed, and they certainly have not gained a voice. Indeed, most people have never even heard of biobanking. And yet the area harbours numerous possibilities for ethical, economic, or political abuses, any of which would undermine public trust in the public agencies administering the system. What if genetic information were to become available to private insurers? Should the information be made available to for-profit pharmaceutical companies? Could tissues be used in ways that violate the religious or traditional norms of aboriginal peoples? More generally, what kinds of processes would provide publics with the confidence that agencies will guard against potential abuses? It does no good to survey the public on such matters, or to convene public hearings or stakeholder meetings, or to develop any other process that depends upon expressions of public interests – voice – for none yet exists.

But it might, especially if the design of biobanks goes wrong in ways that leave the public trust open to abuse.

The minipublic design is well suited for these kinds of problems precisely because it is capable of manufacturing counterfactuals: it can be understood as a simulation of a larger, more inclusive, public discourse that cannot happen, or at least cannot happen in the current period before an attentive, affected public emerges. In such cases, minipublics are not predicting what public opinion might look like if it were more deliberative and better informed. Rather, they are using deliberative methods to manufacture *anticipations* of public concerns, interests, or rationales, which in turn enable future-oriented elites to craft institutions – biobanks in this case – that are worthy of public trust.

It is also worth making a distinction between anticipatory minipublics – of the kind we are describing – and minipublics that are used to 'market test' policy proposals. Goodin and Dryzek (2006) have argued that minipublics can help decision makers determine whether certain policies or approaches will be accepted by affected publics. In some cases, as they observe, the answer will be a resounding 'no'; in other cases the supporters of a policy may 'get a clear and surprising "yes" to the question "Can we sell this to people?"' (Goodin and Dryzek 2006: 229). This account of the potential uses of minipublics is consistent with our own insofar as it focuses on the temporal dimensions of policy-making, and is concerned with the role that minipublics can play in avoiding adverse political outcomes by assessing the legitimacy of policies before they are implemented. We are adding to this analysis by emphasizing the contributions that minipublics can make with respect to resolving *temporal* problems in democracy, and in shaping policies that are more likely to be legitimate for potentially affected publics that *do not yet exist*. We are also pointing to the trust-based functions of this kind of anticipation: it is not just that minipublics might anticipate legitimacy, but that they might also anticipate future conditions of public trust, such that future-affected publics may not mobilize because elites continue to make decisions consistent with their obligations to hold and further a public trust. Indeed, this kind of temporal trust problem is unique in ways that probably *require* some kind of minipublic-like process to solve: for the conditions of trust to be put into place, potentially pivotal public concerns and emergent considerations or values must be anticipated with reasonable accuracy.

For minipublics to function as anticipatory publics, representative sampling is important even if an extensive range of population characteristics cannot be matched in a small-scale deliberative forum. Nonetheless, a minipublic *can* be a description of a population that is sufficiently fine-grained to include potentially unknown issues – though designers will face some guesswork here, as unknown issues cannot serve as a guide. Likewise, the processes of learning and deliberation are necessary. Participants must learn about the issue just because those who are selected to participate are unlikely to know anything about it at all. Then, through deliberation, participants must begin to identify potential issues and to form their opinions around them.

It is worth underscoring that the broader justification of *this* use of minipublics is not 'democratic' or 'participatory' at all. This use speaks to the trust-based dimensions of democratic systems, and their functions are to be found in reproducing public trust in institutions – particularly in the executive functions of government. So the justifications for forming an anticipatory public are twofold. First, basing decisions on the articulated, and deliberatively tested, concerns of an anticipatory public should help to *keep* political issues – in which the interests of affected publics no longer converge – from forming by ensuring that agency policies continue to align with the public interest. If public agencies have an interest in maintaining the trust that is invested in them, they must anticipate the concerns of potential or future publics and incorporate these concerns into their current-period decision-making processes. The point of using a minipublic to represent future publics is that, of the devices available, their combination of representativeness and deliberativeness is most likely to generate anticipations of what future publics will care about. Then present decisions can anticipate what future publics are likely to view as conditions of public trust.

In the second place, select but attentive anticipatory minipublics help underwrite the public trust by ensuring that decisions which are made have been influenced, or at least monitored, by an institution whose interests can be plausibly (and transparently) aligned with the general (inattentive) publics' probable interests. As mentioned above, this is especially important with respect to issues that display temporal complexity: these are precisely the kinds of issues that will initially draw attention from well organized and politically savvy interests. Without processes that model, as it were, potentially affected publics, elites will be more likely to respond to these interests, producing policy path dependencies that will dampen responsiveness to future publics, and generate conditions for warranted mistrust. Indeed, it is likely that the mere presence of minipublics can help insure that decision-making processes on future-oriented issues are worthy of the public trust. Decision-makers may even welcome minipublics as political leverage against organized (but unrepresentative) vested interests. So for these reasons, anticipatory minipublics should be able to function as check-ups on trust, particularly in areas where the conditions of trust are in danger of erosion – that is, on future-oriented issues characterized by uncertainty, unpredictability, and unorganized or yet-to-be-affected publics.

Although the biobanks minipublic, which was conducted at the University of British Columbia's Centre for Applied Ethics in the spring of 2007, was billed as a 'deliberative public engagement' (O'Doherty and Burgess 2009), it may be more appropriate to think of it as a trust-based, and hence limited, participatory exercise. The project convened a relatively small but representatively stratified sample of (twenty-one) British Columbia citizens with the aim of anticipating potential ethical concerns with the idea of establishing a regional biobank in British Columbia. Although the process may not have had a sufficient duration to fully develop the issues – particularly given the steep learning curve for participants – one outcome was significant: participants were less interested in having democratic input into biobanking than they were in constructing institutions that would be self-regulating with respect to the public interest. Thus, participants were primarily concerned that biobanking should have oversight and checks sufficient to align the process with the public interest (O'Doherty and Burgess 2009). This is not a surprising result: the public interest served by biobanking, like many health-related issues, is not complex, in that almost all citizens have a shared interest in advancing the understanding of diseases. The issues, rather, have to do with ethical boundaries, economic trade-offs, the efficient generation of innovation, and the equitable distribution of benefits – all issues with the potential for politicization, but relatively easily addressed in the case of a discrete issue such as biobanking, where a clear public purpose can be identified and served. But because it was not clear to the agencies which of these potential issues might undermine public trust, it made sense to build, as it were, an anticipatory public.

Furthermore, given that the development of a regional biobank in British Columbia is a future-oriented issue which has not (yet) generated organized and articulate publics, the minipublic process can be understood as a means by which to simulate that missing element, particularly as a check to ensure that the decisions made by administrative agencies are aligned with potential public concerns. This check is especially important in terms of generating the conditions for warranted trust to emerge because the issue of biobanking is surrounded by well organized and articulate interests – such as those of for-profit pharmaceutical companies – which may or may not be aligned with the interests of those potentially affected by biobanking, such as tissue donors, patients, taxpayers, or anyone with an interest in continuing advances in medical technology.

We are arguing, then, that *anticipatory* trust-based uses of minipublics might be a necessary part of constructing institutions to manage complex, fast-paced issue areas, in a way that is attentive to potentially affected publics, especially by providing the information that public trust-based institutions need to anticipate trust from their affected publics. In this trust-based use, minipublics underwrite warranted trust judgments, ensuring that citizens' political resources are properly and effectively allocated. For their part, public officials need these kinds of trust checks to avoid potential political gridlock and over-politicization of basic public functions – which can disable democracy by depriving a people of effective collective agents of their purposes.

Conclusion

We know more about how to construct and conduct minipublic exercises than we do about their potential functions within democratic systems. Part of the blame can be laid at the feet of democratic theorists. We have done a poor job of thinking through the implications of the fact that citizens' political resources – their time, attentiveness, and knowledge – are scarce. But when this scarcity is recognized as an inevitable condition of doing politics in modern societies, we are compelled to think about how citizens should divide their political labours. Under conditions of political resource scarcity, a good democratic society should not only support citizens' active political choices by providing opportunities for voice and influence, but should also support their passive choices – their decisions *not* to engage with a particular issue or institution. Once we grant this possibility, it is clear that there are good and bad passive choices. Bad passive choices follow from apathy and disaffection in areas beset by political conflict. Good passive choices are based on warranted trust in areas where citizens' interests align with institutional purposes. A good polity will provide citizens with the means for making these trust-based decisions.

These trust-based needs within a democracy become visible, theoretically speaking, when we understand the ways in which democratic institutions enable citizens to direct their scarce political resources towards the issue areas that are most political, and thus most deserving of their attention, while relating to other, less political, issues through trust. But even this is not enough to enable complex systems to meet democratic standards. In highly complex democratic systems, individuals will be forced to choose between political issues by dividing these among various groups of active citizens. Under these conditions, trust-based judgments play a necessary function in linking together disparate parts of a deliberative system. From this perspective, trust can be understood as the web of social relationships that keep individuals connected even to politicized decisions they are not involved in making, as well as to institutions that affect their interests even though they are not active within them. As deliberative systems become more complex – as the number and variety of their parts multiply – it will become increasingly important to specify the conditions under which warranted trust-based judgments can be made. This is especially true in deliberative systems that are characterized by changing institutional arrangements, *ad hoc* processes, and permeable barriers between legislative and bureaucratic spheres. In these circumstances, and as conditions change, individuals will be under pressure to continually update their own decisions about when to remain passive and when to become active.

Far from being simply another complicating factor in already complex deliberative systems, minipublics can provide some of the means through which citizens can make better judgments about when and where to be passive. They can serve as (1) trusted *information proxies* in political arenas; and (2) *anticipatory publics* to ensure the future conditions of trust in those domains of government (or any other collective organization) that depend on public trust. Minipublics can perform these functions because their composition through representative sampling creates a deliberative body that (ideally) includes all potentially affected interests without the biases of election or self-selection, and because learning- and deliberation-based processes enable these interests to form and become articulate. For certain kinds of problems, such as those that are technically, politically, or temporally complex, this combination of features can produce bodies that fulfil trust functions within complex ecologies of deliberative institutions and practices in ways that no other institution can.

6

On the embeddedness of deliberative systems: why elitist innovations matter more

YANNIS PAPADOPOULOS

Introduction

Experiments in participatory forms of deliberative policy-making are proliferating, not only in Organization for Economic Co-operation and Development (OECD) countries, but also in developing countries. They are so numerous and so different that it is simply not possible to draw any generalizations about their implications, although they have now generated a considerable number of empirical studies on their operation. It is impossible to acquire a thorough knowledge of participatory experiments, especially as most of them take place at the local (small-scale, 'micro') level, and are not widely publicized. Even making an encompassing typology of them would be a Herculean exercise because variation among them is considerable (fifty-seven techniques are listed in Smith 2005). One may say, however, that such mechanisms include 'public inquiries, right-to-know legislation, citizen juries, policy dialogues, impact assessment with public comment, regulatory negotiation, mediation and other kinds of third-party-facilitated conflict resolution' (Dryzek 2000: 164). Urbinati and Warren (2008: 405) list, for their part, 'experiments with citizen juries and panels, advisory councils, stakeholder meetings, lay members of professional review boards, representations at public hearings, public submissions, citizen surveys, deliberative polling, deliberative forums, and focus groups'. They emphasize that, notwithstanding their differences,

As well as the York conference, previous versions of this chapter were presented at the LAGAPE research seminar, University of Lausanne, 15 April 2010, and at the conference on 'Autonomy of institutions', Centre Marc Bloch, Berlin, 24–5 September 2010.

such devices privilege representation by 'lay' citizens and not by professionals, be they experts or interest representatives. Though 'participatory' does not mean that the representation relation is absent (therefore
it would be improper to speak about mechanisms of *direct* democracy),
neither are elected politicians or organized collective actors the key players
in these bodies. The literature usually emphasizes the deliberative character of these mechanisms, as opposed to the traditional aggregative aspect
of voting procedures, but this emphasis should not obscure the fact that
the innovative aspect of deliberative devices also lies in their participatory
properties. What characterizes them is neither their deliberative nor their
participatory components as such, but the combination: the fact that deliberation on policy-making is extended to people who normally are not part
of the policy-making process.[1]

Empirical studies of such devices have significantly contributed to reflection on the virtues and limits of collective deliberation 'in the real world'
(Parkinson 2006a). Most of the empirical work on deliberative democracy
deals with issues related to the quality of deliberation, and sometimes more
generally of democracy, by scrutinizing aspects such as the openness and
degree of inclusiveness of deliberative forums, the nature of exchanged
arguments, the possibly transformative effect of deliberation on preferences, and the collective will, leading to more enlightened, and perhaps also
more consensus-oriented and other-regarding, citizens. This focus is not
surprising, considering that a good many deliberative experiments have,
at best, a tenuous relationship to policy-making – i.e. to the process of the
authoritative allocation of goods and values. Often their primary goal is
to heighten the level of policy-makers' information or, when they emanate
from bottom-up pressure, to reinvigorate civic participation in a context of
distrust for established politics. At the same time, some deliberative experiments are coined instrumentally, resulting from a top-down demand for
public deliberation, and aiming to improve the problem-solving capacity
of political decisions and to facilitate their implementation.[2] Although
these devices are also participatory, in such a case it is the representation
of partisan interests that is privileged (Hendriks *et al.* 2007).

It is widely argued that deliberation is a tool for complexity management.[3] When it involves a plurality of actors, deliberation helps to cope

---

[1] For a discussion of the often ambiguous or unclear relations between deliberative and
participatory theories of democracy, see Bouvier (2007).

[2] Thompson (2008a) even believes that deliberative democracy pertains only to situations
where the deliberative group must produce a collectively binding decision.

[3] One may refer here to the problem, social and institutional dimension of complexity
(Dryzek 1990: 57–76).

better with problem complexity because it allows the grounding of decisions on more accurate knowledge. Being a remedy for uncertainty on the causes of public problems and solutions to them, it is expected that deliberation involving a wide range of participants will contribute to more competent policy-making and that it is, in that respect, a necessary ingredient for the *technical* improvement of policy outputs. Deliberation is also expected to help take account of others' needs and interests, to enhance mutual respect, recognition, tolerance, and empathy. It is seen as the appropriate antidote to the fragmentation of complex societies: as a component of the contemporary 'management of interdependence' (Mayntz 1997: 272), deliberation is deemed to lead to less controversial decisions, reducing the risk of 'pluralized ungovernability' (Warren 2009). Therefore, deliberation is considered to be a necessary ingredient for the *political* feasibility of policy measures, too; and deliberative mediation techniques are used in the case of decisions encountering opposition from social forces that use veto points to manifest themselves. Examples are the management of fears related to technological risk, or the management of the Nimby ('not in my backyard') syndrome that manifests itself in policies with concentrated spatial costs.

Deliberation is thus an instrument both for policy efficiency (knowledge-enhancing) and for the generation of political support. Both goals are expected to enhance policy legitimacy: in the first case 'output legitimacy' (Scharpf 1970) because decisions based on expertise have more chances to attain their objectives and are thus more likely to satisfy policy-takers;[4] in the second case 'input legitimacy' because there are more chances that decisions mirror the preferences of policy-takers (or at least of those with intense preferences) and generate a feeling of ownership if they are involved in their preparation. Hence, part of the empirical work on deliberation (e.g. Papadopoulos and Warin 2007) also focuses on the question of the political decisiveness of deliberative devices.[5] Are official decision-makers

[4] This presupposes that there is broad agreement on policy goals which, however, only exists for the subset of so-called 'efficiency' policies (Majone 1994), on 'valence' issues where the question is only about what is the best way to attain a goal and who is the most competent actor to be in charge of policy-making (e.g. combat a public 'bad' such as pollution), but not about the goal itself (e.g. more or less redistribution).

[5] Dryzek (2010a: 12). On the basis of a cross-national case comparison, Dryzek and Tucker (2008) suggest that the impact of deliberative devices depends on the 'macro' aspects of national political systems, notably their degree and mode of inclusiveness. A precise identification of such effects requires meticulous process-tracing, because participatory devices are only one of the inputs in the policy process, and their effects have a 'diffuse and temporally dispersed character' (Hendriks *et al.* 2007: 375). For a typology of mostly indirect effects on policy-making, see Goodin and Dryzek (2006). An example of indirect impact is the effect through media coverage: see Parkinson (2006b).

responsive to the concerns expressed by their participants, and do such concerns affect the content of collectively binding decisions? Or is participation just 'cheap talk' and symbolic politics, simply promoted because 'battles over public policy and political influence are in part a matter of whether or not one used a good decision technology or not' (Parkinson 2004: 390–1), which is also described in terms of the search for 'throughput' or procedural legitimacy? Answering these questions requires careful empirical scrutiny, but the following two examples are located at the extremes of a continuum on the degree of the policy influence of deliberative and participatory devices. On the one hand, there are experiments such as participatory budgeting – initiated in Pôrto Alegre and widely diffused since then – where collective deliberation clearly aims at the democratization of the decisional process and leads to the formulation of policy options endorsed by public authorities. On the other hand, there are cases such as that of the deliberative poll on *Tomorrow's Europe*, organized by the Notre Europe foundation in October 2007, on pension matters and on European Union (EU) enlargement (Fishkin 2009: 175–89).[6] Such devices, even when they deal with controversial topics, display no influence at all on elite decisions about the fate of the EU.

In this chapter, I would like to argue that in order to come to conclusions on the relevance of participatory and deliberative forms of policy-making in the decisional process, one should take into account the *broader* context of changes in our democracies in which these innovative mechanisms are embedded. The growth of participatory forms of policy-making is not general (it applies to specific policy fields and requires enabling conditions), nor does it take place in a vacuum, as suggested by the systemic approach privileged in this book. In other words, the object is to situate 'deliberative democracy' in the *context of the wider transformation of policy-making itself*, i.e. the emergence of new styles and modes for the production of collectively binding decisions. Therefore, I identify the most important among these changes, and I check to what extent their consequences for our democracies go in the same direction as those expected from participatory forms of policy-making.

I argue that in most (though not in all) of the new trends in policy-making, deliberation is indeed valued for reasons of complexity management: it is expected to allow the 'refinement' of opinions. However, such a refinement is no longer supposed to take place in participatory bodies. It takes place in bodies that are weakly representative or even not representative at all, frequently depoliticized, and operating remotely from the

---

[6] Another deliberative opinion poll was organized as part of the *Europolis* project in connection with the campaign for the elections to the European Parliament in June 2009.

circuit of democratic accountability. Therefore, I suggest that if we ask the question *who participates* (Fung 2006) in deliberative policy-making, the innovations that count the most are of a technocratic or elitist nature and do not go in a participatory direction. To state it bluntly: crucial recent innovations in governance modes and policy-making are indeed deliberative, but undemocratic. This idea goes much further than suggesting, as is often the case in empirical work, that deliberative bodies are insufficiently representative.[7] In some cases representation and participation are not sought at all.

This chapter discusses the following transformations:

- new public management and its derivatives;
- the trend towards cooperative governance mechanisms;
- agencification, the rise of independent regulatory agencies;
- judicialization, the increasing role of courts as policy actors;
- the internationalization of policy-making.

As will be shown in the next sections, we are dealing here with trends in policy-making styles that are alien to the participatory goals of innovative techniques considered by the empirical branch of the deliberative democracy literature, albeit to differing degrees. Especially when we move from the top to the bottom of the list, innovations in policy-making do not appear to be a plus, but rather a minus in terms of the inclusiveness of decision-making, with negative consequences for the democratic quality of the policy process.

Weakly deliberative and weakly participatory: new public management and its derivatives

The growth of deliberative and participatory forms of policy-making largely coincides with a period of considerable administrative reform embodied in 'new public management' (NPM) doctrines and their derivatives (Pollitt and Bouckaert 2004).[8] Both innovations are driven by a 'democratic accountability agenda' that seeks to make policy-making or administrative agencies more 'accessible, accountable, and transparent by ensuring direct participation or representation of citizens in administrative affairs' (Ansell and Gingrich 2003: 165). Like participatory experiments

---

[7] Such as the imperfections in the descriptive representation described as the 'Schattschneider bias': 'The flaw in the pluralist heaven is that the heavenly choir sings with a strong upper-class accent' (Schattschneider 1960: 34–5).

[8] One can also think about the decentralization and devolution processes in some countries, but these are not a general phenomenon.

in policy-making, reforms under the banner of NPM advocate a closer involvement of policy addressees, and administrative proximity to the needs of stakeholders.[9]

However, the intellectual roots of NPM differ: participatory forms of policy-making are often promoted by progressive actors who emphasize the empowerment of ordinary people, whereas in NPM the neoliberal and managerial orientation of right-wing parties and consulting agencies prevails. NPM reforms have a more individualistic tone as they are more targeted at bringing public services closer to users: 'Highly centralised, hierarchical organisational structures have increasingly been replaced by decentralised management environments where decisions on resource allocation and service delivery are made closer to the point of delivery ... Managers and organisational units are given greater freedom in operational decisions and then held accountable ex post' (Hammerschmid *et al.* 2006: 1). Though administrative reforms of the last few decades are heterogeneous, they originate in 'a common sense of the unresponsiveness of highly bureaucratized public administration and the lack of accountability over administrative behaviour', and in 'the desire to make the relationship between citizens and government more *direct* by streamlining or eliminating the layers and complexities of government' (Ansell and Gingrich 2003: 165–6, original emphasis). Reform advocates usually share a concern that public bureaucracies should be more autonomous in their day-to-day operations; become more responsive, efficient, and client-oriented; and operate according to private sector principles, such as competition, management by objectives and setting of performance standards, benchmarking, reliance on indicators, and evaluation of outputs. Audits are conducted; charters stipulating the rights of service users and the obligations of service providers are drafted; and feedback techniques are valued, such as complaints and suggestion schemes or customer surveys aiming to assess satisfaction with services (increasingly labelled as 'products'). Reforms are accompanied by what Djelic and Sahlin-Andersson (2006: 25) nicely describe as 'ritualized performance displays', such as rankings or accreditation processes, which are supposed to facilitate the accountability of bureaucracy and control by its political principals.

In sum, NPM and its derivatives share with deliberative forms of policy-making a concern to take the preferences of policy addressees more into account: 'voice' by individual users of public services is encouraged. However, it should not be taken for granted that users' feedback produces

---

[9] See Harrison and Mort (1998), Parkinson (Parkinson 2004, 2006a: ch. 3), and Rowe and Shepherd (2002) on how deliberative and participatory techniques were implemented to accompany managerial reforms of the National Health Service in the UK.

any policy effect. Besides, the role of deliberation is not central: sometimes deliberative techniques are used; sometimes non-deliberative users' feedback serves as an input for the public debate on policy reforms – serving thus as a sort of indirect macro-deliberative function (Parkinson 2004: 389); and sometimes deliberation takes the form of elite reflection between politicians and high level bureaucrats discussing performance evaluation (when politicians do not simply impose their views based on their ideological beliefs). Although administrative reform is one of the changes in democracies that are driven by concerns to some extent similar to those leading to participatory forms of policy-making, it can by no means be considered as particularly deliberation-friendly, and participation of lay people in their role of service users may be encouraged, but without great ambitions. This situation should be taken into consideration, because public management reform is no less significant a change than those brought about by the wish to promote deliberative democracy.

Deliberative – but in reality elitist? Cooperative governance through policy networks

It is surprising that there is little overlap between the literature on deliberative techniques and the literature on cooperative modes of governance, though both deal with devices emphasizing stakeholder participation and sometimes, moreover, with the common rationale of problem-solving and the search for conflict avoidance.[10]

The diffusion of forms of cooperative governance can be seen as a manifestation of the advent of an 'advocacy democracy' (Dalton 2008: 267ff), where no longer individuals as voters and political parties, but stakeholders and cause groups are the key players in the name of affectedness or, more crudely but less openly, thanks to their blackmailing power.[11] More precisely, cooperative governance can be seen as the output facet of advocacy

---

[10] See, however, Warren (2008b), and works on deliberative modes of governance in the EU, such as 'comitology' (Joerges and Neyer 1997), or more recently 'new' and 'soft' modes of governance, such as the 'open method of coordination' (Sabel and Zeitlin 2008). Interestingly, works on the EU emphasize the deliberative properties of these modes – e.g. the promotion of reflection and mutual learning – but are not much preoccupied by their elitist aspect.

[11] In current normative thinking too – including in theories of democratic deliberation – parties are often regarded with suspicion. They deserve rehabilitation, however (Goodin 2008: 204–23; Mair 2006): parties are not more subject to Michels's 'iron law of oligarchy' than are other organizations; and, in spite of its imperfections, electoral competition remains a necessary condition for democratic accountability because it includes a mechanism of formal ('hard') sanctions, such as removal from office.

democracy because it implies the involvement in decision formulation or implementation of organized stakeholder groups, non-governmental organizations (NGOs), and civil society organizations. This is, by the way, the major difference with the participatory devices mentioned before: cooperative governance implies that deliberation is the job of professional representatives belonging to collective organizations and not of randomly or self-selected lay individuals. Cooperative governance can even take the form of public–private partnerships for service delivery or of delegation of public tasks to private interest government. The growth of policy networks where public and non-public actors collaborate with each other highlights the fact that even though it would definitely be an exaggeration to say that the state is hollowed out (Weller *et al.* 1997), it loses 'its monopoly on collectively binding decision-making and on the production of public goods' (Pauly and Grande 2005: 15) and becomes a sort of *primus inter pares*.

Cooperative policy-making styles are driven by the perception of limits in the vertical steering of social life by the state through coercive means. In our complex and highly differentiated (sometimes even deeply culturally fragmented, or strongly individualized) societies, state bureaucracies seldom control all the resources required to provide adequate and effective responses to social problems in terms of knowledge, organization, or even trust and legitimacy. Hence public bureaucracies must resort to some form of external cooperation in order to pool these resources, and thus become embedded in a complex web of interdependence with other organizations and groups, or even with private actors such as firms. In such a context of interdependence, policy efficiency and acceptability appear to be a function of 'joined-up' state intervention. The establishment of governance networks is considered to be an adequate way to promote policy coordination because in networks, actors communicate and exchange with each other. Networks are a forum of mutual deliberation – it is expected that through reason-giving and the convincing force of justification, actors may be persuaded to change their preferences and include considerations they initially ignored – or at least a negotiation arena where bargaining actors seek to work out policy solutions by taking into consideration a broader set of concerns and interests.

Similar to a number of deliberative experiments, cooperative policy styles are set up primarily in order to enhance governability: engaging, for instance, civil society into more horizontal policy-making is not so much the outcome of a deliberate attempt to democratize decision-making, but rather a piecemeal strategy that primarily results from the pragmatic, functional, and instrumental concerns of policy-makers, the 'governance-driven democratization' of Warren (2009). Bevir (2010: 118) depicts shifts towards more participatory forms of policy-making as 'technocratic responses to worries about the effectiveness and perceived legitimacy of existing political institutions. They are, to put the matter simply, more about systems governance than radical politics'. At the same time, social fragmentation makes systems governance both necessary and delicate. On the one hand, private rent-seeking or simply the rational pursuit of sectoral interest can generate negative externalities, and governments are under pressure to deal with them. Externalities generate, in turn, 'lateral claims for compensation' (Goodin 2008: 152–3), and more generally a social demand to counteract the centrifugal dynamics of interest fragmentation between sectoral, territorial, class, or lifestyle communities. However, such a task cannot be carried out only through coercive public intervention; it also requires interactive coordination among the interdependent actors (Leca 1996: 340). In fragmented societies all sorts of groups claim that their interests should be protected, no matter whether this happens through or against state intervention. Even though public authorities can argue that they are authorized to act, thanks to the electoral legitimacy they enjoy, majoritarian power is not sufficiently authoritative in situations of social fragmentation. Hence public actors often need to include policy-takers as co-producers of binding decisions in order to generate the identification with decisions that is necessary for acquiescence and compliance (Papadopoulos 1995; Pierre and Peters 2005).

In principle, the inclusion in the policy-making of stakeholders and civil society organizations through network governance may be seen as a promising step towards more horizontal and more open processes of decision-making: politically less coercive and socially more pluralistic. However, defining whose claims are legitimate or who can be considered as a credible stakeholder, and hence should deserve recognition, is in reality often a matter of power struggle. One may also suspect that those who achieve a place in governance networks will erect barriers against the participation of newcomers. Even if this is an overly cynical view, there are also structural barriers to participation in policy networks. These barriers first affect the capacity of interests to undertake collective action, with broad interests paradoxically finding it harder to organize than narrow interests (Olson 1965). Further, in order to be included in networks, actors must possess resources that are unevenly distributed. For instance, in order to receive consideration, a high level of professionalism is a crucial resource. Selectivity is caused not only by inequalities, but also by imperatives of governability: the costs for bargaining and for consensus-building increase with the number of actors who have a say, and institutional designers simply must take into account that this situation complicates the policy-making process. What further complicates this process is heterogeneity of views: complexity management may require not only representation, but also reduction of diversity (Papadopoulos 1995: 61–2), and hence a possible reluctance to include non-mainstream actors who are not willing to 'play the game'. If some groups are thus excluded, others might not wish to be part of the networks, and radicals often face a dilemma between entering networks at the price of having to water down their claims, or staying outside at the price of losing policy influence: all this leads to situations of limited pluralism. A consequence of the lack of network pluralism is that if a network is prone to group-think, then horizontal 'peer accountability' (Goodin 2003a) mechanisms among its members, who should control each other, cannot function properly.

Moreover, even if organizational pluralism is safeguarded, this is not tantamount to democracy, because the overall guiding frame of cooperative governance relies more on the respect for interest and value pluralism than on the respect of genuinely democratic policy-making. The opening up of policy processes to civil society lays weight on the principle of affectedness and thus on particular interests. It replaces the egalitarian principle of 'one man one vote' with the principle of stakeholderism, whereby actors eligible for participation are those who can credibly claim that they express strong preferences and defend causes that are of central concern to them. 'Governance *with some of* the people', writes Vivien Schmidt (2006: 28–9), cannot make up for 'the lack of government *by* and *of* the people' (emphases in the original). In other words, 'stakeholders' and 'advocacy groups' are not the citizenry.

After emphasizing the risk of limited and non-egalitarian 'horizontal' pluralism in governance networks, one should add a risk regarding 'vertical' representation relations too. The existence of sufficiently tight links between actors involved in networks and the constituencies they claim to represent should not be taken for granted. It may well be that the network partners of public officials are nothing more than self-proclaimed, 'surrogate' representatives of interests, values, or preferences (Mansbridge 2003). Civil society actors involved in cooperative governance may suffer from external accountability deficits. Not only is it well known that the more interests are broad and diffuse, the more obstacles there are to their organization, but also that even when organizations claim to represent such interests they are seldom accountable to the populations whose concerns they allegedly voice. To this should be added possible internal accountability deficits (Koenig-Archibugi 2004: 236–7): too weak a link not only between self-proclaimed representatives and those they define as their constituencies, but also between organizational leaderships and the rank-and-file.[12]

---

[12] The distinction between internal and external accountability partly overlaps with the distinction between what Gutmann and Thompson (2004: 39) call 'electoral' and 'moral' constituents respectively.

Representation and accountability problems can be aggravated by the proximity of civil society organizations to decision-makers. The attribution of a public status may necessitate concessions to the goals of state bureaucracies and compromises with the demands of other interests that may not find the agreement of militants in organizations (Offe 1981). Moreover, co-opted organizations are expected to provide expertise, so they often have to rely on professional staff whose connections to the rank-and-file are tenuous. All this points to possible contradictions between the 'logic of influence' and the 'logic of members' (Schmitter and Streeck 1999). Given such limitations, it is no surprise if cooperative governance is also affected by the consequences of the loss of faith in public action in general (Peters 2007), even though policy-makers, experts, or academics often perceive it as an alternative to more conventional and dirigiste forms of state action.

Similar to deliberative experiments, the growth of cooperative governance mechanisms aims to enhance the inclusiveness of decision-making processes and to improve policy efficiency, thanks to deliberation in policy networks. However, those who have access to deliberation in network forms of governance are not necessarily representative of the population at large, as they are selected mainly because of the resources they possess, which are necessary for 'steering', and this violates the equality condition of deliberation. Deliberation is favoured, but it is at the level of organizations that participation is broadened, by contrast to managerial reform, which is more oriented towards the individual, but less deliberative. The organizational bias of cooperative governance has important consequences regarding the degree of pluralism, the accountability of policy-makers, and the quality of representation (Papadopoulos 2008). Usually lay citizens do not know much about governance networks, whose establishment and operation are not part of the public discussion on politics, although the diffusion of cooperative policy styles should not be considered a less significant change than the changes brought about by the diffusion of more participatory forms of policy-making involving lay citizens.

Deliberative and elitist 1: agencification and the 'regulatory state'

Empirical studies show that, in spite of its participatory claims, cooperative governance has a technocratic flavour because the key players are still members of public bureaucracies (Schneider 2000: 253–5; Kriesi *et al.* 2006: 354). This, however, is not the result of a deliberate strategy, but rather a consequence of informational asymmetries between specialized public professionals and 'dilettante' elected politicians, which allows the former to assume the crucial second-order task of meta-governance – i.e. of the management and steering of policy networks.

Another change in forms of policy-making in recent decades is much more clearly marked by an openly technocratic rationale. Here I refer to agencification, largely related to the diffusion of policies of deregulation, which resulted from the joint dynamics of globalization and neoliberalism. It soon appeared that deregulation required re-regulation, and nowadays single-purpose independent regulatory agencies (IRAs) issue important binding decisions that clearly affect the market or a policy sector. The EU plays a non-negligible role in the shift to a 'regulatory state' (Majone 1996). Regulatory activities are now largely delegated to independent agencies that receive competencies for issuing and enforcing licences for operating in the market, regulating market operations such as mergers or takeovers, preventing anti-competitive behaviour, supervising financial institutions, setting standards, elaborating directives, imposing fines, and so on. In addition, comparative research shows not only that IRAs are crucial players in regulation, but also that they play a central law-making role in their areas of competence in particular, interestingly (and also alarmingly with regard to accountability), when they face a weak legislature and if they enjoy strong autonomy (Maggetti 2009: 145–96).

It is widely believed today that regulatory authorities must be independent both of government and of the interests that are being regulated in order for them to act efficiently. By being independent, regulatory agencies are more credible in their ability to make long-term consistent commitments that are immune to electoral cycles or governmental changes. The logic of the political game is considered inimical to reasonable and unbiased deliberation: 'partisans make poor deliberators' (Hendriks et al. 2007: 262). Electoral competition generates 'overpromising' and forces politicians to satisfy particular constituencies, while depoliticized bodies are considered more likely to perform for the common good over the long term. Their impartiality and objectivity are supposed to be core ingredients of their legitimacy as opposed to the suspicion of partiality that hangs over representative authorities (Rosanvallon 2008: 22, 130). Delegation to agencies may exceed the normal extension of delegation. In classic principal–agent relations of delegation – such as the periodic delegation of our power to decide to our elected representatives – agents remain under the (theoretical) control of principals who have an interest in monitoring agents' behaviour, in order to avoid the latter's tendency to shirk and to privilege their own interests. In the case of IRAs, by contrast, credibility is so prioritized that much stronger agency autonomy becomes necessary, with IRAs becoming trustees enjoying fiduciary competencies instead of being simple delegates (Majone 2001). Further, being staffed by experts, independent agencies are more credible in their ability to open up the black box of the regulated sector and come to decisions relying on correct causal assumptions. Note also that politicians can have an interest in delegating competencies to agencies if this allows them to shift the blame to the latter in case of problems.

Giandomenico Majone (2005: 37), perhaps the most authoritative specialist on the regulatory state, acknowledges that IRAs are 'constitutional anomalies that do not fit well into the traditional framework of democratic controls'. He maintains that 'the growing importance of non-majoritarian institutions in all democratic countries, in spite of persistent doubts about their constitutional status and democratic legitimacy, shows that for many purposes reliance upon qualities such as expertise, professional discretion, policy consistency, fairness, or independence of judgment is considered to be more important than reliance upon direct democratic accountability' (Majone 2005: 37). Being typical examples of output-oriented organizations, agencies construct their legitimacy on their 'ability to generate and maintain the belief of being, of all feasible institutional arrangements, the most appropriate one for solving a certain range of problems', and it is in this sense that they are primarily accountable for their results (Majone 2005: 38). The problem, however, is that the public at large often ignores even the existence of such bodies, so that accountability forums where deliberation on agency results can take place are mostly constituted by narrow groups of specialized persons such as members of parliamentary committees or representatives of organized interests.

Although not stated explicitly in the literature on agencification, there is no doubt that at least the ideal type of an independent agency is a deliberative institution in which regulatory decisions are based on critically discussed, fact-regarding, and sophisticated arguments. The same applies to transnational regulatory networks of agency members, which are considered as vectors of mutual socialization to norms of 'best practice' (Slaughter 2004). However, the virtuous effects of deliberation can be deployed only if decisions by agencies are produced by a narrow circle of experts isolated from the democratic circuit in order to avoid partisan influence, and from stakeholders of the regulated sector in order to avoid agency 'capture' by vested interests. Compared with cooperative governance, agencification goes a step further in the technocratic direction, which is deliberately promoted, whereas stakeholderism is not welcome, even in the filtered form of surrogate representation. Expert deliberation is most likely positive for the technical quality of policy outcomes, yet it remains a decision-making mode in which broad participation is judged undesirable.[13] Agencification

---

[13] However, Gilardi (2002) has shown that the cross-national diffusion of IRAs has more to do with bounded rationality and imitation, and there is no *a priori* reason to believe that regulatory networks promote critical self-reflection and learning from 'best practice' rather than uncritical adhesion to a mainstream policy paradigm (*'pensée unique'*).

is deliberative, but not participatory, and the same applies to the next shift in policy-making modes considered in this chapter.

Deliberative and elitist 2: judicialization

Judicialization refers to the fact that courts have acquired a more influential role in decision-making and have become policy actors in their own right, challenging the formal principle of separation of powers. Court activism has dramatically increased: in the past thirty years, French, Italian, and German courts have invalidated more pieces of legislation than during their whole previous history (Bellamy 2007: 11). Virtually all new democracies in Central and Eastern Europe have constitutional courts, as their communist past generated a culture of suspicion *vis-à-vis* power holders. Although judicialization is a more long-term evolution than administrative reform, there are some commonalities in the rationales underlying judicialization and agencification. The common foundation is a belief, probably mirroring a *Zeitgeist* of distrust of politics, that partisan decisions may be arbitrary and subject to particularistic capture, including by political majorities. They may as a result cause prejudice to the common good and the long-term interest (hence the need for IRAs), or to minority and individual rights (protected by the courts).

Nevertheless, contrary to agencification, which may appear to be a constitutional anomaly, gains in fairness expected from judicialization are justified on the grounds of classic principles of the rule of law. What distinguishes judicialization is that it results from an explicit wish to develop counter-powers to governmental discretion, and not simply from a functional logic of self-restraint and delegation for efficiency reasons. Courts are part of the checks and balances system by which institutions should ensure that the government and administration do not exceed their power and do not violate fundamental rights. Judicialization implies that courts and citizens can increasingly appeal to constitutional, statutory, or European law for different reasons: to ensure at a fundamental level that majoritarian excesses are checked or to remedy practices of maladministration when regulations are implemented, including non-compliance with the supranational order of the EU. Similarly to agencification, but more ambitiously, judicialization embodies a will to create a depoliticized sphere of counter-power limiting the latitude of politicians. Liberal political philosopher Benjamin Constant, referring then to the power of the monarch, called this a '*pouvoir neutre*', which today can dispute the constitutionality of legislation, decide the legality of administrative action, and have a say on the power balance in multilevel systems. Needless to say, experiences with totalitarianism in the twentieth century had a strong influence on the desire to safeguard rights, though 'how much self-rule we are willing to sacrifice in order to keep the Leviathan within tolerable limits' (Dorf 2006: 302) is not an issue that can be definitely settled.

The problem of rights is also closely related to the socio-cultural fragmentation of our societies, which we found at the origin of more cooperative forms of governance. The aggregative principle of majoritarian democracy is insufficiently complex and imperfectly legitimate in differentiated societies (Zolo 1992): why should a political order decided by virtue of sheer numbers be accepted by all others, and especially by social groups, able to claim convincingly that they have intense preferences or particular characteristics that should be recognized? In order to gain legitimacy, political majorities must be other-regarding, and acting in the shadow of judicial oversight offers a favourable incentive structure for that.

The culmination of fragmentation is individualization, and a consequence thereof is the 'constitutionalization' of fundamental individual rights and freedoms, with the role of the European Court of Human Rights being significant in that respect. Individuals feel now that they deserve to be well protected against state authorities and that they can appeal to the courts as well as to non-judicial bodies like ombudsmen by invoking violation of their rights. Personal respect, equity, and non-discrimination become core elements of the social demand (Rosanvallon 2008: 109). There are widespread claims for impartiality, and courts are seen as promoters thereof, unlike majoritarian politics. A sort of precautionary principle is introduced in policy-making, with the shadow of court rulings expected to act as a deterrent to the temptation for majorities to abuse their power. Legislators have to anticipate possible court vetoes when drafting pieces of legislation and in a sense to internalize possible objections by the judiciary. Thus courts become part of policy: for example the French Constitutional Council is widely seen as a sort of third, unelected chamber, given the fact that parties defeated in parliament frequently challenge the constitutionality of major bills and that such actions have to be anticipated by decision-makers. If constitutional courts can be used as a veto point with reasonable chances of success by opponents to reforms, then political majorities will tend to make compromises in the shadow of court rulings in order to avoid the invalidation of legislation by the judiciary. In the words of Austrian public lawyer Hans Kelsen (1928), courts are a 'negative legislator' or, in the contemporary political science jargon, 'veto players'.

Courts are important for policy-making in yet another respect. Seen not from the top but from below, appeals to the courts can be considered as the functional equivalent of lobbying, with the courts providing an additional access point to promoters and opponents of policy causes. Such an access point is particularly attractive, as 'the judicial route to policy reform can

be maximally efficacious, since judicial law-making grounded in an interpretation of a constitutional right is immune from legislative override;
such rulings can be changed only through a subsequent judicial decision
or by constitutional amendment' (Cichowski and Stone-Sweet 2003: 197).
This means that political actors have an obvious interest in appealing to
the courts in order to achieve their policy aims. Yet appealing to a court
requires resources in terms of expertise, staff, and finance. As a result,
even though individuals also use litigation, it is mainly used by interest-
group organizations backed by legal experts, so that it strengthens 'advocacy' democracy. A vibrant support structure in society is needed for legal
mobilization, and this can exist only if rights-advocacy organizations, professional lawyers educated in appropriate schools eager to engage in 'cause
lawyering', sympathetic state agencies, and legal aid schemes are part
of the landscape. As Epp (1998: 18) puts it, 'The judicial process is time-
consuming, expensive, and arcane; ordinary individuals typically do not
have the time, money, or expertise necessary to support a long-running
lawsuit through several levels of the judicial system.' Consequently, even
if stigmatized and marginalized groups can benefit from judicialization,
individuals and even organizations unfamiliar with courts fare poorly in
comparison with well resourced organizations that are repeat players in
this game.

The role of the courts is seen by some as a welcome addition of reflexiv-
ity in the policy process (Rosanvallon 2008: 222, 231–2). The initial deliberate intention of the advocates of judicialization was to 'remove certain
decisions, for example concerning fundamental rights, from the electoral
process and thus to tie the hands of the current majority' (Majone 2005:
196). Rosanvallon (2008: 26–30) claims that nowadays the 'subjective'
sphere of electoral, partisan, and representative politics is coupled with
the 'objective' sphere of institutions of indirect democracy, notably courts
and independent agencies. The legitimizing principles are not the same for
courts and agencies, which do not have the same functions in a framework
of separation of powers. Their coupling with a democratic constitutional
order is not equally tight either: agencies have legitimacy thanks to their
expertise, but courts have legitimacy grounded on the rule of law. However,
with agencification and judicialization alike, deliberative forums are created in which it is expected that more objective discourse based on expert
knowledge or on legal reasoning will tame the negative effects of partisan
politics, which is strongly characterized by ideological or short-term electoral considerations. Hence, even though judges must listen to the voices
of those that come before the court (Bevir 2010: 172), with judicialization
it is the least representative branch of government that gains decisional
power (Cichowski and Stone-Sweet 2003: 216). One cannot avoid then the

question as to why 'judges, who (typically) are unelected and (typically) are insulated from the bureaucratic control of those who are elected, should be permitted to impose their own views about liberty, equality, and the like, upon the public as a whole' (Dorf 2006: 301).

In a recent book Richard Bellamy (2007) raised fundamental questions as to the legitimacy of the role of courts in the policy process. Judicialization relies, according to him, on an idealized view of the role of the judiciary. First, counter-majoritarianism 'is biased towards the privileged and well-organized' (Bellamy 2007: 42): in the case of courts not only is access to them selective, but also judges are even less representative of social and ideological pluralism than MPs because of insufficient descriptive representation. Bellamy (2007: 16) also argues that judicial decisions themselves may appear arbitrary, simply because 'despite widespread support for both constitutional rights and rights-based judicial review, theorists, politicians, lawyers and ordinary citizens frequently disagree over which rights merit or require such entrenchment, the legal form they should take, the best way of implementing them, their relationship to each other, and the manner in which courts should understand and uphold them'. It is also questionable whether the judicial process is more prone to consider all the dimensions of rights-related questions than is the democratic process in which, after all, more diversity is ensured because the various constituencies are better represented: 'the need to represent broad constituencies enlarges the range of experiences with which law-makers must acquaint themselves and seek to address' (Bellamy 2007: 34). Because access to courts is limited, they may be more vulnerable to social bias and less open to minority interests than the representative process, although perhaps Bellamy views the latter in too positive terms: he fails to consider that both participation in elections and representation in legislative bodies are often socially stratified, too. Finally, courts do not escape pressure from the mass media or public opinion, nor are they insensitive to the latter's fluctuations.

Today the self-restraint of democratically elected authorities to the advantage of non- or counter-majoritarian institutions has come to touch on many more fields than the protection of fundamental rights and liberties. As a result, the issue of the power and lack of democratic accountability of such bodies has gained prominence. Like agencification, judicialization favours deliberation, but only within a professional community of peers, thus signalling the 'rise of the unelected' (Vibert 2007).[14]

---

[14] Judicial bodies are often explicitly mentioned as deliberative *par excellence* in the literature. The connection of agencification to the quest for deliberation is less explicit, but it is clearly distinguishable in works focusing on mechanisms of mutual learning within transnational networks of regulators (Slaughter 2004).

To state it a bit more forcefully, such bodies are deliberately deliberative and non-participatory in order to attain objectivity. They would be normatively legitimized in the name of their role as guarantors of objectivity only if this role were validated through enlightened consent following a public deliberative process, but this is very unlikely. Few citizens are aware of the degree of agencification and judicialization processes, and they have few concrete opportunities to evaluate their outcomes.

Deliberative and elitist 3: cooperative, informal, and private governance at the transnational level

The internationalization of policy-making does not favour participatory policy-making. The 'democratic deficit' of the EU is notorious; but in transnational governance the traditional features of a democratic polity are even less discernible than in the EU (Benz and Papadopoulos 2006). Nothing reminiscent of a democratically elected assembly exists. Beyond the European level the chain of delegation is lengthier and more complex so that people usually do not know that decisions affecting them are made at global level too, and this lack of visibility impedes accountability.

International relations are increasingly institutionalized and codified in sector-specific regulatory 'regimes' – regimes with a functional orientation towards trade, environmental regulation, and so on. The accountability of officials participating in these regimes is, to a large extent, fictitious because the accountors seldom possess the necessary information to hold decision-makers effectively accountable. International rules are prepared by top-rank administrators and officially negotiated by members of national executives, with government officials forming transnational government networks, such as in trade policy (in the World Trade Organization [WTO]) or in financial policy (in the World Bank and International Monetary Fund [IMF]). The interplay between the network members who form a global elite and the public at large is weak, so that control of networks by affected groups becomes illusory. Accountability problems are accentuated by the fact that most international organizations are hybrids incorporating a global body acting autonomously, and a negotiation system composed of representatives from national governments (Mayntz 2008: 52).

The existence of international regimes shows that the international arena is the realm of cooperative governance *between* governments in the absence of a global government habilitated to issue collectively binding decisions. Arguing and bargaining are key elements of the international cooperative order. The access of broader concerns to deliberative forums and bargaining arenas is primarily – and increasingly – ensured by international NGOs and advocacy networks, who 'claim to represent a wide variety of goods: human rights and security, health, education, animals, rainforests, community, spirituality, safety, peace, economic development, and so on' (Urbinati and Warren 2008: 403). Urbinati and Warren notice that self-authorized representatives 'function beyond borders' and 'in areas where no electoral democracy exists'. Deliberation with NGOs, which exemplify this kind of representation, is viewed as a remedy to the lack of input through democratic channels. If advocacy democracy develops in parallel to electoral democracy in national settings, at the transnational level the former replaces the latter.

NGOs and advocacy networks acquire a capacity to define the problems that preoccupy them as related to the public interest, and to set them on the political agenda. They thus induce the establishment of a transnational public sphere where public policy-makers as well as global private firms face justificatory burdens. Both are pressed to engage in issues that they would otherwise ignore and to give reasons for their choices. Critical scrutiny of the reasons advanced and deliberation on them can take place thereafter (Nanz 2006: 80–1). As described by Steffek (2008: 2), 'Organized civil society is instrumental in exposing current governance to wider public scrutiny and in detecting and denouncing pathologies of governance that some of the actors involved would prefer to silence; in translating the highly technical and specialized discourses of regulatory policies into a language accessible to lay people; in flagging new issues and formulating alternatives to the choices made by policy-makers'. In a nutshell, NGOs and transnational activist movements are proactive agenda-setters as well as reactive watchdogs, and their claims force the international system to become more self-reflexive. Their increasing participation has indeed changed the debate, not only on substantive decisions – by making it more pluralist through the inclusion of minority expertise or stakeholders' concerns – but also on the policy process (Zürn 2003: 248–52). Changes have ensued in the structure of international regimes and organizations: to varying degrees, they are opening up to groups expressing concerns about peace, the environment, human rights, consumer interests, feminist issues, and the like.

However, the participation of organizations representing civil society in global policy-making remains weakly codified: who is selected to participate is important for the representation of diversity, and in that respect international organizations remain the gatekeepers and shapers of what is defined as global civil society (Woods 2007: 38). In addition, though they are considered to be the most efficient channels for the democratization of global policy-making, civil society organizations may themselves suffer from accountability deficits: as noted before, they do not escape problems of opacity, elitism, and lack of authorization to represent; indeed, such problems are probably aggravated at the transnational level. The internal accountability of NGOs to their members may be weak, and NGOs often speak in the name of groups who are not represented in the organization and to whom organizational leaders do not have to justify their options. A well known phenomenon at the global level is the so-called 'suitcase' NGO, 'made up of one person who travels from conference to conference' (Jordan and Maloney 2007: 152). It may happen that the represented are not informed at all about the activists' action in their name. They may even be unaware of the existence of such representatives of their cause.

Moreover, transnational governance takes place not only in international organizations and functional regimes, but also in less formalized, specialized institutions like the Basel Committee on Banking Supervision (BCBS), the International Organization of Securities Commissions (IOSCO), or the International Association of Insurance Supervisors (IAIS). These organizations 'tend to operate with a minimum of physical and legal infrastructure; most lack a foundational treaty, and operate only along a few agreed upon objectives or bylaws' (Slaughter 2004: 48). Such institutions do not have the capacity to issue binding decisions, but their national members – who do have such a capacity – are strongly influenced by their debates and by the exchange of information therein. Such transnational networks of experts produce norms of 'best practice' and thus act as socialization forums for their national members, who are inclined to follow these 'soft' norms of conduct for fear of loss of reputation among their peers. Reference has been made, for example, to a global 'mercatocracy' (Cutler 2003) engaged in unifying, harmonizing, and globalizing private international trade law, and composed of a mix of private and public actors, such as transnational merchants, international lawyer firms and their associations, government officials, and international organizations. Considering their influence in cross-national policy coordination and convergence, the fact that such networks are composed of transnational elites raises questions about their accountability similar to those raised about formal international regimes. But the fact that informal networks operate in a sort of 'grey zone' and may not be composed of formal representatives is a supplementary source of concern.

Informal modes of governance are problem-solving oriented and deliberative, but they remain technocratic and are not penetrated by civil society organizations. The same applies to privatized governance, which is particularly developed at the transnational level (Cutler 2003; Ronit 2007). Private international regulatory regimes exist today in fields as different as the regulation of the internet or intellectual property; the international minerals, insurance, or maritime transport industries; or industrial production standard-setting (Hall and Biersteker 2002: 30). For instance, the

International Organization for Standardization (ISO) was little known until the 1980s, issuing few standards. At that time it worked under the shadow of powerful national standardization organizations, such as those in Germany or Britain. The situation changed with market globalization which gave the ISO a prominent role. Its annual output has almost doubled compared with the beginning of the 1980s, and as of January 2003 it had produced more than 13,700 standards (Mattli and Büthe 2003: 7). ISO funding is private, and states cannot be members, although membership is by country.

Such an international NGO is best described as a global network comprising hundreds of technical committees from all over the world and involving tens of thousands of experts representing industry and other groups. The institutional backbone of these networks is formed by private sector standards bodies at the national level. Domestic bodies are thus part and parcel of the international institutional architecture (Mattli and Büthe 2003: 4). Part of the ISO consists of about 180 technical committees, 550 subcommittees, and 2,000 working groups involving several thousands of representatives selected by national organizations and coming mostly from industry. ISO standards are voluntary, and the organization has no formal capacity to enforce them. However, countries increasingly adopt this form of 'soft' law, which tends to be hardened by the fact that if states stick to their own standards despite the existence of international norms, they can be found as constituting an unnecessary obstacle to trade and thus in violation of WTO law (Mattli and Büthe 2003: 2). Again, the ISO is a deliberative body composed of experts representing mostly economic interests and thus not mirroring diversity. Even consumer influence is marginal, let alone citizens' influence more broadly. And it is only one example of 'islands of private governance' (Stone-Sweet 2004) from which the idea of stakeholder participation is absent.

Conclusion

In a recent article, Thompson (2008a) pleaded for better knowledge of the ways in which deliberation relates to other decision-making modes, and this book focuses on the interdependence of the various deliberative sites. This chapter has suggested that participatory experiments of deliberative democracy have been introduced at the same time as several other deliberative but non-participatory policy-making modes, modes which have more influence on policy output, and probably in more important (i.e. less local) policy areas, beyond the small scale of minipublics. Therefore, it may happen not only that 'people find themselves deliberating about topics that are constrained by larger forces over which they have no control' (Parkinson

2004: 392), but also that these uncontrolled forces will undermine popular participation and favour the confinement of deliberation within elitist circles. Stated differently, not only do participatory deliberative devices have their own limitations, but also their (undeniable) development is offset by *counteracting* tendencies in the wider policy-making context. These trends are characterized by the limited inclusiveness of the decision-making process, the weakness of democratic modes of accountability, and, in the cases of cooperative or privatized governance, lack of formal authorization.

Among the changes surveyed, only in NPM-inspired reforms are lay citizens included, but even there the extent of their intervention is limited, with uncertain possibilities for influence. Moreover, the deliberative dimension is reduced and remains, at best, indirect. In all other changes – in cooperative forms of governance, including at the transnational level, in agencification, judicialization, or in privatized governance – deliberation is valued, but only in narrow elitist circles, even when it is extended beyond technocrats to representatives of stakeholder interests, who are often professionals and sometimes self-proclaimed. The situation is reminiscent of the trade-off between equality, non-tyranny, and deliberation that preoccupied James Fishkin (1991). He was, above all, concerned with the US trend towards 'direct-majoritarianism' which inhibits deliberation. Today it can be said that the *global* trend has been reversed towards *deliberative elitism*.[15] Innovative experiments seek to reconcile deliberation with participation, but deliberative elitism is a sign that decision-makers continue to find that deliberation cannot be reconciled with the equal participation of all (Mutz 2006).

With the partial exception of the new public management reforms, the devices considered in this chapter can be viewed as deliberative, but not as participatory: either they are purely technocratic, or they entail problems of truncated representation. At best, representation relations are weak and indirect, or arbitrarily constructed as such by the designers of the policy process; at worst, they are fictitious or even considered a nuisance, as in cases of purely technocratic policy-making. Although it would be wrong to argue that participatory experiments simply do not matter, putting them into context allows us to better assess *to what extent* they matter (Fung 2006) as part of the transformations in decision-making modes experienced by contemporary democracies.

Party specialists argue that parties are increasingly 'presidentialized' which, as regards decision-making, means that power is increasingly

---

[15] Note that, unlike Joseph Schumpeter's *democratic* elitism (1962), *deliberative* elitism does not consider democratic competition as necessary (and sometimes not even as desirable).

concentrated at the level of the core executive (Webb and Poguntke 2005). Though the trends identified here rather point out that power can also be fragmented, it appears that it can be fragmented among narrow and closed decision-making communities. Elitist deliberative processes such as those here described have insidiously become important games in town. Pessimism of the mind demands that we ask ourselves, then, whether participatory forms of deliberative policy-making appear to be more than *quantité négligeable*. Some observe a trend towards 'post-parliamentary' (Andersen and Burns 1996) – or post-representative – governance, but one may consider this simply as a trend towards 'post-democratic' governance.[16] Yet optimism of the will should induce us to reflect also on strategies to make participatory forms of deliberation matter more (Parkinson 2006a: 166–73), considering that deliberation is only meaningful if it is consequential (Dryzek 2010a: 10). This means making these forms less dependent on the needs of power-holders and transforming the instrumental ontology of deliberative policy-making into a genuinely participatory ontology. To conclude, therefore, I would like to suggest a few possible strategies for these purposes.

First, the potential of already existing participatory devices is not fully exploited. In Chapter 1, Mansbridge *et al.* correctly consider the degree of coupling between the various sites of deliberation within a deliberative system to be an important issue. In this case, it seems reasonable to advocate a tighter coupling of participatory devices to the formal decision-making circuit. The tighter coupling allows better transmission between public (deliberative) and empowered (decision-making) sites, to use Dryzek's (2010a: 11) terms. In a recent book, Smith (2009) cites a few cases where such a coupling has been achieved. A first example is the participatory budgeting process in Pôrto Alegre, Brazil, where part of the budget is more or less directly decided by 'ordinary' citizens, who thus become *de facto* co-decision-makers. Another example is the Citizens' Assembly for the reform of the electoral system in the Canadian province of British Columbia. The state authorities first established a randomly selected deliberative citizens' assembly. This assembly drafted a reform proposal that was thereafter submitted to a referendum vote with binding effects. At the other end, there are cases such as that of the deliberative opinion polls on European integration, which were not expected to have any influence on (elite) decisions pertaining to the integration process. It would be worth pushing EU authorities to take seriously their own concern about bringing

---

[16] Hermet (2007) speaks about the 'winter' of democracy and the emergence of a 'new regime', and Crouch (2004) – albeit relying on a different line of thinking – about the advent of 'post-democracy'.

citizens 'back to Europe', and to provide accounts of how they intend to give consideration to the reflective preferences expressed in such polls concerning important policy issues. Otherwise, these polls risk remaining 'political curiosities' (Culpepper *et al.* 2008: 33). It is worth considering here, for instance, the proposal that this kind of poll be formally authorized to formulate at least inputs to legislative processes, coupled with obligations to account publicly for any substantial deviation from the formulated proposals (Hoppe 2011: 172).

In addition, one should seek to emulate the experiments that have a more direct impact on decision-making. Participatory budgeting has been widely emulated, not only in numerous other Latin American and West European cities, but also within the Brazilian state of Rio Grande do Sul, where attempts have been made to apply the process on a larger political scale. As to the British Columbia process, it has been replicated in the State of Ontario within the context of electoral reform as well. There is then no reason why randomly selected citizens' assemblies could not draft or scrutinize some of the reform proposals that are subject to referendum votes in Switzerland, a country that is by far the world champion as regards formal popular consultations at the national level. Furthermore, in some cases, NPM and agencification have led to the establishment of micro-deliberative bodies composed of policy-takers (such as stakeholder or citizen panels) and endowed them with an advisory function on the operation of administrative segments and individual agencies. This can be considered a good practice that administrative reformers and agency designers should generalize. A broader diffusion of this kind of deliberative body would be welcome, provided that such bodies ensure a sufficient level of inclusiveness and equity in participation, and that they are endowed with sufficient expertise to make sound judgments. A suitable format could be a combination of pluralist representation of stakeholder interests with a representation of randomly selected lay citizens. This does not solve the problem of the uncertain influence of such bodies on policy-making and regulation. It would be unrealistic to expect – and also in all likelihood undesirable – that they take over a decision-making role. However, deliberation between the executive levels of the administration (or agency management) and these bodies should be intensified, a closer interface between decision-making and deliberative sites facilitating the process of mutual learning. Here, one should privilege forms of 'loose coupling' (Benz 1998) that is, mutual empathy that facilitates communication and coordination should be encouraged, while avoiding too much mutual identification that inhibits critical reflection on one another's preferences.

What about judicialization and the role of courts in policy-making? Courts are a necessary part of the political system to check abuses of power by democratically authorized bodies, but with the increasing judicialization of policy-making there is indeed a shifting balance to a liberal constitutionalist version of democracy where the concern to check majority rule prevails over respect for popular sovereignty (Meny 2010). Should one wish to counterbalance such a shift, there would be no *a priori* reason, then, to exclude the courts from implementation of the democratization strategies envisaged for other bodies. Bevir (2010: 172), for instance, suggests extending the role of popular juries, but this would not be accepted by those valuing the impartiality of the judiciary, considering that they are already alarmed by the more indirect popular pressure exerted over professional judges when they are subject to election and recall. Similarly to the loose coupling of minipublics and stakeholder boards with agency management, one could plead for more intense deliberations between popular juries (which would have a consultative voice) and professional judges (who would retain the competence to pronounce judgments).

Now, panels that are a microcosm of society are not a one-size-fits-all solution to the problem of elitism or truncated representation in deliberation, and it would be naïve to think that they could be established everywhere. Take, for example, the case of cooperative governance networks: safeguards should be set to avoid trading off pluralism for the sake of their deliberative role, but it is not possible to create a minipublic for each network, simply because networks are often mere analytical constructs referring to amorphous entities that have no institutional existence. In order to preserve democratic governance, networks should have sufficient democratic 'anchorage points' (Sørensen and Torfing 2009: 244). This means that the following necessary conditions are fulfilled: their degree of inclusiveness should allow equity and a fair amount of pluralism in participation and deliberation; transparency, which allows effective accountability, consent, and contestation from outside should be secured in their operation; and the direct presence of or indirect supervision by elected officials should prevent formally authorized representative bodies from being 'hollowed out' in the process of cooperative governance.[17] For instance, eager to gain legitimacy, the EU has recently made considerable progress in all of these aspects. The inclusion of civil society organizations in the policy process is contingent on the fulfilment of criteria of representation and accountability; the participation of organized interests is increasingly codified and subject to more stringent requirements of transparency; and the legislative role of the directly elected assembly, the European Parliament, has

---

[17] Dryzek (2010a: 130–2) formulates this as a requirement of internal differentiation and discursive representation for networks.

been strengthened through the 'co-decision' process (Greenwood 2007; Saurugger 2010).

As already noted, the prospects for democratic anchorage are worse in the case of opaque forms of informal and private governance at the transnational level. I have suggested that participatory deliberative procedures should be more tightly coupled to the formal decision-making process. In the case of elitist deliberative procedures in transnational governance, what is required is their tighter coupling with the circuit of democratic institutions that are formally authorized to issue collectively binding decisions. Interestingly, networks of national parliamentarians have emerged with the aim of checking the activity of international organizations, such as the Parliamentary Network on the World Bank and International Monetary Fund. For the time being, legislators remain laggards with respect to their international networking, so there is much potential for increased activity (Slaughter 2004).

In a nutshell, current developments in the wider context of governance go in the direction of deliberative elitism, and cause prejudice against self-determination, democratic control, and equal participation. However, there is no fatality in such a trend: deliberative elitism can be counteracted by other deliberative devices likely to cope with the double challenge of being truly participatory and truly influential in political decision-making.

7

Democratizing deliberative systems

JOHN PARKINSON

Deliberation occurs in many different kinds of social system; but not all deliberative systems are democratic. Deliberation might occur in enclaves that are cut off from formal decision-makers; it might occur within a limited elite; and the inputs into elite deliberation might be technical-legal ones rather than the reflective preferences of those affected.

As Papadopoulos emphasizes in Chapter 6, deliberation is just one value among several that drive modern governance. Even if the formal institutions of government are reasonably democratic, there are other systems of power that can pull in different directions and that are resistant to democratic control: the judicial system, the administrative system, the economic system, and so on.

Furthermore, there may be features of the systemic account of deliberation that weaken its democratic credentials – that weaken the ability of the demos to fight back against economic, technical, or juridical power. For example, if Chambers (Chapter 3) is right, and social science surveys can count as valid inputs in a deliberative system, then how do real, flesh and blood people get their voices heard? If the processes by which a system gives voice to its citizens becomes yet another preserve of technical experts, then public debates can become battles over who possesses the right technology rather than the substantive merits of cases made in less technically sophisticated ways (Mort *et al.* 1996; Parkinson 2004). In such settings, public participation can easily become passive rather than active, the result of a random selection process or a privilege bestowed by the powerful, not a right that one can claim against the powerful (cf. Cooke and Kothari 2001; Gaventa 2006).

This would be ironic indeed. As was pointed out in the introduction, one of the key motivations behind the systemic turn in deliberative theory is to put the democracy back into deliberation because of concerns about the democratic possibilities of isolated minipublics both in principle and in practice in modern technocratic states. Indeed, it has been thought for some time now that the deliberative and democratic desiderata pull in opposite directions, with deliberative criteria being maximized in small-scale settings and the democratic being maximized in large. While Goodin and Dryzek (2006) have been cited frequently as presenting reasons to be cheerful, Papadopoulos presents a more complex picture in which deliberation becomes yet another tool for exclusion. This book has been focused on rethinking the deliberative criteria to see how they can be made to work at the large scale. But we should not just assume that the democratic criteria hold too.

The aim of this concluding chapter is, therefore, to ask whether it really makes sense to speak not just of macro deliberation, but of macro deliberative democracy. It analyses this question in two broad themes – democratizing rationality and the question of decisiveness – and while it focuses on the answers that the volume's contributors provide, it does not restrict itself to those. Along the way, it raises four caveats to do with the way that deliberative systems are likely to work in context, especially the context of states under the influence of Papadopoulos's administrative imperatives, features of mediatized communication systems, changes in the nature of citizenship, and two political features that still should play more of a role in deliberative scholarship than they often do: power and interests. The analysis gives cautious support for the idea that a democratic deliberative system is workable in principle, but with some important specifications about procedures. Whether the empirical objections can be overcome is another matter, and the chapter ends with a call to analytic and empirical action.

The conclusions are ones that echo this volume's overall pluralism: there are many different possible configurations of sites, actors, and roles that will achieve deliberatively democratic outcomes, but 'many different' is not the same as saying 'infinite'. What is recommended here is what I call a 'stepped pluralism', coupled to a fluid, relationship-based account of representation, more demanding criteria for deliberative justification at the empowered end of deliberative systems, institutional referees, and a central role for decisiveness.

Public reason and equal treatment

The purpose of a deliberative system remains to place public reasoning at the heart of politics, although what public reason demands has changed in important ways over the last decade of deliberative scholarship. Christiano (Chapter 2) pushes the hardest line on this point, arguing that the purpose of a deliberative system is to produce epistemically better outcomes, and the best means to achieve that is to have a division of labour between experts and citizens: citizens providing the basic aims of society and experts debating the means. However, citizens' legitimate concerns are often about means, not just ends. Citizens very often agree that they do not want riots and looting in the streets, to take an example highly salient in the UK at the time of writing, but disagree passionately about the means to achieve those ends, partly on the basis of their differing experiences. To rule those views out of bounds would be to rule out much of what citizens want to say and want to be heard in a deliberative system, limiting their empowered communication in unjustifiable ways. Thus a more expansive view of what makes a system democratic includes the extent that it is sensitive to *all* that is said in the public sphere. Whether that makes it deliberative is another question, but that is the heart of the issue: can a system be both deliberative and democratic in more than Christiano's limited sense?

An alternative approach starts by distinguishing between modes of reasoning, such as Chambers (2005: 207) who draws a line between the Socratic ratiocination of philosophers and Supreme Court justices on the one hand, and the public reason-giving embodied in the publicity principle on the other, a distinction that Chambers labels 'public *reason*' versus '*public* reason' (original emphases). Still others focus on the narrative forms of deliberation, the primary mode that deliberators use in the real world: telling stories, helping others feel what it is to be in another's shoes, and making public claims on the basis of those experiences.[1] Public reason, in this sense, is not about achieving universal objectivity; it is about figuring out what to do at a given moment for a given people with particular concerns, experiences, desires, and preferences, things that Bohman (Chapter 4) bundles into the category 'perspectives'. Public reasoning should still include reason-giving – the justification and probing of reasons behind proposals – but these reasons are often couched in terms of lessons drawn from lived experience and must be offered in terms that others can accept before they can be taken as determinative (Niemeyer 2011). Thus deliberative scholarship has come full circle, returning to Habermas's more sociological concerns in *Between Facts and Norms* (1996) after spending some time focused on more technical issues of institutional design and the analysis of contained moments of decision-making.

This loosening of what it might mean to 'reason together' is one of the critical intellectual moves that have allowed the deliberative systems

---

[1] Parkinson (2006a: 138–40), with debts to Rorty (1998) and Young (2000).

approach to re-emerge. Walzer's (1999: 68) criticism that '100 million [people], or even 1 million or 100,000 can't plausibly "reason together"' depends on a Socratic understanding of reasoning. For what I call macro deliberative theorists, millions of people can indeed reason together if by 'reason' we mean narrating and claim-making in a way that is 'decision-oriented' (to use Chambers's term); and if by 'together' we mean 'on the same topic' and 'in the same, broad communicative system'. An important objection arises: that by redefining public reason in this way, macro deliberative theorists have thrown the deliberative baby out with the bath water. If everything is deliberation, then deliberation means nothing any more, and contributes nothing to our understanding of democracy: deliberation risks becoming 'directionless, or worse, pointless' (Bächtiger *et al.* 2010: 48). Now, that objection is clearly overstated in this form. The 'reasons' criterion filters out a great deal of everyday talk (Niemeyer 2011), but it does not remove problems of insincerity and manipulation, so a modification of the objection still stands.

Chambers suggests that a way of distinguishing deliberation from mere talk is that the former needs to be 'decision-oriented', but that does not address the objection either. Instead, one might apply Bohman's analysis (Chapter 4) to argue that the objection misses the point of the systemic turn. A system with a division of labour is deliberative to the extent that it increases the pool of perspectives, claims, narratives, and reasons available to decision-makers, and whether those perspectives are generated deliberatively or not is neither here nor there so long as the decision-makers' processes themselves are deliberative – and this is indeed the line that Bächtiger *et al.* (2010) take, distinguishing between communication that is an input into deliberation and deliberation itself (see also Parkinson 2006a: 171). Thus Chambers is right to argue that public opinion research, something that is not itself deliberative, can be an important input into a deliberative system if it provides a channel for the perspectives of those who have no other channel. Similarly, Mansbridge *et al.* (Chapter 1) can argue that the openly partisan and clearly interested play an important role in a deliberative system when they alert citizens to issues and increase the pool of available perspectives, increasing the system's overall deliberative quality, without needing to claim that this represents the sum total of deliberation in a system.

Here I want to raise the first of my caveats. In the real political world, decision-makers make decisions to trust others to come up with quality inputs into their processes, just as citizens do. Following MacKenzie and Warren (Chapter 5), those judgments are made on the basis of assessments about the participants' motivations and competence. This has an important side-effect: perspectives that have been generated by more reliable technologies weigh more in public deliberation than those that have not. Here, 'reliable' means processes that are likely to be free of the distortions of instrumental rationality that have long exercised public managers, including narrow self-interest and cognitive limits on knowledge (Simon 1947; Papadopoulos, Chapter 6) – i.e. bad motivations and limited competence. Furthermore, there is a hierarchy of technologies, with unmanaged public discourse near the bottom, qualitative social science higher, survey research further up, deliberative minipublics higher still, and so on. Where economics, lobbying, constituency views, and party members come in that hierarchy varies by setting.

The result is that not every contribution to the pool of perspectives is treated equally. Contributions are sorted into reliable (good motivations and competence), unreliable (poor motivations and competence), and mixed. Indeed, it may be that the deliberative turn makes equality less likely in such a context: one of the reasons why some advocates of deliberative minipublics have been promoting them (e.g. Fishkin 2009), and why the British government in particular took to minipublics with such fervour in the mid- to late 1990s, is because they promised a competent, disinterested public voice rather than an ill-informed or partisan public voice.[2]

This is crucial. Christiano's account aside, the democratic credentials of a deliberative system rest on the degree to which it includes all perspectives equally (see Mansbridge *et al.*, Chapter 1: 12). If deliberation itself introduces features into a communicative system that ensure that perspectives are *not* treated equally, then the deliberative systems approach is doomed to failure. The riposte to Walzer's (1999) 'reasoning together' objection seems to include the seeds of its own undoing.

Bohman and Chambers both offer a normative way out. For Bohman, a good deliberative system is one in which there is a plurality not just of inputs but of *kinds* of input, and in which those kinds are treated with equal respect. It is not that we should sort the pool of perspectives into a hierarchy according to the mechanisms that generated them, but that we should (1) use a variety of mechanisms to ensure that we have increased our pool to the widest possible extent; and (2) that each perspective is then treated on its own merits. Chambers says something similar: she emphasizes the point that epistemic quality is not the sum total of deliberative legitimacy; inclusion is important too, and mass, aggregative methods are an important way of ensuring full inclusion. MacKenzie and Warren, meanwhile, argue that it is crucial that, in their terms, there are *both* institutions of trust and institutions of distrust, and that judgments about when to use which are

---

[2] Harrison and Mort (1998); Parkinson (2004); Papadopoulos (Chapter 6). See also Hogg and Williamson (2001) for a critique of the ideal of the disinterested citizen.

partly based on the features of the relevant publics: where a defined public exists on a topic, then it is right to consult that public directly; where it does not, then a deliberative minipublic can be used to anticipate the reactions of publics to proposals.

At this point, my second caveat arises. The anticipatory role of mini-publics is greatly overstated, because there is no such thing as a perfectly anticipatory *context*. Deliberation in the real world takes place in a context of power and interests (Shapiro 1999). The decisions and deliberations of real minipublics impact on established interests and preconceptions, sometimes significantly. When confronted by deliberated agreements that contradict their positions, organized interests react in three ways: by putting forward opposing perspectives; by calling into question the motivation and competence of the minipublic, often by sowing doubts about such 'quaint, think-tanky experiments', as one senior UK government policy advisor once said to me in an interview (Parkinson 2006a: 82); and by applying other kinds of political pressure via routes to which they have privileged access (see Hendriks 2002, 2006b), doing end-runs around the minipublic. Likewise, the casually observing public – the great majority – frequently dismiss counterintuitive results of deliberation as the ravings of madmen. Fishkin (1997: 1–2) opens with exactly such a story about the town of Grandview from the movie *Magic Town*, in which deliberators come up with 'such a preposterous departure from conventional opinion that they become an object of national ridicule'. It is precisely this feature of deliberative minipublics that the opponents of abolition of the monarchy used in Australia in 1999 to undermine confidence in the motivations and competence of a deliberative poll (Uhr 2000). MacKenzie and Warren acknowledge this problem (Chapter 5), as does Fishkin (1997), but do not pursue its implication, which is that the anticipatory function is most reliable on issues that lack political salience. Elsewhere, I have argued that such a lack of salience renders deliberative minipublics less attractive motivationally, and makes them less likely to attract attentive publics (let alone the inattentive), robbing them of some of their legitimating power (Parkinson 2006a).

It is worth noting here that Bächtiger *et al.* (2010: 49) make a related objection to the 'any old input + deliberation' solution. They argue that rational consensus and sincerity are preconditions of deliberation itself. That is, it is the expectation that a rational consensus will emerge, and the expectation that one's interlocutors are sincere, that motivates one's own deliberative behaviour. We can apply this to systems thinking as a way of restating my caveat: if decision-makers think that the pool of perspectives has been generated by those who are insincere or self-interested, then *they themselves* may not behave deliberatively. Bächtiger (2005) reports evidence of this in a micro setting; whether it applies across settings in a system is an important empirical question.

Now, one response to this caveat is to recommend institutional arrangements that minimize the ability of powerful interests to do end-runs, restricting the formal public sphere (Hendriks 2002; Parkinson 2006a: 157–8). Likewise, Papadopoulos recommends coupling minipublics and empowered decision-making sites: not so tight that the former become co-opted, not so loose that they are ignored. However, that is not the recommendation that emerges from the other contributions. Bohman, for one, recommends institutional pluralism 'in which there is a variety of overlapping and mutually checking procedures, each formulated according to its contribution to the division of decision-making and epistemic labour within the deliberative system as a whole' (Chapter 4, 88; see also Mansbridge *et al.*, Chapter 1, 20 and Christiano, Chapter 2, 40 on competition). However, that solution is under-specified as it stands. Once again, not all access points are created equal: some have more communicative power than others. In that case, what may be required is not just competitive pluralism, but a set of strong institutions that are both connected to the broad public sphere and empowered to perform a scrutiny and checking role – Thompson's 'tribune', for example (Thompson 1999) – as well as the media, interest groups, and citizen networks. Just as it has long been recognized that formal, small-scale deliberation works best with a trained moderator (e.g. Dryzek 1987), so it might also be the case that large-scale deliberative systems require empowered referees to control the game.

In constitutionalist democratic theory this is the role of the courts, but again Papadopoulos's objections are important here. In real-world politics, constitutionalism becomes judicialization, the shift of power away from the players to the referee and those with the resources needed to access the referee. Judicial judgments involve deliberation of a kind, certainly, but not the 'public reasoning' that was emphasized earlier in this section, and certainly not of an inclusive kind. Nor does judicial reasoning match Christiano's democratic criteria: the judiciary is drawn from a very narrow slice of society, even taking the limited exception of magistrates at the bottom of the judicial hierarchy in the UK into account. This highlights the normative importance of Christiano's 'groundedness' criterion: in a democratic deliberative system, experts and institutional power brokers should themselves come from a broad base, sharing solidarity and overlapping understanding with other citizens.

Of course, it is clearly the case that these caveats and objections are mainly to do with the implementation of deliberative ideals in an imperfect world, and thus do not necessarily tell critically against the norm itself – although see Gunnell (1986) for a sustained critique of the separation of theory and practical politics. But it might just be the case that it is impossible to make abstract judgments about what kinds of reasoning count in a deliberative system. This is the final possible response to the challenge posed at the start of this section. As Mansbridge *et al.* argue, partisanship and self-interest might be destructive of the deliberative system in some instances but constructive in others, just as numerous political theorists over the years have argued that some situations call for suits and sober miens, while others require throwing the toys out of the cot (Parkinson 2006a). I, and I suspect many other deliberative democrats, feel somewhat uncomfortable making such a recommendation, because at the end of the day the deliberative movement, if we can call it that, is in large part about replacing power plays and political tantrums with 'the mild voice of reason' (Bessette 1994). Not only that, but deliberative democrats, deep down, judge deliberative systems by their substantive outcomes as much as their procedures. Political legitimacy involves not just doing things right, but doing the right things (Beetham 1991; Chambers 1996; Parkinson 2003)

This points in the direction of a refinement to this solution, one that comes from Fung (2005). In brief, Fung's view of deliberation 'before the revolution' is that unreasonable acts are justified to the extent that political circumstances are unequal, and failures of reciprocity abound. In other words, talk first, but if one meets a stone wall, ramp up the pressure until one is heard, and feels heard.[3] This fits with Chambers's point: public opinion is a valuable input into the deliberative system if – and only if – there are failures elsewhere in the system that mean it is the only way for some voices to be heard. So, a deliberative system is more democratic when it *hears* what (the inclusive) people say – that is, takes their communication seriously – but in an imperfect context it may (often) be necessary that people try different means of communicating, even deliberately disruptive means, before decision-makers start listening. It is yet more democratic when the decision-makers themselves are authorized and accountable, or chosen in a random way that improves judgments about good motivations and thus trust.

This is not a general, non-specific pluralism; it is a stepped pluralism. It has a default setting – reason together calmly, *à la* Bessette (1994) and Gutmann and Thompson (1996) – but it also has different communication channels and modes appropriate to a given context, with referees and Christiano's 'groundedness' requirement. It is also a pluralism with formal decision-making sites that are accountable, either electorally or

---

[3] Readers familiar with game theory will recognize the echoes of Axelrod's (1981) 'cooperate, then tit-for-tat' strategy in this formulation: first 'cooperate', but if the response is 'defect', then 'defect' in turn.

deliberatively (Roche 2003), to the rest of the public. This, I think, is one good response to the problem of democratizing reason in real deliberative systems. 'Deliberation' on this account still has some analytic bite – it is not all things to all people – but it becomes a means to an end rather than an end in itself. Sometimes non-deliberative means will be required in order to make the deliberative system as a whole more responsive. Whether that is a sufficient response will be seen shortly.

Responsiveness, determinacy, and communication

The word 'responsive' in the last section brings us to the next set of democratic challenges for a deliberative systems account. For some theorists, the democratic credentials of a deliberative system rest on the 'responsiveness rule' (Goodin 2003b; May 1996; Saward 1998). Christiano (Chapter 2, 34) takes a variant of this line, claiming that systems are democratic to the degree that they 'faithfully implement the basic aims of citizens'. At the same time, it has been a standard line in democratic theory that systems are democratic to the extent that public wishes are determinative in some way. If consulting public opinion is a merely formal requirement, and government action is actually driven by powerful interests, then we do not have democracy (Beetham 1994; Dryzek 1996; Papadopoulos, Chapter 6). Furthermore, all the classic electoral definitions of democracy have a simple mechanism for handling disagreement: majority rule. While some deliberative accounts also have a determinacy requirement (e.g. Cohen 2007; Thompson 2008a), others do not. Indeed, in the early phases of deliberative theory it was a standard criticism that deliberative democrats had no account of decision-making at all, let alone a decision rule, once the highly problematic consensus requirement was watered down or dropped entirely (Dryzek 2000). For some years now, most scholars have therefore thought that deliberative democracy must be a system of 'talk, then vote' (Chambers, Chapter 3; Goodin 2008).

But the deliberative systems approach throws this into question once more, thanks to the very moves it makes to open up what counts as 'reasoning together'. In electoral democracy, the link between citizens' preferences and electoral decisions is relatively direct: although mediated by the party and electoral systems, voters' choices determine the outcome. In classic deliberative democracy, citizens' preferences are constructed *in* deliberation – they do not pre-exist it – and so the idea that there is a gap between initial preferences and outcomes simply does not arise (List and Koenig-Archibugi 2010). But in deliberative systems, at least as articulated here, there need be no direct link between citizens' perspectives and outcomes. Nor could there be: only a small number of citizens are going to have well formed and well informed preferences on any given topic, which is one of the reasons why there is a division of labour and a need for institutions of trust in the first place. The great mass of people are going to have bits of argument and bits of experience, many of which will compete with each other. Some participate only minimally, trusting others to do it maximally; some contribute only in the form of aggregate data in opinion surveys; others may have come to conclusions in one corner of the deliberative system that are at odds with the conclusions reached in another. It is the role of decision-makers (elected, randomly selected, or self-appointed) in empowered sites (whether traditional assemblies or democratic innovations, as in Smith 2009) to put the pieces together into a coherent whole, leaving out some pieces and reconfiguring others in order to resolve disagreements. So there is always going to be a gap between opinions and preferences in the broader public sphere and the agreements that deliberative systems deliver, a degree of indeterminacy about public opinion. Can the deliberative systems approach bridge that gap?

There are several different ways of attacking this problem. We might think that responsiveness is the right criterion, but that the system should respond to the common good, or to citizens' expressed aims (Christiano, Chapter 2), or to preferences that have been 'laundered' in deliberation itself (Goodin 1986) rather than to perspectives or raw preferences. I have already distanced myself from the 'aims' formulation, and 'the common good' is not a terribly effective evaluative standard because in most cases it is something that is discovered or created in deliberation, not an external, pre-existing standard against which we judge deliberation (Parkinson 1999; cf. Estlund 1993). The laundered preferences response simply restates the problem – citizens need to be able to recognize the laundered results and, as already discussed, there are reasons to doubt that would happen in the real world.

Another response might be to extend MacKenzie and Warren's (Chapter 5) analysis and argue that responsiveness is the wrong criterion, and that trust is a better central principle. As use makes them familiar, citizens will come to trust that minipublics, minidemoi (Bohman, Chapter 4), or other small-scale deliberative processes are the right way to solve political controversies, and so any correspondence between their wishes or perspectives and the *outcome* does not matter. What matters instead is that the system be systematically sensitive to citizens' *inputs* – i.e. back to the account of democracy in the previous section. We should then want the institutions of a deliberative system to be organized in such a way as to give citizens good reasons for trusting decision-makers based on assessments of motivations, competence, and, crucially, respect, adding to that institutions of distrust in which those assessments are carefully and publicly scrutinized.

But surely it is problematic to rely on institutions of trust in democratic contexts where trust in all sorts of institutions is declining (Papadopoulos, Chapter 6). One might argue that the institution itself will create trust; but trust in MacKenzie and Warren's exemplars of trusted institutions – legal juries – is also declining. Although it is easy to forget this in moments of institutional crisis, it is not just the design of political institutions that is causing a loss of trust, but fundamental shifts in technology and the citizenry as well. All over the world, citizens are better educated, more informed, more critical, and less deferential. They not only have access to better information, they are themselves the producers of information, and are therefore much more likely to rate their own information-processing abilities more highly than the abilities of those who produce what to them are counterintuitive results. It seems unwise to put all, or even a significant proportion, of the democratic burden on institutions whose social and psychological foundations are being eroded.

Still another response is to take more seriously the 'social decisions' point made by Mansbridge *et al.* (Chapter 1), and this is a response in which the changing nature of citizens' interaction with each other and with power is a positive feature rather than a negative. The idea here is that the broad fields of citizens' decision-oriented discourse in the public sphere often – not always, but often – act as a significant driver of and constraint on formal decision-making. Rae (2003: x), in his preface, gives an excellent account of how this feels from inside local government, which is relatively weak in the face not just of the usual array of interests, agencies, and representatives but '"forces" as ineffable as popular culture – from its veneration of green lawns on quiet streets to its hypnotic fascination with firearms – [which] form part of the power environment in which city government must operate'. One of the clearest accounts of how these 'ineffable' forces can be democratized comes from Dryzek (1990, 2000, 2006), who uses examples of decentred, flat-structured, diffuse yet participatorily controlled social networks to show how citizens can be not just the unthinking mass-generators of discourse but the reflexive, critical, deliberative creators of discourse. His normative yardstick for a democratic deliberative system is one in which agreements come about through the contestation of such reflexive discourses. Now, of course, Dryzek is not so naïve as to believe that all discursive contestation in real politics is conducted in this reflexive way; but he does believe that important strands of modern politics can be understood in this way, particularly the environmental and anti-globalization movements.

One of the traditional weaknesses of such approaches is that they lack a clear account of how that contestation is translated into acts of governance. Habermas (1996) has provided one such account, with his 'two track model' in which opinions formed in the informal public sphere are translated into law in the formal public sphere by mediating institutions like minipublics, the news media and social networks, and automatically by virtue of the fact that decision-makers are themselves participants in discursive contestation. But this can mean that the precise linkages between discussion and action are opaque to citizens, and thus open to manipulation by powerful insiders (Papadopoulos, Chapter 6). Compared with aggregative processes, in which there is a clear story about how individual preferences are added together to choose governments; and compared with MacKenzie and Warren's or Christiano's proposals, where there are publicly visible sites for deliberation, discursive processes are much harder to pin down. It is hard to hold anyone to account for their actions and reasons, hard to judge the presence of hidden agendas and interests, and hard to judge the strength of support for a proposal if there are no clear sites of power, no clear lines of responsibility and accountability, and no clear institutional boundaries.[4]

Dryzek himself has come up with a modest proposal for a transmission mechanism, the 'chamber of discourses', in which discourse representatives are chosen by means of a social scientific procedure, the Q methodology.[5] I am not a fan of the chamber of discourses approach: its highly technical selection method is too opaque to allow citizens to make good trust judgments. But there are many, many more options available than just that, and some of them are both familiar and fit the need for decisiveness. Most obviously there is the referendum device, which can be used to send precise proposals (rather than more-or-less vague problem statements) to the people for a vote when other institutions have not been able to reach an agreement. The referendum process has many anti-deliberative features, especially when used as an agenda-setting tool or when it is expected to reveal consensus among citizens that is lacking among representatives (Parkinson 2001, 2009). However, when used to legitimate a course of action, it is useful indeed because of its broad franchise and (ideally) decisive force. This is one of the features of the British Columbia Citizens' Assembly (BCCA) case that is not given enough discussion. Writers citing the case tend to focus on the Assembly itself, forgetting the referendums that followed and all the communication that surrounded the decision over more than five years. And yet the interesting feature of the case from a *democratic* point of view is that the Assembly made no binding collective decision; the decision was made by citizens in

---

[4] March and Olsen (1995); Savoie (2004). For an extended argument for the importance of single, physical stages for democratic scrutiny and accountability, see Parkinson (2012).
[5] Dryzek and Niemeyer (2008). On Q methodology, see Brown (1980).

two referendums, one in 2005 and another in 2009 (Carty *et al.* 2009). So while the BCCA itself was not decisive, and had no direct responsiveness mechanisms, the system as a whole was. Smith (2009) notes other benefits of the referendum device in a deliberative context (see also Budge 1996), along with several other 'innovations' which connect the informal public sphere with empowered decision-making moments.

Dryzek (2009) has also argued that participation in minipublics is itself a tool of democratization, because it builds the capacity to exercise communicative freedom and power (to use Bohman's terms) in other spheres as well, a variant of the spillover thesis long advocated by participatory democrats from Pateman (1970) to Mansbridge (1983) and on (e.g. Gastil *et al.* 2010; see also Carter 2006). In other words, small-scale deliberation can have large-scale impacts not just in a formal, mechanistic way, but because it helps to create the very kinds of empowered citizens that make discursive democracy at the large scale work (Goodin and Dryzek 2006). Those empowered citizens then choose their fights in an active fashion. Thus democracy could be enhanced in a deliberative system not just by mechanisms that hardwire linkages between the formal and informal public sphere, but also by a plurality of participatory institutions that encourage active citizenship – an active citizenship that demands responsiveness in a bottom-up fashion rather than a formal, institutional design approach that generates responsiveness in a top-down fashion.

This might well be right, but it cannot be sufficient. The same objections that arose with regard to radical pluralism in the previous section apply again here. A final response is to have a more nuanced view of what representation in a deliberative system demands. Representation scholarship has recently undergone something of a revival and recasting after being stuck for many years in the highly influential but problematic analytics of Pitkin (1967). From Young (2000) and Urbinati (2000), to Mansbridge (2003), Rehfeld (2005), and Saward (2010), representation theory now emphasizes both 'representation as relationship', to use Young's term, and the idea that constituencies are not fixed entities determined by identity and borders but are fluid things called into being by representative claims (see also Bohman 2007; Iveson 2007; List and Koenig-Archibugi 2010). These two moves transcend the limits of traditional principal–agent thinking, in which the problems of responsiveness are cast as difficulties of identifying fixed, pre-existing constituencies and knowing what they want, and creating bonds of authorization and accountability such that representatives do those things. Instead, representatives call constituencies into being by their claims – appeals to 'right thinking people' or 'urban youth' – such that citizens identify and engage with different representatives on different topics in different contexts. This is both more normatively useful and more empirically accurate. Empirically, partisan dealignment has been a long-noted phenomenon, with citizens supporting more specific causes, perspectives, and arguments rather than simply identifying with or deferring to party lines or members of parliament.[6] Normatively, it helps us see responsiveness as a matter of mutual co-creation of perspectives and problems between citizens and representatives, even where decision-making power is delegated to trusted institutions. The problems then become ensuring not that representatives do as they are told, but that representatives are grounded in and give voice to the wide variety of perspectives that might be relevant on any given topic (Christiano, Chapter 2; Young 2000: 148).

This view of representation helps reconcile the deliberative ideal that citizens' views are created in deliberation with the systemic approach that creates a deliberative division of labour, because rather than seeing deliberative authenticity as being either a top-down or a bottom-up affair, it sees it as both, and shares the responsibility between citizens and representatives. But we should not think that the problems of responsiveness and determinacy magically vanish in such a conception. As discussed in the previous section, and as Chambers insists at the end of her chapter, it needs to be remembered that sometimes raw opinion reflects 'what citizens actually think, believe and care about'. This means that despite the best communicative efforts of representatives and citizens, there is always going to be some gap between demands and outcomes in a deliberative system. Thus while a revised account of representation means that Papadopoulos's concerns about formal bonds of authorization and accountability are probably overstated, they are not irrelevant.

Caveats three and four arise at this point. Number three is if deliberative systems theory is going to place the democratic burden on communication between representatives and citizens, then there needs to be a very great deal more work done by deliberative democrats to understand the channels of communication. In a complex society, the burden of communication between citizens and representatives is going to be carried in three ways: face-to-face or one-to-one, in relatively small networks; via the traditional mass media; and via online social networks, some of which are large-scale, some of which are quite small.

---

[6] For a critical review of dealignment in the UK context, see Dunleavy (2005). This is not to say that identity issues are unimportant, especially when it comes to the recursive and rhetorical construction of identities: 'right-thinking people' and 'patriots', or 'urban youth' and 'hard-working families'. Perhaps one blind spot of some new representation theory is that it does not take the performative and rhetorical construction of representation seriously enough, with the notable exception of Saward (2010: 66–70).

Deliberative democrats have long recognized the limitations of face-to-face engagement, although part of the point of the deliberative systems approach is to reactivate interest in the myriad conversations around kitchen tables and online that make up the informal deliberative system (Chambers, Chapter 3; Jacobs *et al.* 2009; Mansbridge 1999; Mansbridge *et al.*, Chapter 1), while others have pointed out the benefits of deliberative enclaves for subaltern groups (Fraser 1992; Sunstein 2002). However, deliberative democrats continue to present an unrealistically rosy view of both traditional and new media, treating both as perfect transmission mechanisms instead of institutions that have incentives and filters, like any other institution. The traditional media introduce systematic distortions into deliberative systems: even putting aside 'pre-revolution' (Fung 2005) problems with the political economy of news, their audience and narrative requirements, and physical features mean that the personalistic, unusual, and conflictual dominates over the impersonal, the usual, and the harmonious, while much of the story that deliberative democrats want to tell falls into the latter category, not the former (Parkinson 2006b). This introduces incentives to focus on the dramatic features of an issue at the expense of the more mundane. Certainly the traditional media are good at conveying 'perspectives', and if that is all we judge the quality of deliberative systems by then the problem is relatively minor. However, that is not all we judge deliberative systems by: we also want them to be good at communicating reasons for agreements, and details about macro-political forces. This means that the problem is still significant. Research on the deliberative quality of social media, meanwhile, is still in its infancy, with analysis focusing largely on micro-deliberative criteria rather than systemic inputs (Janssen and Kies 2005; Wright and Street 2007; although a partial exception is Hajer 2009). Again, there are reasons to be cheerful: citizen-journalists are now much more effective at communicating perspectives and telling stories that traditional media, for various reasons, do not cover well; or, as in the Arab Spring, set the agenda for traditional media, formal institutions, and informal deliberation alike. But there are also reasons to be extremely cautious, to do with the loss of civility that occurs online; the tendency for online communication to strip situations and arguments of their subtleties; the increasing technical ability of the powerful to restrict content and dialogue online, given the dependence of online networks on hardware that is outside the network members' control; and the very proliferation and fragmentation of media that makes it relatively easy to reach particular groups but much harder to reach citizens in general without significant resources going into attracting attention to a story. This is to say nothing of the rhetorical, symbolic, and performative tools needed to attract attention (Edelman 1988), things which lead unmediated public deliberation to be conducted in largely symbolic rather than reasonable terms (Niemeyer 2011), features which have led many deliberative democrats to be extremely wary of rhetoric.[7]

All this calls into question the ability of citizens and representatives not to *talk* but to be *heard*. Deliberative systems that rely on mediated communication might feature a lot of talk, but only a limited number of sites of talking *together* let alone reasoning together. The sites that do have desirable features might have a limited impact on the rest of the public sphere. Perhaps the best that can be hoped for in a deliberative system is that it uses lots of different channels, including a mix of face-to-face, small network, social network, and traditional media outlets; and that at least some of that communication concerns the grounds of trust between decision-makers and publics, as well as the substantive detail of the reasons underlying agreements reached. Even that stripped-down norm demands a great deal. To return to the BCCA case, evidence reported by Thompson (2008b) suggests that more than two-fifths of respondents to a pre-referendum survey could barely recall the Assembly, if at all, just a few months after its final report was released. While the Assembly clearly had an impact on the vote of those who knew about it, large numbers were untouched. That seems a little disappointing in a process that is frequently held up as a paragon of macro deliberation in action.

The fourth and final caveat relates to deliberative democrats' great faith that deliberative processes result in epistemically better, procedurally better, or just decisions. There is remarkably little empirical evidence to go on here – most of it is anecdotal at best, and even that which is not is generated in the rather limited, controlled environments of minipublics (Ryfe 2005). Using that as evidence of the deliberative capacities of citizens is fine (Niemeyer 2011), and to be warmly welcomed. There is no point discussing deliberative systems if citizens do not even have the capacity to act in accordance with deliberative norms. But using that evidence to think that deliberative *systems* will have the same effects is just a mistake. An entirely different set of outcomes is possible under different institutional constraints (Bächtiger and Hangartner 2010). Perhaps, having opened up normative room for many different sites and modes of expression, systems come to be dominated by perspectives that are narrowly constructed, unreflective or self-interested. Perhaps the powerful just exercise power in whatever way they can. Perhaps discourses that are generated in the right

---

[7] See, for example, Chambers (1996). Not all deliberative theorists dismiss the role of rhetoric, including Dryzek (2000, 2010b) and O'Neill (1998). See Parkinson (2006a) for further discussion.

way have no correlation with right content. This is something that troubles students of the Tea Party movement in the US: disaffected conservatives have borrowed the grassroots and online networking techniques of the progressives to forge a more powerful anti-progressive alliance (Williamson *et al.* 2011).

Summary: the criteria for a democratic deliberative system

Let me sum up the tensions and implications discussed in the last two sections before offering an in-principle answer to the question that opened this chapter.

The first major point is that the deliberative systems approach is based on a loosening of what counts as 'reasoning together', based on dispersed narration and opinion generation oriented to public decisions, and making claims for public action or inaction. However, that loosening opens up room for trouble in real-world systems of governance. The normative vision calls for the equal treatment of perspectives, but introduces into real political systems a technical hierarchy, based on the very criteria that are used to make trust judgments, that ensures that perspectives are not treated equally. While the norm might seem attractive in the abstract, its effect in governance is to restrict greatly the sources that count and thus to impose its own kind of restrictions on the range of voices that can be heard. It may even impact on the willingness of decision-makers to behave in accordance with deliberative norms.

Three solutions are offered, two of which are opposites. Most of the contributors to this volume recommend institutional pluralism that encourages competition between techniques and voices, while another approach is to insist on a carefully constrained formal public sphere in which deliberative norms are more strictly enforced and the number of access points is strictly limited, combined with what I have called 'stepped pluralism' in which it becomes legitimate to move away from deliberative norms the less one is treated with like regard. Perhaps it is no accident that those advocating the former are North Americans, used to a system of institutional pluralism, checks, and balances, while the latter are Europeans and Australasians, used to a more structured, controlled institutional approach. Which produces better deliberation or more legitimate outcomes, however one measures those things (Bächtiger and Hangartner 2010), is an empirical question, although I have leaned towards the 'managed' approach for reasons to do with the resources required to be effective in a pluralistic environment. The third recommendation is to ensure the groundedness of decision-makers in the perspectives they are meant to represent and adjudicate between.

Whether equal treatment requires anything more than being treated with respect is another area of disagreement. While some kind of determinacy in deliberation seems to be required to make it democratic, the deliberative systems move makes that very difficult. The discussion began by presenting the problem as being to do with the degree to which collective decisions fitted with citizens' preferences. For the most part, deliberative theory conceives citizens' preferences as constructed in deliberation, not pre-existing it, but the deliberative systems move makes that a more problematic conception: not everyone has their preferences transformed by the 'better argument' because not everyone is exposed to all the arguments. Some participate only minimally, trusting others to do it maximally; some contribute only as aggregate data in opinion surveys. Mediated communication introduces further filters on what information people are exposed to. So there is always going to be a gap between what citizens want and what deliberative systems deliver, and yet deliberative systems need to take those wants – 'an opinion', to use Chambers's phrase – seriously, not just those generated by the most sophisticated technique.

A frequent response is that the system should be responsive to laundered preferences or the contingent results of reflexive discourse, but both of these responses recreate the problem – it is an empirical question whether citizens will recognize their inputs after the laundering, or grant legitimacy to the ideas of those (relatively few) reflexive discussants. I think that unlikely without a great deal of change in the broader communicative system. Another response is to argue that new institutions will create new habits, and that trust will emerge as citizens start to see deliberative forums as the right way of doing things. That presupposes a limited formal public sphere rather than a competitive pluralist one, outlined above – only the 'right kind' of institution, such as minipublics or minidemoi, are likely to generate trust on MacKenzie and Warren's account, while I have warned against relying too heavily on trust when trust in institutions generally is in marked decline.

The response that seems to work best is to think of good deliberative systems as being richly representative ones, hitched to a combination of direct and indirect decision-making institutions like referendums, minidemoi, and elected assemblies where appropriate. Representation should be an ongoing relationship based on flexible constituencies rather than a fixed, positional relationship between principals and agents. Representatives can be elected – and elected representation brings with it a kind of accountability that other modes cannot replicate (Parkinson 2006a) – but in deliberative systems representative roles can be performed by the self-appointed and the randomly selected as well, especially in settings like the international financial system where there are no formal, fully democratic institutions to act as focal points. The key criterion for judging representatives in a deliberative systems account is that they are 'grounded' in the experience of those they represent: that the 'pool of perspectives' available to decision-makers is broadly inclusive, and that the representatives themselves are diverse in their experiences. No one group of representatives can do this, so a good deliberative system will feature a range of sites, a range of perspectives, and a range of communicative modes along with some public decision-making mechanism. Nonetheless, to maintain its deliberative character there should be a 'default mode' of reasonable, respectful discussion which, while having more of the character of public reasoning than the Socratic mode (Type II more than Type I, in Bächtiger *et al.*'s terms, 2010), imposes more justificatory demands at the formal end of the public sphere, leaving the relatively powerless free to try other means when they find their claims, arguments, or agency dismissed without respectful consideration. To aid the powerless and increase the pool of perspectives there might need to be a macro deliberative moderator: perhaps Thompson's tribune or some other kind of watchdog. Marketized media do not in themselves provide the necessary diversity of perspective (Street 2001). Whether the powerful should be given the same right to turn to non-deliberative means is not something I have gone into here, but the answer is probably 'no'. One of the pathologies of deliberation (Stokes 1998) is when the powerful circumvent reasonable processes in order to get what they want, and as Bohman (Chapter 4) argues, one of the purposes of a deliberative system is to empower citizens against powerful interests.

This account has many points of similarity with the more state-focused, formal deliberative system outlined in Parkinson (2006a). There is no need to go into detail here, but the present account is meant to be more broadly applicable to *ad hoc* systems that come into being to address specific issues, as well as to state-focused, formal deliberative systems, as well as to transnational systems and more. But it is worth stressing that both schemes meet the sequencing criteria that Bächtiger *et al.* (2010) propose as a way of reconciling the tight rationality requirements of deliberation with the loose requirements of democracy. They do this by emphasizing the wild public sphere as the 'grounds' of any democracy, giving a role to minidemoi (noting Bohman's distinction between that and minipublics) in the technical appreciation of arguments; a service role to experts; and a role to representatives of all kinds in presenting perspectives, communicating reasons, and making decisions where appropriate, with the latter decisiveness function performed by referendums where necessary.

Given all that, I think we can answer the question of whether it makes sense to talk of a deliberative democratic system in the affirmative, at least in principle. How closely real political systems match this ideal is another question, and the challenges of measuring the fit between theory and practice are considerable (Bächtiger and Hangartner 2010; Bächtiger *et al.* 2010). Focusing just on the issue of responsiveness and decisiveness, the key problem is recognizing when inputs have been treated seriously and integrated into the decision-making process. Bächtiger *et al.* (2010) back away from making the attempt, for good reasons, and argue for an empirical approach that examines opportunities and procedures rather than examining whether there is a substantive gap between public claims and acts of governance, while recognizing that this is a relatively poor proxy for real influence. But part of the problem here might be their positive political science methodologies. Alternative methods exist, including discursive, qualitative methods, computerized network analysis, and so on – methods that may be more interpretive but need not be less rigorous. This is not the place for a detailed methodological discussion, however – that is something for future work.

Conclusion

I want to close with some general reflections on the application of the deliberative systems approach. While they did not say this in so many words, the authors of the introduction (Chapter 1) talked of the 'larger goal of deliberation' as being to improve the legitimacy of democracy by making democratic institutions systematically responsive to reasons, not just the weight of numbers or the power of interests. The systems approach was taken up because no single institutional innovation can achieve that goal on its own. While the study of deliberation in parliaments and democratic innovations has been very rich and rewarding, it has become obvious that all institutions do their work in context. Indeed, increasingly scholars of minipublics justify those efforts not just in terms of the effects on participants or the rationalization of a particular decision-making moment, but in terms of their connections with other institutions and with systems of governance more broadly. While sometimes one comes across statements that equate deliberative democracy with deliberative polls or citizens' juries, say, few scholars now justify those institutions in isolation. It is the impacts that they have – or fail to have – on binding collective decisions that matter. Because the failures have much to do with the broader systemic context in which such innovations operate, it behoves deliberative democrats to look up from their microscopes and examine those interactions more seriously.

It is clear that some branches of academic deliberative scholarship are looking up, and have been looking up for some time. It is not so clear that practitioners are doing the same. For example, a deliberation industry has sprung up (Hendriks and Carson 2008) which, while having some features that are broadly positive for the future of deliberative democracy, has some damaging ones as well. Not the least of these is the tendency to reduce deliberative democracy to a consultants' toolkit of trademarked techniques rather than something grounded in the public sphere. In government, Papadopoulos alerts us to the fact that deliberation becomes just another tool of depoliticization, the attempt to take the politics out of politics and replace it with impersonal analysis, treating people as mere bearers of values with an uncertain grasp of facts rather than citizens with the agency and cognitive abilities that allow them to practise self-government.

If deliberative democracy is a normative, emancipatory project – and the authors in this volume have certainly presented it as such – then such considerations matter. The approach needs to consider not just the questions of how citizens might deliberate together in a differentiated system, but how that system is itself embedded in a political economy, in an administrative system, in a culture, in ideologies, power relations, and interests. It is one of the strengths of this volume that the contributors are aware of these constraints, although only just beginning to think through responses that are not just analytically satisfying, but workable in the real world.

There are three next steps. The first is to subject the framework to critical scrutiny, although I would caution against the view that finding contradictions necessarily condemns the entire project to the dustbin. All our political ideals have tensions; a tidy ideal is one whose adherents have forgotten something important, usually something human. The second task is to take up the empirical challenges that have been presented, deepening our understanding of macro deliberative realities and possibilities. The third step is to take good quality empirics and build them back into the theory.

One of two broad conclusions will result: the deliberative systems approach is hopelessly contradictory and utopian on both principled and practical grounds; or it offers a way forward both as a framework of analysis and as a practical vision of how democratic societies should work. This volume has, I hope, demonstrated that the approach has some analytic usefulness, although there is much work to be done to make that demonstration more robust. As for its success as a practical vision, it would be easy to make some wearily cynical remark to close, but that would be neither justified nor helpful. We already know that, even though Habermasian ideal discourse is an extremely demanding ideal, there are islands of rational discourse in the ocean of everyday praxis (Habermas 1983; cited by Bächtiger *et al.* 2010: 37). Even were the majority of real deliberative systems found to be not terribly deliberative nor terribly democratic, it might be that scholars find examples of reasonably good practice, all things considered. Perhaps those islands are more likely to be found in small communities rather than the very large, or perhaps the opposite is true. Perhaps the state provides an essential focal point for deliberative democracy, or perhaps states are too entangled with inimical powers to be as deliberative or democratic as other kinds of system. We do not know yet. We have an analytic framework, and we have bits of evidence. Now is the time to systematize what we know, and start filling in the gaps.

References

Ackerman, Bruce 1991. *We The People. Vol. I.* Cambridge University Press.
Ackerman, Bruce and James S. Fishkin. 2004. *Deliberation Day.* New Haven, CT: Yale University Press.
Addams, Jane. 1902. *Democracy and Social Ethics.* London: Macmillan.
Agarwal, Bina. 2001. Conceptualizing environmental collective action: why gender matters. *Cambridge Journal of Economics* 24: 283–310.
    2010. *Gender and Green Governance.* Oxford University Press.
Andersen, Svein and Tom Burns. 1996. The European Union and the erosion of parliamentary democracy: a study of post-parliamentary governance. In *The European Union: How Democratic Is It?*, edited by S. Andersen and K. Eliassen. London: Sage. 226–51.
Anderson, Elizabeth. 2006. The epistemology of democracy. *Episteme* 3 (1–2): 6–22.
Ansell, Christopher and Jane Gingrich. 2003. Reforming the administrative state. In *Democracy Transformed? Expanding Political Opportunities in Advanced Industrial Democracies*, edited by B. Cain, R. Dalton, and S. Scarrow. Oxford University Press.
Axelrod, Robert. 1981. The emergence of cooperation among egoists. *American Political Science Review* 75 (2): 306–18.
Bächtiger, André. 2005. *The Real World of Deliberation: a Comparative Study of its Favorable Conditions in Legislatures.* Bern: Paul Haupt.
Bächtiger, André and Dominik Hangartner. 2010. When deliberative theory meets empirical political science: theoretical and methodological challenges in political deliberation. *Political Studies* 58 (4): 609–29.
Bächtiger, André, Simon Niemeyer, Michael Neblo, Marco R. Steenbergen, and Jürg Steiner. 2010. Disentangling diversity in deliberative democracy: competing theories, their blind spots and complementarities. *Journal of Political Philosophy* 18 (1): 32–63.
Banfield, Edward C. 1961. *Political Influence.* Glencoe, IL: Free Press.

Bartels, Larry M. 2008. *Unequal Democracy: the Political Economy of the New Gilded Age*. Princeton University Press.

Beetham, David. 1991. *The Legitimation of Power*. Basingstoke: Macmillan.

ed. 1994. *Defining and Measuring Democracy*. London: Sage.

Bellamy, Richard. 2007. *Political Constitutionalism: a Republican Defence of the Constitutionality of Democracy*. Cambridge University Press.

Benz, Arthur. 1998. Ansatzpunkte für ein Europafähiges Demokratiekonzept. *Politische Vierteljahresschrift* (special issue) 29: 345–68.

Benz, Arthur and Yannis Papadopoulos. 2006. Actors, institutions and democratic governance: comparing across levels. In *Governance and Democracy: Comparing National, European, and International Experiences*, edited by A. Benz and Y. Papadopoulos. London: Routledge.

Bessette, Joseph M. 1994. *The Mild Voice of Reason: Deliberative Democracy and American National Government*. University of Chicago Press.

Bevir, Mark. 2010. *Democratic Governance*. Princeton University Press.

Blais, André, Kenneth Carter, and Patrick Fournier. 2008. Do citizens' assemblies make reasoned choices? In *Designing Deliberative Democracy: the British Columbia Citizens' Assembly*, edited by M. Warren and H. Pearse. Cambridge University Press. 127–44.

Bohman, James. 1998. The coming of age of deliberative democracy. *Journal of Political Philosophy* 6 (4): 400–25.

1999. Democracy as inquiry, inquiry as democratic: pragmatism, social science, and the cognitive division of labor. *American Journal of Political Science* 43 (2): 590–607.

2000. The division of labour in democratic discourse: media, experts, and deliberative democracy. In *Deliberation, Democracy, and the Media*, edited by S. Chambers and A. Costain. Oxford: Rowman and Littlefield. 47–64.

2003. Deliberative toleration. *Political Theory* 31 (6): 757–79.

2007. *Democracy across Borders: from Demos to Demoi*. Cambridge, MA: MIT Press.

2009. Living without freedom: democracy and the cosmopolitan constitution. *Political Theory* 37 (4): 539–61.

Bouvier, Alban. 2007. Démocratie délibérative, démocratie débattante, démocratie participative. *Revue Européenne des Sciences Sociales* 45 (136): 5–34.

Brown, Mark B. 2006. Survey article: citizen panels and the concept of representation. *Journal of Political Philosophy* 14 (2): 203–25.

Brown, Phil. 1992. Popular epidemiology and toxic waste contamination: lay and professional ways of knowing. *Journal of Health and Social Behavior* 33 (3): 267–81.

Brown, Stephen. 1980. *Political Subjectivity: Applications of Q Methodology in Political Science*. New Haven: Yale University Press.

Budge, Ian. 1996. *The New Challenge of Direct Democracy*. Cambridge: Polity Press.

Cain, Bruce and Kenneth P. Miller. 2001. The populist legacy: initiatives and the undermining of representative government. In *Dangerous Democracy? The Battle over Ballot Initiatives in America*, edited by L. J. Sabato, H. R. Ernst, and B. A. Larson. New York: Rowman and Littlefield. 33–65.

Cain, Bruce, Russell Dalton, and Susan Scarrow, eds. 2003. *New Forms of Democracy? The Reform and Transformation of Democratic Institutions*. Oxford University Press.

Caplan, Brian. 2008. *The Myth of the Rational Voter: Why Democracies Choose Bad Policies*. Princeton University Press.

Carter, Neil. 2006. Political participation and the workplace: the spillover thesis revisited. *British Journal of Politics and International Relations* 8 (3): 410–26.

Carty, R. Kenneth, Fred Cutler, and Patrick Fournier. 2009. Who killed BC-STV? *The Tyee*, 8 July 2009.

Chambers, Simone. 1996. *Reasonable Democracy: Jürgen Habermas and the Politics of Discourse*. Ithaca, NY: Cornell University Press.

2001. Constitutional referendums and democratic deliberation. In *Referendum Democracy: Citizens, Elites, and Deliberation in Referendum Campaigns*, edited by M. Mendelsohn and A. Parkin. New York: Palgrave Macmillan.

2003. Deliberative democratic theory. *Annual Review of Political Science* 6: 307–26.

2005. Measuring publicity's effect: reconciling empirical research and normative theory. *Acta Politica* 40 (2): 255–66.

2009. Rhetoric in the public sphere: has deliberative democracy abandoned mass democracy? *Political Theory* 37 (3): 323–50.

Checkel, Jeffrey. 2005. It's the process, stupid! Process tracing in the study of European and international politics. *ARENA Working Paper No. 26*. Oslo: ARENA Centre for European Studies, University of Oslo.

Christiano, Thomas. 1996. *The Rule of the Many*. Boulder, CO: Westview Press.

2008. *The Constitution of Equality: Democratic Authority and its Limits*. Oxford University Press.

2009. Must democracy be reasonable? *Canadian Journal of Philosophy* 39 (1): 1–34.

Cichowski, Rachel and Alec Stone-Sweet. 2003. Participation, representative democracy, and the courts. In *Democracy Transformed? Expanding Political Opportunities in Advanced Industrial Democracies*, edited by B. Cain, R. Dalton, and S. Scarrow. Oxford University Press. 192–220.

Coady, David. 2006. When experts disagree. *Episteme* 3 (1–2): 68–79.

Cochran, Molly. 2008. *The Normative Power of International Publics: the Case of the Women's International League for Peace and Freedom*. Paper given at the annual meeting of the American Political Science Association, 28–31 August, Boston, MA.

Cohen, Joshua. 1989. Deliberation and democratic legitimacy. In *The Good Polity: Normative Analysis of the State*, edited by A. Hamlin and P. Pettit. Oxford: Blackwell. 17–34.

1996. Procedure and substance in deliberative democracy. In *Democracy and Difference*, edited by S. Benhabib. Princeton University Press. 95–119.

2007. Deliberative democracy. In *Deliberation, Participation, and Democracy: Can the People Govern?*, edited by S. W. Rosenberg. New York: Palgrave Macmillan. 219–36.

Cohen, Joshua and Charles Sabel. 1998. Directly deliberative polyarchy. In *Private Governance, Democratic Constitutionalism, and Supranationalism*, edited by C. Joerges and O. Gastenberg. Florence: European Commission.

Cook, Fay Lomax, Michael X. Delli Carpini, and Lawrence Jacobs. 2007. Who deliberates? Discursive participation in America. In *Deliberation, Participation, and Democracy: Can the People Govern?*, edited by S. W. Rosenberg. New York: Palgrave Macmillan. 25–44.

Cooke, Bill and Uma Kothari, eds. 2001. *Participation: the New Tyranny?* London: Zed Books.

Corburn, Jason. 2005. *Street Science: Community Knowledge and Environmental Health Justice.* Cambridge, MA: MIT Press.

Crosby, Ned. 1995. Citizens' juries: one solution for difficult environmental questions. In *Fairness and Competence in Citizen Participation: Evaluating Methods for Environmental Discourses*, edited by O. Renn, T. Webler, and P. M. Wiedemann. Dordrecht: Kluwer. 157–74.

Crouch, Colin. 2004. *Post-democracy.* Cambridge: Polity Press.

Culpepper, Pepper, Elena Fagotto, Archon Fung, and Taeku Lee. 2008. *Beyond Elections? Deliberation and Democracy in the European Union.* Paper given at the annual meeting of the American Political Science Association, 28–31 August, Boston, MA.

Cutler, Claire. A. 2003. *Private Power and Global Authority.* Cambridge University Press

Cutler, Fred and Patrick Fournier. 2007. Why Ontarians said no to MMP. *Globe and Mail*, 25 October 2007.

Cutler, Fred, Richard Johnston, R. Kenneth Carty, André Blais, and Patrick Fournier. 2008. Deliberation, information, and trust: the British Columbia Citizens' Assembly as agenda setter. In *Designing Deliberative Democracy: the British Columbia Citizens' Assembly*, edited by M. Warren and H. Pearse. Cambridge University Press. 166–91.

Dahl, Robert Alan. 1970. *After the Revolution? Authority in a Good Society.* New Haven, CT: Yale University Press.

1989. *Democracy and its Critics.* New Haven, CT: Yale University Press.

1999. Can international organizations be democratic? A skeptic's view. In *Democracy's Edges*, edited by C. Hacker-Cordon and I. Shapiro. Cambridge University Press.

Dalton, Russell. 2008. *The Good Citizen: how a Younger Generation is Reshaping American Politics.* Washington, DC: Congressional Quarterly Press.

Dienel, Peter and Ortwin Renn. 1995. Planning cells: a gate to 'fractal' mediation. In *Fairness and Competence in Citizen Participation*, edited by O. Renn, T. Webler, and P. M. Wiedemann. Dordrecht: Kluwer. 117–40.

Djelic, Marie-Laure and Kerstin Sahlin-Andersson. 2006. Introduction: a world of governance: the rise of transnational regulation. In *Transnational Governance: Institutional Dynamics of Regulation*, edited by M.-L. Djelic and K. Sahlin-Andersson. Cambridge University Press. 1–28.

Dorf, Michael C. 2006. Problem-solving courts and the judicial accountability deficit. In *Public Accountability: Designs, Dilemmas and Experiences*, edited by M. Dowdle. Cambridge University Press. 301–28.

Downs, Anthony. 1957. *An Economic Theory of Democracy.* New York: Harper & Row.

Druckman, James. 2004. Political preference formation: competition, deliberation, and the (ir)relevance of framing effects. *American Political Science Review* 98 (4): 671–86.

Druckman, James and Kjerston Nelson. 2003. Framing and deliberation: how citizens' conversations limit elite influence. *American Journal of Political Science* 47 (4): 729–45.

Dryzek, John. 1987. Complexity and rationality in public life. *Political Studies* 35 (3): 424–42.

1990. *Discursive Democracy*. New York: Cambridge University Press.

1996. *Democracy in Capitalist Times: Ideals, Limits, Struggles*. New York and Oxford: Oxford University Press.

2000. *Deliberative Democracy and Beyond: Liberals, Critics, Contestations*. Oxford University Press.

2006. *Deliberative Global Politics*. Cambridge: Polity.

2009. Democratization as deliberative capacity building. *Comparative Political Studies* 42 (11): 1,379–402.

2010a. *Foundations and Frontiers of Deliberative Governance*. Oxford University Press.

2010b. Rhetoric in democracy: a systemic appreciation. *Political Theory* 38 (3): 319–39.

Dryzek, John and Simon Niemeyer. 2008. Discursive representation. *American Political Science Review* 102: 481–93.

Dryzek, John and Aviezer Tucker. 2008. Deliberative innovation to different effect: consensus conferences in Denmark, France, and the United States. *Public Administration Review* 68 (5): 864–76.

Dryzek, John, David Downes, Christian Hunold, David Schlosberg, and Hans-Kristian Hernes. 2003. *Green States and Social Movements: Environmentalism in the United States, United Kingdom, Germany, and Norway*. Oxford University Press.

Dunleavy, Patrick. 2005. Facing up to multi-party politics: how partisan dealignment and PR voting have fundamentally changed Britain's party systems. *Parliamentary Affairs* 58 (3): 503–32.

Dworkin, Ronald. 1985. Civil disobedience and nuclear protest. In *A Matter of Principle*, edited by R. Dworkin. Cambridge, MA: Harvard University Press. 104–15.

Edelman, Murray. 1988. *Constructing the Political Spectacle*. Chicago: University of Chicago Press.

Epp, Charles. 1998. *The Rights Revolution: Lawyers, Activists, and Supreme Courts in Comparative Perspective*. University of Chicago Press.

Epstein, Steven. 1996. *Impure Science: AIDS, Activism, and the Politics of Science*. Berkeley, CA: University of California Press.

Estlund, David. 1993. Making truth safe for democracy. In *The Idea of Democracy*, edited by D. Copp, J. Hampton, and J. E. Roemer. New York: Cambridge University Press. 71–100.

2000. Political quality. *Social Philosophy and Policy* 17 (1): 127–60.

2001. Deliberation down and dirty: must political expression be civil? In *The Boundaries of Freedom of Expression and Order in American Democracy*, edited by T. R. Hensley. Kent, OH: Kent State University Press.

2002. *Democratic Authority*. Princeton University Press.

Ferejohn, John. 2008. Conclusion: the citizens' assembly model. In *Designing Deliberative Democracy: the British Columbia Citizens' Assembly*, edited by M. Warren and H. Pearse. Cambridge University Press. 192–213.

Fishkin, James S. 1991. *Democracy and Deliberation*. New Haven: Yale University Press.

1997. *The Voice of the People: Public Opinion and Democracy*. 2nd edn. New Haven: Yale University Press.

2009. *When the People Speak: Deliberative Democracy and Public Consultation*. Oxford University Press.

Fishkin, James S. and Peter Laslett. 2003. *Debating Deliberative Democracy*. Malden, MA: Blackwell.

Fishkin, James S. and Robert Luskin. 2005. Experimenting with a democratic ideal: deliberative polling and public opinion. *Acta Politica* 40: 284–98.

Fraser, Nancy. 1992. Rethinking the public sphere: a contribution to the critique of actually existing democracy. In *Habermas and the Public Sphere*, edited by C. Calhoun. Cambridge, MA: MIT Press. 109–42.

Freeman, Samuel. 2000. Deliberative democracy: a sympathetic comment. *Philosophy and Public Affairs* 29 (4): 371–418.

Fung, Archon. 2003. Survey article: recipes for public spheres: eight institutional design choices and their consequences. *Journal of Political Philosophy* 11 (3): 338–67.

2004. *Empowered Participation: Reinventing Urban Democracy*. Princeton University Press.

2005. Deliberation before the revolution: toward an ethics of deliberative democracy in an unjust world. *Political Theory* 33 (2): 397–419.

2006. Varieties of participation in complex governance. *Public Administration Review* 66 (s1): 66–75.

2007. Minipublics: deliberative designs and their consequences. In *Deliberation, Participation, and Democracy: Can the People Govern?*, edited by S. W. Rosenberg. New York: Palgrave Macmillan.

Garrett, Elizabeth and Matthew D. McGubbins. 2008. When voters make laws: how direct democracy is shaping American cities. *Public Works Management and Policy* 13 (1): 39–61.

Gastil, John. 2008. *Political Communication and Deliberation*. Thousand Oaks, CA: Sage.

Gastil, John and Katie Knobloch. 2011. *Evaluation Report to the Oregon State Legislature on the 2010 Oregon Citizens' Initiative Review*. Seattle: Department of Communications, University of Washington.

Gastil, John, E. Pierre Deess, Philip J. Weiser, and Cindy Simmons. 2010. *The Jury and Democracy: how Jury Deliberation Promotes Civic Engagement and Political Participation*. Oxford University Press.

Gaventa, J. 2006. Finding the spaces for change: a power analysis. *IDS Bulletin – Institute of Development Studies* 37 (6): 23–33.

Gilardi, Fabrizio. 2002. Policy credibility and delegation to independent regulatory agencies: a comparative empirical analysis. *Journal of European Public Policy* 9 (6): 873–93.

Goldman, Alvin I. 2001. Experts: which ones should you trust? *Philosophy and Phenomenological Research* 63 (1): 85–110.

Goodin, Robert. 1986. Laundering preferences. In *Foundations of Social Choice Theory*, edited by J. Elster and A. Hylland. Cambridge University Press.

2003a. Democratic accountability: the distinctiveness of the third sector. *European Journal of Sociology* 44 (3): 359–96.

2003b. *Reflective Democracy*. Oxford University Press.

2005. Sequencing deliberative moments. *Acta Politica* 40: 182–96.

2007. Enfranchising all affected interests, and its alternatives. *Philosophy and Public Affairs* 35 (1): 40–68.

2008. *Innovating Democracy: Democratic Theory and Practice after the Deliberative Turn*. Oxford University Press.

Goodin, Robert and John Dryzek. 2006. Deliberative impacts: the macro-political uptake of mini-publics. *Politics and Society* 34 (2): 219–44.

Greenwood, Justin. 2007. Review article: organized civil society and democratic legitimacy in the European Union. *British Journal of Political Science* 37 (2): 333–57.

Gunnell, John G. 1986. *Between Philosophy and Politics: the Alienation of Political Theory*. Amherst: University of Massachusetts Press.

Gutmann, Amy and Dennis Thompson. 1996. *Democracy and Disagreement*. Cambridge, MA: Belknap Press of Harvard University Press.

2004. *Why Deliberative Democracy?* Princeton University Press.

2010. The mindsets of political compromise. *Perspectives on Politics* 8 (4): 1,125–38.

Habermas, Jürgen. 1975. *Legitimation Crisis*. Translated by T. McCarthy. Cambridge, MA: Beacon Press.

1983. *Moralbewusstein und Kommikatives Handeln*. Frankfurt: Suhrkamp.

1995. Reconciliation through the public use of reason: remarks on John Rawls's *Political Liberalism*. *Journal of Philosophy* 92 (3): 109–31.

1996. *Between Facts and Norms: Contributions to a Discourse Theory of Law and Democracy*. Translated by W. Rehg. Cambridge: Polity Press.

2001. *The Postnational Constellation*. Cambridge, MA: MIT Press.

2006. Political communication in media society: does democracy still enjoy an epistemic dimension? The impact of normative theory on empirical research. *Communication Theory* 16 (4): 411–26.

Hajer, Maarten. 2009. *Authoritative Governance: Policy-making in the Age of Mediatization*. Oxford University Press.

Hajer, Maarten and Hendrik Wagenaar, eds. 2003. *Deliberative Policy Analysis: Understanding Governance in the Network Society*. Cambridge University Press.

Hall, Rodney Bruce and Thomas Biersteker. 2002. The emergence of private authority in the international system. In *The Emergence of Private Authority in Global Governance*, edited by R. B. Hall and T. Biersteker. Cambridge University Press. 3–22.

Hammerschmid, Gerhard, Renate Meyer, and Christoph Demmke. 2006. *Balancing Decentralisation and Accountability: Different Paths and National Understandings in EU Countries*. Paper given at the conference of the International Public Management Network, June, St. Gallen University, Switzerland.

Hardin, Russell. 1999. Do we want trust in government? In *Democracy and Trust*, edited by M. Warren. Cambridge University Press. 22–41.

2009. Deliberative democracy. In *Contemporary Debates in Political Philosophy*, edited by T. Christiano and J. Christman. Oxford: Wiley-Blackwell. 231–46.

Harrison, Stephen and Maggie Mort. 1998. Which champions, which people? Public and user involvement in health care as a technology of legitimation. *Social Policy and Administration* 32 (1): 60–70.

Hendriks, Carolyn. 2002. Institutions of deliberative democratic processes and interest groups: roles, tensions and incentives. *Australian Journal of Public Administration* 61 (1): 64–75.

2006a. Integrated deliberation: reconciling civil society's dual role in deliberative democracy. *Political Studies* 54 (3): 486–508.

2006b. When the forum meets interest politics: strategic uses of public deliberation. *Politics and Society* 34 (4): 571–602.

Hendriks, Carolyn and Lyn Carson. 2008. Can the market help the forum? Negotiating the commercialization of deliberative democracy. *Policy Sciences* 41 (4): 293–313.

Hendriks, Carolyn, John Dryzek, and Christian Hunold. 2007. Turning up the heat: partisanship in deliberative innovation. *Political Studies* 55 (2): 362–83.

Hermet, Guy. 2007. *L'hiver de la Démocratie ou le Nouveau Régime*. Paris: Armand Colin.

Hogg, Christine and Charlotte Williamson. 2001. Whose interests do lay people represent? Towards an understanding of the role of lay people as members of committees. *Health Expectations* 4 (1): 2–9.

Hoppe, Robert. 2011. Institutional constraints and practical problems in deliberative and participatory policy making. *Policy and Politics* 39 (2): 163–86.

Inglehart, Ronald and Christian Welzel. 2005. *Modernization, Cultural Change, and Democracy: the Human Development Sequence*. Cambridge University Press.

Iveson, Kurt. 2007. *Publics and the City*. Malden, MA: Blackwell.

Jacobs, Lawrence and Benjamin I. Page. 2005. Who influences US foreign policy? *American Political Science Review* 99 (1): 107–23.

Jacobs, Lawrence, Fay Lomax Cook, and Michael X. Delli Carpini. 2009. *Talking Together: Public Deliberation and Political Participation in America*. University of Chicago Press.

Janis, Irving L. 1982. *Groupthink: Psychological Studies of Policy Decisions and Fiascos*. Boston, MA: Houghton Mifflin.

Janssen, D. and R. Kies. 2005. Online forums and deliberative democracy. *Acta Politica* 40 (3): 317–35.

Joerges, Christian and Jürgen Neyer. 1997. Transforming strategic interaction into deliberative problem-solving: European comitology in the foodstuffs sector. *Journal of European Public Policy* 4 (4): 609–25.

Jordan, A. G. and William A. Maloney. 2007. *Democracy and Interest Groups: Enhancing Participation?* Basingstoke; New York: Palgrave Macmillan.

Kelsen, Hans. 1928. La garantie juridictionnelle de la Constitution. *Revue du Droit Public et de la Science Politique en France et à l'Étranger* 45: 1–61.

Kitcher, Philip. 2001. *Science, Truth and Democracy.* Oxford University Press.

Koenig-Archibugi, Matthias. 2004. Transnational corporations and public accountability. *Government and Opposition* 39 (2): 234–59.

Krause, Sharon. 2008. *Civil Passions: Moral Sentiment and Democratic Deliberation.* Princeton University Press.

Kriesi, Hanspeter, Silke Adam, and Margit Jochum. 2006. Comparative analysis of policy networks in western Europe. *Journal of European Public Policy* 13 (3): 341–61.

Leca, Jean. 1996. La 'gouvernance' de la France sous la Cinquième République: une perspective de sociologie comparative. In *De la Cinquième République à l'Europe: Hommage à Jean-Louis Quermonne,* edited by F. d'Arcy and L. Rouban. Paris: Presses de Sciences. 329–65.

List, Christian and Mathias Koenig-Archibugi. 2010. Can there be a global demos? An agency-based approach. *Philosophy and Public Affairs* 38 (1): 76–110.

Loka Institute. 2009. *Danish-style, Citizen-based Deliberative Consensus Conferences on Science and Technology Policy Worldwide.* 9 June. Available from www.loka. org/TrackingConsensus.html.

Lupia, Arthur. 2001. Dumber than chimps? An assessment of direct democracy voters. In *Dangerous Democracy? The Battle over Ballot Initiatives in America,* edited by L. J. Sabato, H. R. Ernst, and B. A. Larson. New York: Rowman and Littlefield. 66–70.

Lupia, Arthur and Mathew McCubbins. 1998. *The Democratic Dilemma: Can Citizens Learn what They Need to Know?* Cambridge University Press.

Mackie, Gerry. forthcoming. Travelling to the village of knowledge. In *Deliberation for Development,* edited by V. Rao and P. Heller. Washington, DC: World Bank.

Maggetti, Martino. 2009. Regulation in practice: the *de facto* independence of regulatory agencies and its consequences for policy making and regulatory outcomes. PhD thesis. Political Science, Université de Lausanne, Lausanne.

Mair, Peter. 2006. Ruling the void. *New Left Review* 42 (Nov–Dec): 25–51.

Majone, Giandomenico. 1994. Décisions publiques et délibération. *Revue Française de Science Politique* 44 (4): 579–98.

1996. *Regulating Europe.* London: Routledge.

2001. Two logics of delegation: agency and fiduciary relations in EU governance. *European Union Politics* 2 (1): 103–22.

2005. *Dilemmas of European Integration: the Ambiguities and Pitfalls of Integration by Stealth.* Oxford University Press.

Maliks, Reidar. 2009. Acting through others: Kant and the exercise view of representation. *Public Reason* 1 (1): 9–26.

Manin, Bernard. 1987. On legitimacy and political deliberation. *Political Theory* 15 (3): 338–68.

Mansbridge, Jane. 1983. *Beyond Adversary Democracy.* 2nd edn. University of Chicago Press.

1986. *Why We Lost the ERA.* University of Chicago Press.

1999. Everyday talk in the deliberative system. In *Deliberative Politics: Essays on 'Democracy and Disagreement',* edited by S. Macedo. New York: Oxford University Press. 211–39.

2003. Rethinking representation. *American Political Science Review* 97 (4): 515–28.

2009. A 'selection model' of political representation. *Journal of Political Philosophy* 17 (4): 369–98.

Mansbridge, Jane, James Bohman, Simone Chambers, David Estlund, Andreas Føllesdal, Archon Fung, Cristina Lafont, Bernard Manin, and José Luis Martí. 2010. The place of self-interest and the role of power in deliberative democracy. *Journal of Political Philosophy* 18 (1): 64–100.

March, James G. and Johan P. Olsen. 1995. *Democratic Governance*. New York: Free Press.

Mattli, Walter and Tim Büthe. 2003. Setting international standards: technological rationality or primacy of power? *World Politics* 56 (1): 1–42.

May, John. 1996. *Keeping it Together: the Role of Peak Bodies in a Civil Society*. Canberra: Australian Council of Social Service.

Mayntz, Renate. 1997. Politische Steuerung: Aufstieg, Niedergang und Transformation einer Theorie. In *Soziale Dynamik und Politische Steuerung: Theoretische und Methodologische Überlegungen*, edited by R. Mayntz. Frankfurt: Campus. 263–92.

2008. Von der Steuerungstheorie zu Global Governance. *Politische Vierteljahresschrift* (special issue) 41: 44–60.

Meny, Yves. 2010. Democracy in troubled times. *European Political Science* 9 (2): 259–68.

Mill, John Stuart. 1975. Considerations on representative government. In *Mill: Three Essays*, edited by R. Wollheim. Oxford University Press.

Mort, Maggie, Stephen Harrison, and Gerald Wistow. 1996. The user card: picking through the organisational undergrowth in health and social care. *Contemporary Political Studies* 2: 1,133–40.

Muirhead, Russell. 2006. A defense of party spirit. *Perspectives on Politics* 4 (4): 713–27.

Mutz, Diana. 2006. *Hearing the Other Side: Deliberative versus Participatory Democracy*. Cambridge University Press.

Nanz, Patrizia. 2006. Democratic legitimacy and constitutionalisation of trans-national trade governance: a view from political theory. In *Constitutionalism, Multilevel Trade Governance and Social Regulation*, edited by C. Joerges and E.-U. Petersmann. Oxford: Hart. 59–82.

National Research Council. 2008. Public participation in environmental assess-ment and decision making. In *Panel on Public Participation in Environmental Assessment and Decision Making*, edited by T. Dietz and P. C. Stern. Washington, DC: Committee on the Human Dimensions of Global Change, Division of Behavioral and Social Sciences and Education, The National Academies Press.

Neblo, Michael. 2010. *A Research Agenda for Deliberative Consultation on Health Care and Bioethics*. Paper given at the Harvard Bioethics Conference, 22 April, Harvard University, Cambridge, MA.

New America Foundation. 2009. *Is There a Constitutional Convention in California's Future? An Opportunity for Political Reform*. 10 June. Available from www.newamerica.net/programs/political_reform/citizens_assembly.

Niemeyer, Simon. 2011. The emancipatory effect of deliberation: empirical lessons from mini-publics. *Politics and Society* 39 (1): 103–40.

O'Doherty, Kieran and Michael Burgess. 2009. Engaging the public on biobanks: outcomes of the BC Biobank Deliberation. *Public Health Genomics* 12 (4): 203–15.

O'Neill, John. 1998. Rhetoric, science and philosophy. *Philosophy of the Social Sciences* 28 (2): 205–25.

Offe, Claus. 1981. The attribution of public status to interest groups. In *Organized Interests in Western Europe*, edited by S. Berger. Cambridge University Press. 123–58.

Olson, Mancur. 1965. *The Logic of Collective Action: Public Goods and the Theory of Groups*. Cambridge, MA: Harvard University Press.

Page, Benjamin I. 1994. Democratic responsiveness? Untangling the links between public opinion and policy. *PS: Political Science and Politics* 27 (1): 25–9.

Page, Benjamin I. and Lawrence Jacobs. 2009. *Class War? What Americans Really Think about Economic Inequality*. University of Chicago Press.

Page, Benjamin I. and Robert Y. Shapiro. 1992. *The Rational Public: Fifty Years of Trends in Americans' Policy Preferences*. University of Chicago Press.

Page, Scott. 2008. *The Difference: How the Power of Diversity Creates Better Groups, Firms, Schools, and Societies*. Princeton University Press.

Papadopoulos, Yannis. 1995. *Complexité Sociale et Politiques Publiques*. Paris: Montchrestien.

2008. Assessing the claims of 'post-parliamentary' governance: few certainties, much more open questions. In *Changing Images of Civil Society*, edited by B. Jobert and B. Kohler-Koch. London: Routledge. 177–94.

Papadopoulos, Yannis and Philippe Warin, eds. 2007. Innovative, participatory, and deliberative procedures in policy-making: democratic and effective? *European Journal of Political Research* (special issue) 46 (4).

Parkinson, John. 1999. *The Definition of Good Decisions*. Paper read at Conference of the Australasian Political Studies Association, University of Sydney, Australia.

2001. Deliberative democracy and referendums. In *Challenges to Democracy: Ideas, Involvement and Institutions*, edited by K. M. Dowding, J. Hughes, and H. Margetts. London: Palgrave. 131–52.

2003. Legitimacy problems in deliberative democracy. *Political Studies* 51 (1): 180–96.

2004. Why deliberate? The encounter between deliberation and new public managers. *Public Administration* 82 (2): 377–95.

2006a. *Deliberating in the Real World: Problems of Legitimacy in Deliberative Democracy*. Oxford University Press.

2006b. Rickety bridges: using the media in deliberative democracy. *British Journal of Political Science* 36 (1): 175–83.

2009. *Beyond Technique: the Role of Referendums in the Deliberative System*. Paper presented to the Referendums and Deliberative Democracy conference, 8 May, University of Edinburgh.

2012. *Democracy and Public Space: the Physical Sites of Democratic Performance*. Oxford University Press.

Pateman, Carole. 1970. *Participation and Democratic Theory*. Cambridge University Press.

Pauly, Louis W. and Edgar Grande. 2005. Reconstituting political authority: sovereignty, effectiveness, and legitimacy in a transnational order. In *Complex Sovereignty: Reconstituting Political Authority in the Twenty-first Century*, edited by E. Grande and L. W. Pauly. Toronto University Press. 3–21.

Peters, B. Guy. 2007. Virtuous and vicious circles in democratic network governance. In *Theories of Democratic Network Governance*, edited by E. Sørensen and J. Torfing. Basingstoke: Palgrave Macmillan. 61–76.

Pierre, Jon and B. Guy Peters. 2005. *Governing Complex Societies: Trajectories and Scenarios*. Basingstoke: Palgrave.

Pierson, Paul. 2004. *Politics in Time: History, Institutions and Social Analysis*. Princeton University Press.

Pincione, Guido and Fernando Teson. 2006. *Rational Choice and Democratic Deliberation: a Theory of Discourse Failure*. Cambridge University Press.

Pitkin, Hanna. 1967. *The Concept of Representation*. Berkeley and Los Angeles: University of California Press.

Pollitt, Christopher and Geert Bouckaert. 2004. *Public Management Reform: a Comparative Analysis*. 2nd edn. Oxford University Press.

Rae, Douglas. 2003. *City: Urbanism and its End*. New Haven: Yale University Press.

Rawls, John. 1971. *A Theory of Justice*. Oxford University Press.

Rehfeld, Andrew. 2005. *The Concept of Constituency: Political Representation, Democratic Legitimacy and Institutional Design*. Cambridge University Press.

Richardson, Henry. 2002. *Democratic Autonomy: Public Reasoning about the Ends of Policy*. Oxford University Press.

Roche, Declan. 2003. *Accountability in Restorative Justice*. Oxford University Press.

Ronit, Karsten, ed. 2007. *Global Public Policy: Business and the Countervailing Powers of Civil Society*. London: Routledge.

Rorty, Richard. 1998. Human rights, rationality and sentimentality. In *Truth and Progress: Philosophical Papers. Vol. III*. Cambridge University Press. 167–85.

Rosanvallon, Pierre. 2008. *La Légitimité Démocratique*. Paris: Editions du Seuil.

Rosenblum, Nancy. 2010. *On the Side of the Angels: an Appreciation of Parties and Partisanship*. Princeton University Press.

Rousseau, J. J. 1987. *Social Contract, Book III*. Indianapolis: Hackett.

Rowe, Rosemary and M. Shepherd. 2002. Public participation in the new NHS: no closer to citizen control? *Social Policy and Administration* 36 (3): 275–90.

Ruggie, Gerald. 2000. *Constructing the World Polity*. London: Routledge.

Ryfe, David M. 2005. Does deliberative democracy work? *Annual Review of Political Science* 8: 49–71.

Sabel, Charles and Jonathan Zeitlin. 2008. Learning from difference: the new architecture of experimentalist governance in the EU. *European Law Journal* 14 (3): 271–327.

Sanders, Lynn. 1997. Against deliberation. *Political Theory* 25 (3): 347–76.

Saurugger, Sabine. 2010. The social construction of the participatory turn: the emergence of a norm in the European Union. *European Journal of Political Research* 49 (4): 471–95.

Savoie, D. J. 2004. Searching for accountability in a government without boundaries. *Canadian Public Administration – Administration Publique du Canada* 47 (1): 1–26.

Saward, Michael. 1998. *The Terms of Democracy*. Cambridge: Polity Press.

2010. *The Representative Claim*. Oxford University Press.

Scharpf, Fritz W. 1970. *Demokratietheorie zwischen Utopie und Anpassung*. Konstanz: Universitätsverlag.

Schattschneider, Elmer E. 1960. *The Semi-sovereign People*. Hinsdale, IL: Dryden Press.

Schlozman, Kay Lehman, Sidney Verba, and Henry A. Brady. 2010. Weapon of the strong? Participatory inequality and the internet. *Perspectives on Politics* 8 (2): 487–509.

Schmidt, Vivien. 2006. *Democracy in Europe: the EU and National Polities*. Oxford University Press.

Schmitter, Philippe and Wolfgang Streeck. 1999. *The Organization of Business Interests: Studying the Associative Action of Business in Advanced Industrial Societies*. Köln: Max Planck Institute for the Study of Societies.

Schneider, Volker. 2000. Organisationsstaat und Verhandlungsdemokratie. In *Gesellschaftliche Komplexität und Kollektive Handlungsfähigkeit*, edited by R. Werle and U. Schimank. Frankfurt: Campus. 243–69.

Schudson, Michael. 1978. *Discovering the News: a Social History of American Newspapers*. New York: Basic Books.

Schul, Yaacov, Ruth Mayo, and Eugene Burnstein. 2004. Encoding under trust and distrust: the spontaneous activation of incongruent cognitions. *Journal of Personality and Social Psychology* 86 (5): 668–79.

Schumpeter, Joseph. 1962. *Capitalism, Socialism and Democracy*. 3rd edn. New York: Harper and Row.

Searing, Donald D., Frederick Solt, Pamela Johnston, and Ivor Crewe. 2007. Public discussion in the deliberative system: does it make better citizens? *British Journal of Political Science* 37 (4): 587–618.

Shapiro, Ian. 1999. Enough of deliberation: politics is about interests and power. In *Deliberative Politics: Essays on 'Democracy and Disagreement'*, edited by S. Macedo. New York: Oxford University Press. 28–38.

Simon, Herbert. 1947. *Administrative Behavior*. New York: Macmillan.

Slaughter, Anne-Marie. 2004. *A New World Order*. Princeton University Press.

Smith, Graham. 2005. *Beyond the Ballot: 57 Democratic Innovations from Around the World*. London: The Power Inquiry/Short Run Press.

2009. *Democratic Innovations*. Cambridge University Press.

Sørensen, Eva and Jacob Torfing. 2009. Making governance networks effective and democratic through metagovernance. *Public Administration* 87 (2): 234–58.

Steffek, Jens. 2008. Public accountability and the public sphere of international governance. In *RECON Online Working Papers*. Oslo: Reconstituting Democracy in Europe, ARENA – Centre for European Studies, University of Oslo.

Steiner, Jürg, André Bächtiger, Markus Spörndli, and Marco Steenbergen. 2004. *Deliberative Politics in Action: Analysing Parliamentary Discourse*. Cambridge University Press.

Stokes, Susan C. 1998. Pathologies of deliberation. In *Deliberative Democracy*, edited by J. Elster. Cambridge University Press. 123–39.

Stone-Sweet, Alec. 2004. Islands of transnational governance. In *Restructuring Territoriality: Europe and the United States Compared*, edited by C. K. Ansell and G. Di Palma. Cambridge University Press.

Street, John. 2001. *Mass Media, Politics and Democracy*. Basingstoke: Palgrave.

Sunstein, Cass. 2002. The law of group polarization. *Journal of Political Philosophy* 10 (2): 175–95.

2003. *Why Societies Need Dissent*. Cambridge, MA: Harvard University Press.

Sztompka, Piotr. 1999. *Trust: a Sociological Theory*. Cambridge University Press.

Thompson, Dennis. 1999. Democratic theory and global society. *Journal of Political Philosophy* 7 (2): 111–25.

2008a. Deliberative democratic theory and empirical political science. *Annual Review of Political Science* 11: 497–520.

2008b. Who should govern who governs? The role of citizens in reforming the electoral system. In *Designing Deliberative Democracy: the British Columbia Citizens' Assembly*, edited by M. Warren and H. Pearse. Cambridge University Press: 20–49.

Uhr, John. 2000. Testing deliberative democracy: the 1999 Australian republic referendum. *Government and Opposition* 35 (2): 189–210.

Urbinati, Nadia. 2000. Representation as advocacy. *Political Theory* 28 (6): 758–86.

Urbinati, Nadia and Mark Warren. 2008. The concept of representation in contemporary democratic theory. *Annual Review of Political Science* 11: 387–412.

van Gunsteren, Herman. 1998. *A Theory of Citizenship: Organizing Plurality in Contemporary Democracies*. Boulder, CO: Westview Press.

Vibert, Frank. 2007. *The Rise of the Unelected. Democracy and the New Separation of Powers*. Cambridge University Press.

Walzer, Michael. 1981. Philosophy and democracy. *Political Theory* 9 (3): 379–99.

1999. Deliberation, and what else? In *Deliberative Politics: Essays on 'Democracy and Disagreement'*, edited by S. Macedo. New York: Oxford University Press. 58–69.

2002. Equality and civil society. In *Alternative Conceptions of Civil Society,* edited by S. Chambers and W. Kymlicka. Princeton University Press. 34–49.

Warren, Mark. 1996. Deliberative democracy and authority. *American Political Science Review* 90 (1): 46–60.

1999. Democratic theory and trust. In *Democracy and Trust*, edited by M. Warren. Cambridge University Press. 310–45.

2002. What can democratic participation mean today? *Political Theory* 30 (5): 677–701.

2006. Democracy and deceit: regulating appearances of corruption. *American Journal of Political Science* 50 (1): 160–74.

2008. Citizen representatives. In *Designing Deliberative Democracy: the British Columbia Citizens' Assembly*, edited by M. Warren and H. Pearse. Cambridge University Press. 50–69.

2009. Governance-driven democratization. *Critical Policy Studies* 3 (1): 3–13.

Warren, Mark and Hilary Pearse, eds. 2008. *Designing Deliberative Democracy: the British Columbia Citizens' Assembly*. Cambridge University Press.

Webb, Paul and Thomas Poguntke. 2005. The presidentialization of contemporary democratic politics: evidence, causes, and consequences. In *The Presidentialization of Politics: a Comparative Study of Modern Democracies*, edited by T. Poguntke and P. Webb. Oxford University Press. 335–56.

Weiler, Joseph H. H. 1999. *The Constitution of Europe*. Cambridge Univerity Press.

Weller, Patrick Moray, Herman Bakvis, and R. A. W. Rhodes. 1997. *The Hollow Crown: Countervailing Trends in Core Executives, Transforming Government*. New York: St. Martin's Press.

White, Jonathan and Lea Ypi. 2011. On partisan political justification. *American Political Science Review* 105 (2): 381–96.

Williamson, Vanessa, Theda Skocpol, and John Coggin. 2011. The Tea Party and the remaking of Republican conservatism. *Perspectives on Politics* 9 (1): 25–43.

Woods, Ngaire. 2007. Multilateralism and building stronger international institutions. In *Global Accountabilities. Participation, Pluralism, and Public Ethics*, edited by A. Ebrahim and E. Weisband. Cambridge University Press. 27–44.

Wright, S. and J. Street. 2007. Democracy, deliberation and design: the case of online discussion forums. *New Media and Society* 9 (5): 849–69.

Young, Iris Marion. 2000. *Inclusion and Democracy*. Oxford University Press.

Zolo, Danilo. 1992. *Democracy and Complexity*. Cambridge: Polity Press.

Zürn, Michael. 2003. Global governance in der Legitimationskrise? In *Demokratisierung der Demokratie*, edited by C. Offe. Frankfurt: Campus. 232–56.

Index